COURAGE
AND
DEVOTION

COURAGE
AND
DEVOTION

A HISTORY OF BANKHEAD'S/SCOTT'S TENNESSEE
BATTERY IN THE AMERICAN CIVIL WAR

Bruce R. Kindig

ARPress
ILLUMINATING IDEAS
EMPOWERING VOICES

ARPress

45 Dan Road Suite 5

Canton MA 02021

Hotline:	1(888) 821-0229
Fax:	1(508) 545-7580

Ordering Information:

Quantity sales. Special discounts are available on quantity purchases by corporations, associations, and others. For details, contact the publisher at the address above.

Printed in the United States of America.

ISBN-13:	Paperback	979-8-89356-482-2
	eBook	979-8-89356-480-8
	Hardback	979-8-89356-482-2

Library of Congress Control Number: 2024904581

CONTENTS

━━━◗◉◖━━━

CONTENTS

ACKNOWLEDGMENTS

I would like to thank Glenda Riggs, who is a third cousin four times removed to Smith P. Bankhead, for the vast amount of material she provided on the Bankhead family. I would also like to thank the various librarians who helped me find materials; and I would like to thank the many park rangers and employees who gave me guidance and assistance in my quest. One such employee, Joe Hadley, at Fort Pillow State Park continued to answer my questions that went far beyond my expectations, and I am truly grateful. I have met many descendants of the veterans of Bankhead's/Scott's Tennessee Battery and have incorporated some of their family histories in this book. Some of them are listed in the bibliography.

I am also grateful to the Reverend Walter Gordon of St. James Episcopal Church in Bolivar, Tennessee, for allowing me access to the stained glass window that started me on my quest, and for explaining the symbolism of the window.

This book could not have been written without the support of my wife, Connie, who accompanied me in all of my travels. When I visited libraries, she often sat alone for hours in another room reading magazines. Sometimes she would sit in the car at battlefields while I tramped through the woods. At home, when I went to the basement to write, she left me alone with my thoughts. Her love and devotion are truly exceptional.

I also want to thank my old friend, Ed Reiter, whose technical support saved me hours of work.

PREFACE

—◉—

In Bolivar, Tennessee, at the corner of Lafayette and Washington is St. James Episcopal Church. It is a small church built in an old gothic style in 1869. There are several memorial windows in the church, one of which is a tribute to General Otho Strahl and Lieutenant John Marsh, who were both killed at the Civil War Battle of Franklin, Tennessee, in 1864. Why is there a memorial to these men at this church? Before the American Civil War began, Strahl had been the teacher of young Marsh at a rural country school outside of Bolivar. Strahl had been instrumental in getting Marsh an appointment to West Point, because he saw something in the character of this very bright pupil of his. Strahl went on to become the commander of the Fourth Tennessee Infantry Regiment, and Marsh went into the artillery and was badly wounded at Chickamauga. Never fully recovering from his wound, Marsh rejoined his old teacher as an aid on his staff, and they both met their end at the Battle of Franklin in 1864. Charles T. Quintard was responsible for the memorial window. He had served as a chaplain during the war and was a good friend of Strahl's, and he had helped Marsh when he was in the hospital. Quintard became the Episcopal Bishop of Tennessee after the war and paid for the memorial window from the proceeds of a horse Strahl had given to him. How many people know about this window? How many times have people of the church looked at it without knowing its significance?

My decision to write this book goes back many years before I even knew about the memorial window in Bolivar. I had always been an avid reader on the subject of the American Civil War. When I was in eighth grade, I think I read every Civil War book in the public library where I grew up in Cedar Falls, Iowa. So how does a Northern boy become a passionate Southerner? As a young reader, I admired Robert E. Lee and Stonewall Jackson and the military campaigns of the Army of Northern Virginia. So I began to read more about the Civil War in the West. I developed an interest in the Army of Tennessee and began to focus on the artillery. When I read about John Marsh at Chickamauga and Franklin, I wanted to know more. When I found out about the memorial window, I wanted to put together a history so that Marsh and the men who fought with him would not be forgotten. Strahl, who is also named in the window, was well known in the Army of Tennessee, but Marsh and Bankhead's/ Scott's Battery had their own story of courage and devotion that this book will tell.

John Marsh had commanded Scott's Tennessee Battery at Chickamauga, and so I began my odyssey to find out more about Marsh by taking on the task of reading about the battery. So where is the unit history? No one had written one. William L. Scott wrote a brief history that was published in 1886 in John Berrien Lindsley's *Military Annals of Tennessee*. Scott wrote only five pages, mostly from memory. His generalizations of the campaigns did not satisfy my desire for detail. Scott wrote about the officers, and not much about the men. In Scott's narrative was one statement that I knew would make my task difficult, "It is impossible at this distance of time, and when all records of the company's history have long been destroyed."[1] Scott could not write from facts, because the records of the war were destroyed. I decided to look for records that Scott did not have.

Scott's Battery was disbanded after Missionary Ridge in 1863, and the men were dispersed to other units. Scott admitted that he still had the company records in October of 1864 when there was an inquiry about one of the officers. I had hoped that they would be found in someone's attic or that a diary had been written. I have not found any letters, but I have spent over thirty years gathering material. I decided that, if I did not put this book together, all my work would be lost.

In my journey to gather the story, I have met some wonderful people. These are people like me who want to know about a single soldier. Some want to know about their Civil War ancestors; I unfortunately do not have one. My interest in Marsh is really an interest in the men of the battery of which he was a gallant commander. Just as my father rarely talked about his World War II experiences, so too the Civil War soldier were reluctant to talk. It was my mother who told me about my father's wounds from Anzio, and so I decided to turn to the relatives who might tell the story of the Civil War soldier. I remember traveling to Madison, Wisconsin, to talk to Phil Talty about his Civil War ancestors. The Talty brothers had been in Bankhead's Battery (the predecessor to Scott's Battery), and I wanted to know what Phil knew. Phil was a widower in his sixties and had done some genealogy on his family. It turned out Phil wanted to know what I knew. He had a few newspaper clippings and some family history, but

---

[1] John B. Lindsley, ed., *The Military Annals of Tennessee* (Nashville: J. M. Lindsley & Co., Publishers, 1886), 793.

they all dealt with his Union ancestors. His cousin, Jim Carey, who lived in Atlantic, Iowa, filled in a great deal about the family, and so I decided that I would try to include in this book some personal touches about the men in the battery. There are some selected biographies of the officers and men in the last chapter.

Most people know about Robert E. Lee, Stonewall Jackson, and Nathan Bedford Forrest. Why shouldn't we know about Smith P. Bankhead, James T. Morris, or Burrill B. Battle? Whose story should be told? Or not told? This book will try to tell the stories of common men. Why is one man a patriot and another a coward? Why would one man desert and another fight on to the last battle? The answers may not be obvious, but at least we may look into the nature of humans and be filled with either pride or shame.

In my journey I met several descendents of Scott's Battery veterans who have helped me find my way. I realized the diary I am looking for may not exist, as most of the men were illiterate. Those who did write were well educated, and their prose was excellent. The diaries and letters used in this book usually come from members of units that were brigaded with Scott's Battery. Sometimes the battery was camped with other artillery units or fell under the command of an infantry brigade. I have not changed any of the quotes with modern spelling or punctuation corrections. I have left out the use of (sic) and left in the ampersand (&), as that was in common use during that time.

Scott was wrong about the battery records, because they were not all destroyed after all. Some of them are in the National Archives and are easily accessible. The collection and publication of the records wasn't finished until 1901. These records are called The Official Records of the War of the Rebellion, and I will cite them in the footnotes as the ORs. These were published in 128 volumes. I used to go to the Davenport Public Library, where I had a teaching job, and go through them for information. I had to request the volumes I wanted, and library staff members would bring them up from the basement four books at a time. Later I bought a CD ROM of all 128 volumes for about $75. Now they are all accessible online for free. I bought my first roll of microfilm from the National Archives and Records Administration in 1986. I acquired a used microfilm reader and searched the records that Scott would be astounded still exist today. Now they can be found online too.

I wrote this book with the purpose of having the historical narrative separate from stories of the men. If the reader wants to know about an individual, there are sections within the chapters about the officers and enlisted men. There are two lists on the first page of each chapter. The list on the left is the chain of command, or who had authority over the battery. The list on the right is the men who commanded the battery from the captain to the corporals. The sergeants and corporals are listed alphabetically instead of by length of service. Unlike modern times, these noncommissioned officers were promoted and demoted at the whim of the captains. Also listed are the men who held the rank of quartermaster sergeant or ordnance sergeant, although they would serve at a higher level such as battalion, brigade, or division. The lists are set at the time frame of the beginning of the chapter.

It is the intention of this book to describe the battery's place in the large scheme of things. On the maps in this book are marks that show the location of the battery at each battle. In each chapter, after the narrative, there are descriptions of the officers and what they were doing, followed by information about the enlisted men. At the end of the book, there are several appendices that present lists of men for various times. The names are listed chronologically first and then alphabetically. Genealogists may have to search several appendices to follow a single person.

I know that this story is incomplete. Maybe someone will find that diary in the attic, and my next project will be to edit it. I could not find any photographs of Smith P. Bankhead or William L. Scott, but I will continue to look. Any errors in this book are strictly mine, and I apologize if you find any, but if you do I would appreciate hearing about it with your documentation. E-mail me at scotts_battery@hotmail.com, and maybe we can take the next journey together.

Chapter 1

———◉———

Memphis
April–May 1861

Provisional Army of Tennessee	First Tennessee Artillery Regiment Battery B
Governor Isham Harris Major General Gideon Pillow Colonel John McCown First Tennessee Artillery Regiment	Captain Smith P. Bankhead

Memphis in 1861 was a bustling town with packet boats and railroads always busy. Cotton was the main product exported, but other businesses were booming as well. This commerce needed a strong work force. Slaves from Africa and their descendents contributed to the economic prosperity by providing cheap labor for cotton production. Because of the value of a good slave hand, many slave owners would not let their slaves work in dangerous jobs such as railroad construction; therefore, a need for additional labor attracted people to Memphis.[2]

Irish immigrants filled the need for workers. Most of them were unskilled laborers. They often did the tedious or dangerous work that slaves did not do. The Irish remained poor, and prejudice put them in the social position between blacks and the Anglo-Southerners. They enjoyed an American freedom that they had not found in their native Ireland. The Irish immigrant could be induced to volunteer in the army to keep his position in society or for wages.[3]

Germans made up another immigrant labor force. Although they comprised a smaller work force than the Irish, many of them created small businesses. They could be induced to volunteer for the army for economic reasons.[4]

The newspapers also stirred up patriotism for Southern rights. Editorials in the *Memphis Daily Appeal* supported the Union in 1860, supported compromise in January and February 1861, and in March favored secession. April is full of editorials in favor of secession and about the tyranny of Lincoln. Discounts were offered for advertisements for military units, and in May the paper published the Confederate Constitution. Memphians were well aware of the news of the day, albeit from the view of the *Memphis Daily Appeal*. The idea that states had the right to secede and for Abraham Lincoln to say they didn't was tyranny.[5]

Federal tyranny or Northern aggression also figured into the willingness of Tennesseans to join the new Provisional Army of Tennessee. Lincoln's call for 70,000 volunteers to stop the Confederate states from seceding

---

[2] John E. Harkins, *Metropolis of the American Nile* (Woodland Hills, California: Windsor Publishing, Inc., 1982), 69.

[3] David T. Gleeson, *The Irish in the South 1815–1877* (Chapel Hill: University of North Carolina Press, 2001), 78.

[4] Harkins, *Metropolis of the American Nile*, 66–67.

[5] Ibid., 70–72.

was considered an oppressive invasion by a foreign foe. West Tennessee had strong ties to the Confederate states and refused to supply troops for Northern aggression, but would supply troops to defend their homes and families. The *Memphis Daily Appeal* carried articles in April and May about federal troop activities in Maryland and Virginia and particularly the build up at Cairo, Illinois. This was clearly a threat to Memphis and all free men of the South.[6]

In April and early May, some fifteen companies of infantry and cavalry were formed in Memphis. The Irish joined because they saw the federal army much as they saw the British in Ireland—as tyrants and oppressors. The German immigrants saw an oppressor who would put down their newfound democracy. Others joined because they needed work, and army pay was better than nothing. Some were coerced to join by the patriots, many of whom had formed committees of safety and vigilance. These groups of vigilantes were very small but very vocal. They chased strangers out of town and encouraged army enlistment. One example of a Kentuckian passing through Memphis shows the power of such committees:

> A policeman handed him a letter from the chairman, suggesting that he enlist in the Provisional Army of Tennessee. The note strongly advised it was in his interest to volunteer because; "Several members of the committee think if you do not see fit to follow this advice, you will probably stretch hemp ... an infuriated mob ... may hear that you came from the North." It was clearly apparent, the Kentuckian wrote, "that the military power in the city resolved to *compel* me to *volunteer*, and in my friendliness I could think of no way to escape ... I wrote my name and thus volunteered."[7]

As this suggests, some volunteers were not exactly eager to join as able-bodied men, but not joining could put one under scrutiny.[8]

---

[6] *Memphis Appeal*, April and May 1861.

[7] James B. Jones Jr., "The Reign of Terror of the Safety Committee Has Passed Away Forever: A History of Committees of Safety and Vigilance in West and Middle Tennessee, 1860–1862," The West Tennessee Historical Society Papers, vol. LXIII, 2009), 3.

[8] Ibid.

With Memphis arming to defend itself, the Provisional Army of Tennessee was formed to organize the state volunteers. Although Tennessee was not in the Confederacy yet, there were close connections with army commanders in Tennessee and President Jefferson Davis' administration. General Gideon Pillow was appointed to command the army, and other officers were soon to be appointed. In Memphis more artillery units needed to be formed to fulfill the needs of the army.

On Monday, May 13, 1861, Smith P. Bankhead left his home on Washington Street and walked the six blocks to his office at Main and Madison. He had arranged a meeting that morning with William Y. C. Humes and James C. McDavitt. Bankhead, age thirty-seven; Humes, age thirty; and McDavitt, age twenty-seven, were all lawyers in Memphis. By the authority of the state Army Bill of May 6, Bankhead had been appointed a captain of artillery by Governor Isham Harris, although this information would not be made public until the May 21 issue of the *Memphis Daily Appeal*, and the meeting was set up to organize Company B of the First Tennessee Artillery Regiment.[9]

Of the three, Bankhead was the only man with any military experience, having served in the Mexican War. Humes would hold the rank of first lieutenant and McDavitt would be second lieutenant. The meeting started with the men signing the state commission papers, which would then have to be approved by the state legislature. As officers they were required to obtain their own uniforms and horses. Bankhead listed his horse as having a value of $250; Humes listed his at $200. McDavitt would try to procure uniforms and any other equipment, while Bankhead and Humes would recruit as many men as possible. The governor would procure artillery equipment, such as guns, limbers (two-wheeled vehicles for guns and ammunition), and caissons (ammunition chests). They had a short time line, as they were to bring their company to Fort Pillow by the end of the month for artillery training.[10]

The original Tennessee infantry uniform was gray with red trim, and several companies had already been mustered in with these uniforms. General Pillow had recently changed the uniform to be without the red trim. There were still quantities of these uniforms with red trim to be had,

---

[9]   *Memphis Appeal*, May 21, 1861; Consolidated Confederate Service Record (CCSR), Washington DC, National Archives, Series 268 microfilm roll 98.

[10] *Memphis Appeal*, April 27–May 23, 1861.

and McDavitt wasted no time in securing them. These uniforms would satisfy the initial recruitment, but over time additional recruits often wore a uniform without the red trim. Many of the recruits would join the battery with their own clothing. Bankhead and Humes realized that the infantry and cavalry recruiters had already taken the most eager men into the army. They decided to canvass the town and individually find men throughout Memphis. They did not put any notices in the newspapers; neither did they put up any signs at a recruiting station. They went to the hotels, boarding houses, cafes, drinking establishments, and, in particular, to the docks along the river and the pinch area of northern Memphis. The pinch area was full of boarding houses, and most of the Irish immigrants lived there.[11]

Bankhead also knew that he needed more second lieutenants and set about filling his staff. He succeeded in enlisting William B. Greenlaw Jr., age twenty, who came on board on Wednesday, May 15. Greenlaw was also a lawyer and the son of William B. Greenlaw Sr., who was a successful contractor and one of the benefactors of the Memphis and Charleston Railroad. He would assist McDavitt in procuring uniforms and other supplies. Another second lieutenant was William L. Scott, a lawyer in Knoxville and a friend of Humes. Humes had contacted him, and he agreed to join with Bankhead. He was closing up his law practice and would soon be en route to Memphis. Scott was twenty-seven years old.[12]

Wednesday, May 15, also brought the first two privates to join the unit. They were Michael Nason, age seventeen, and J. W. Harrison, age twenty-three. Nason was born in County Cork, Ireland, and lived in the pinch area. Harrison was a native Tennessean, married, and the father of one child. They were told to pass the word to friends and neighbors about Bankhead's Battery and to get their affairs in order. A sergeant would come to them before the month was out to inform them of when to report for muster. The men had volunteered with no bounty offered, only wages of eleven dollars a month. On that day the *Appeal* ran a story about Irish recruitment thanking them for their "commendable zeal." The next day four more men joined the unit. One of them was twenty-six-year-old Samuel Brown, whom Bankhead made the first sergeant. Lewis Merchant

---

[11]   Ibid.

[12]   CCSR m268 roll 97.

was also made a sergeant, and he and Brown would help canvass the town for Bankhead.[13]

Saturday proved to be the best recruitment day yet. Twelve men were recruited, all from the pinch area. Bankhead made two of them sergeants and one a corporal. As the first week of recruitment ended, there were eighteen men in Bankhead's Battery, but the goal was sixty to seventy men, and there was more work to do the next week.[14]

On Monday, May 20, 1861, twelve more men were recruited; most of them were Irish immigrants, but a few were native Tennesseans. One of them was Nicholas Schriner, whom Bankhead made artificer. Schriner was skilled in metal work, and his services would be necessary if equipment needed repair. Also joining were four brothers, Patrick, George, John, and Simon Talty. At age thirty-two, Patrick was the oldest and was made corporal. The brothers had been working the docks, but work was declining as shipping to the north was almost nonexistent. There were twenty-three more recruits throughout the week, bringing the total so far to fifty-two.[15]

On Monday, May 27, Bankhead held a meeting with his officers. Plans were made to muster the men and move to Fort Pillow, about sixty miles north of Memphis, where all of the artillery companies would come together to drill and learn about artillery. They would move by steamboat. Only three more men were recruited before they left—Jerry Crowley and Albert Sailhorst on May 28, and David Ennis on May 29. Then they left Memphis. A few days later, William L. Scott arrived from Knoxville to find that the unit was gone. He arrived at Fort Pillow on June 4, signed his commission papers, and listed the value of his horse at $200. On June 8, 1861, Tennessee seceded from the Union.[16]

---

[13]   Ibid., Historical Data Systems, comp., American Civil War Soldiers, Provo UT, ancestry.com Operations Inc. 1999; CCSR m231 roll 32. *Memphis Appeal*, May 19, 1861. See Appendix 1 for a list of all of the recruits enrolled by Bankhead in May 1861.

[14]   CCSR m268 roll 97–98.

[15]   Ibid.

[16]   Ibid.

The Officers

All of the officer's of Bankhead's Battery were educated men with professional occupations. They were all lawyers. They gave up their law practices to go off to war for $90 to $100 per month. It is assumed that these men were patriots fighting for the rights they believed were threatened. However, William Greenlaw may not have been as much of a patriot as the others. It would come out later that he was more of an opportunist, trying to get rank and the privileges that went with it. These men were also property owners defending their homes and were slave owners. Bankhead had owned several house servants that set his lifestyle. Humes had owned slaves before, but it is uncertain if he owned any at this time, as he had sold a slave prior to moving to Memphis. Greenlaw came from a wealthy family that owned domestic servants. It does not appear that Scott ever owned slaves. They did support the social system prevalent in the South, and they were willing to risk their lives and fortunes to maintain the system.[17]

Smith Pyne Bankhead was born on August 20, 1823, at Fort Moultrie, South Carolina, while his father, Brigadier General James Bankhead, a career army officer from Virginia, was stationed in South Carolina. Smith Bankhead grew up in Virginia. graduated from Hampden Military School, and attended Georgetown University and the University of Virginia. During the Mexican War, he was a captain in the Virginia volunteers and served under his father who commanded the US troops at Vera Cruz after the city fell. After the war, Bankhead went to California hoping to cash in on the gold rush. He didn't strike it rich and found life difficult in California. Bankhead decided to return east and, in 1851, chose to settle Memphis, as he had been there briefly during the Mexican War. In Memphis he founded and edited the *Memphis Whig*, a political newspaper. After a short time, he sold the newspaper and decided to practice law. He was elected the city attorney of Memphis in 1852 and built a reputable private law practice. He married Susan Adeline "Ada" Garth in 1851, and they had a daughter, Ada Pyne Bankhead, born in 1852. Bankhead lived at 224 Washington Avenue and had property valued at $20,000. Mrs. Bankhead and Ada remained in Memphis throughout the war. He was

---

[17] Shelby County Death Records 1842–1899, 88; W. Y. C. Humes to O. P. Temple, March 17, 1861, University of Tennessee, Digital Library Initiatives.

described as "A reliable man and well-instructed officer." His job was to train the men and continue to recruit more men into the battery.[18]

William Young Conn Humes was born on May 1, 1830, in Abington, Virginia. He was the son of John Newton Humes, who originally lived in Knoxville, Tennessee. He attended Virginia Military Institute (VMI) and graduated second in his class of 1851. His VMI studies gave him some military background, but he never served in the military. He married Margaret Preston White and moved to Knoxville after graduation where he took the bar exam and began practicing law. They had two children, but only his son Newton survived childhood. Humes had done some work in Memphis and decided to practice law there. He arrived in 1858, but his family remained in Knoxville. He sold a female slave who had been a domestic servant before he left, but was planning to buy another female and her two boys when he planned to move his family to Memphis in the fall of 1861. Humes would be a strong proponent favoring segregation after the war.[19]

James Clare McDavitt was born November 25, 1834, in Shelby, County Kentucky. He was the son of George McDavitt and Linnie Nowlin from a distinguished family of Kentucky. He attended Ashbury University in Indiana (today DePauw University) and then studied law under Judge T. W. Brown of Shelbyville, Kentucky. He moved to Memphis in 1857 and was a partner of the law firm of Kortrecht and McDavitt. He was not married and politically was a Whig, as was Smith Bankhead. McDavitt shared similar views about race relations and the economics of the South with Bankhead, and became the first second lieutenant of Bankhead's Battery.[20]

William Bowden Greenlaw Jr. was born in May 1841 in Memphis to William B. Greenlaw Sr. one of the financial barons of early Memphis. Greenlaw's father invested heavily in construction and railroad development in the 1840s and 1850s. The Greenlaw block was on Main Street between

---

[18]   U.S. Seventh Census; The Official Records (OR), VIII pt. 2, 760; Lindsley, *The Military Annals of Tennessee*, 793.

[19]   Ibid; Humes to Temple, March 17, 1861; Family Data Collection-Births, Individual Records (Humes). ancestry.com, 1999.

[20]   U.S. Sixth Census; Memphis City Directory, 1860; Eloise LaFont Pullen Bible, hand-written family record, 1822–1900; Family Data Collection.

Union and Gayoso Streets. Here was located the Law Office of William B. Greenlaw and Company. Greenlaw's father financed his education and established his law office for the young twenty-year-old. William B. Greenlaw Sr. and his brother, J. Oliver Greenlaw, were contractors in many enterprises. They controlled $290,000 worth of real estate and $100,000 in personal property. Greenlaw was not married and still lived in his parents' home on Union Street when he joined Bankhead's Battery. He was not a slave owner but subscribed to the racial relations of the time. He was a young man whose family had influence. Perhaps this could be helpful to Bankhead in the future.[21]

William Luther Scott was born to James Scott and Eliza Ramsey in Knoxville, Tennessee, in 1834. He came from a large family, his great-great grandfather having settled in Connecticut after arriving from England around 1750. Scott was not married but had established his law practice in his hometown of Knoxville and was a friend of Humes. He was not a slave owner but supported the social structure of the South and was a proponent of states' rights and the second amendment to bear arms against tyranny. Although he had no military training, Humes trusted the abilities of Scott and asked him to join with Bankhead in Memphis. Leaving his assets with his family, he set off to complete the leadership team led by Smith P. Bankhead.[22]

The Enlisted Men

A total of fifty-one men had been recruited in Memphis in about two weeks. There were thirty-nine men who were foreign born (70.9 percent). However, thirty-seven of these men were born in Ireland. It was economic opportunity that proved to be the biggest incentive, as most of the men had recently become unemployed. These hungry men looking for work found employment in the army. That the Irish made up 67 percent of Bankhead's Battery should not be surprising. The most politically minded native-born Memphians had already joined infantry and cavalry units that had been organized before Bankhead ever started recruiting.[23]

---

[21]   Memphis City Directory 1860; U.S. Seventh Census; Family Data Collection.

[22]   Family Data Collection.

[23]   CCSR Record Group 109 rolls 6, 9, 10, 12, 24, 27, 29, 30, 31, 35, 36, 38 and m268 rolls 97–98.

An example of Irish recruits would be the Talty brothers. In 1853 Michael and Catherine Talty arrived in the United States from Ireland with their six children. The brothers, Patrick, Simon, George, and John, and two sisters, Katie and Bridget, were all born in County Clare, Bridget being only five at the time of their arrival. It is not clear where they settled at first. Irish immigrants often knew others who had come before them. They may have spent time in Memphis, but eventually the family settled in Davenport, Iowa. Here work could be found at the lumber mills or on the Mississippi River trade. Steamboats were constantly going up and down the river between St. Paul and New Orleans. The parents had settled in the west end or Irish section of Davenport. The four boys had traveled to Memphis and found work as laborers in Memphis in 1860. Patrick, the oldest, was married. The other three brothers were not married and lived with him in the first ward. The men had become unemployed in the spring of 1861 when they met Smith P. Bankhead. They were offered rations and wages, which for poor, hungry men became the main reason for enlistment. What could be a concern for these men was that their parents and sisters lived in the North.[24]

Another reason to join with Bankhead could be to escape from the law. Michael Mahoney, a twenty-one-year-old Irish immigrant, joined the battery on May 23. The *Memphis Daily Appeal* carried his story in the May 25 edition of the paper. He had been charged with passing a counterfeit $10 bill from a Virginia bank at a local business. By declaring patriotism and volunteering to defend Memphis, he received leniency from the court, and he soon left town with the battery.[25]

Other recruits were born in the North (7.3 percent) and in the South (7.3 percent). One of the men born in New York was Nicholas Schriner. Nicholas and his brother, James, lived with an uncle, John Schriner, in a boarding house in Memphis. Nicholas worked as a blacksmith in his uncle's blacksmith shop in the Second Ward. With work down, Nicholas Schriner joined Bankhead with the rank of artificer and the prospect of steady work and perhaps no requirement to drill with the other men. He had skills needed for keeping equipment in shape. None of the records

---

24   Phil Talty (descendant of the Talty brothers), interview with the author, March 6, 2003; James Carey (descendant of the Talty brothers), personal correspondence with author, March 2003; Davenport City Directory 1863.

25   *Memphis Daily Appeal*, May 25, 1861.

indicate that he was a second-generation German immigrant, but he may have been. Albert Sailhorst was the other German recruit.[26]

Samuel Brown, who was made first sergeant, was also from New York. The two men born in Virginia, Lewis Putney and James Welsh, were also made sergeants. A fourth sergeant was Lewis Merchant, who had been born in Paris, France. There is no indication that he was a French immigrant. Four noncommissioned officers, Sergeant John Purcell and Corporals James McLaughlin, Patrick Talty, and Miles Kehoe were Irish immigrants.[27]

The occupations of the recruits varied. Of the twenty-three men who listed their occupations, twelve claimed to be laborers. All of them were Irish except Samuel Brown. Sergeant Merchant had been a tailor, and Sergeant Putney had been a clerk. John Hayes had been a railroad worker, and John Murphy had been a drayman at the docks. Two men had worked on riverboats. Martin Lyon had been a steward, Patrick Mathews had been a col'd hostler (coal heaver), and Nicholas Schriner was a blacksmith. The majority of men were working-class wage earners.[28]

Of the fifty-one men recruited, we know the ages of fifty of them. The youngest recruit was Michael Nason, age seventeen, and the oldest recruit was Philip Sullivan, age forty-five. However there were only two men under age twenty (4 percent) and five men over age forty (10 percent). Most of the men were in their twenties (62 percent) and thirties (24 percent). The average age of Bankhead's initial recruitment was twenty-eight. Only five of the men were married. Most of them had lived in boarding houses and seldom owned property. It could be concluded that most of the men in Bankhead's Battery were single, blue-collar Irish immigrants in their late twenties with no property. Of course this is a generalization, and the battery was never thought of as an Irish unit.[29]

Bankhead's Battery was not up to full strength, and more recruitment was needed. For now the Memphian recruits would have to pull together to form a fighting unit.

---

[26]   U. S. Seventh Census.

[27]   CCSR Record Group 109 rolls 6, 9, 10, 12, 24, 27, 29, 30, 31, 35, 36, 38 and m268 rolls 97–98.

[28]   Ibid.

[29]   Ibid.

CHAPTER 2

FORT PILLOW
JUNE–JULY 1861

Provisional Army of Tennessee	First Tennessee Artillery Regiment Company B
Governor Isham Harris Major General Gideon Pillow Colonel John McCown First Tennessee Artillery Regiment	Captain Smith P. Bankhead First Lieutenant W.Y.C. Humes Second Lieutenant James C. McDavitt Second Lieutenant William B. Greenlaw Jr. Second Lieutenant William L. Scott First Sergeant Samuel Brown Second Sergeant Lewis Putney Sergeant Lewis Merchant Sergeant John Purcell Sergeant James Welsh Corporal Miles Kehoe Corporal James McLaughlin Corporal Patrick Talty 48 privates

At the time Bankhead and his men were proceeding to Fort Pillow for artillery training, the Provisional Army of Tennessee had not been absorbed into the Provisional Army of the Confederate States. The troops would have to rely on state assistance until Governor Harris and the government in Richmond could work this out.

Captain Smith P. Bankhead and his newly recruited men ascended the sloping ground just south of the First Chickasaw Bluff and arrived at an open field with woods to the east and what would become Fort Pillow to the west. Some of the men were wearing their new gray uniforms with the red trim, while others were still in their civilian clothing. A few carried some of their belongings in carpetbags or empty flour sacks, while others had no personal effects of any kind. As they drew closer to Fort Pillow, they saw several work parties of slaves working on the fortifications. Fort Pillow had been designed to accommodate as many as fifty heavy guns overlooking the Mississippi River. Already several of them were at the fort, but none had yet been emplaced.

Fort Pillow commanded an excellent view of the Mississippi, and at 200 feet above the river could deliver a plunging fire upon federal ironclad gunboats now under construction up river. Fort Pillow had been designated the artillery training camp for Tennessee and was under the command of Colonel John McCown. The infantry training camp was just a few miles south at the Second Chickasaw Bluff. Fort Wright was being constructed there, with the town of Randolph nearby. Memphis itself sat above the Fourth Chickasaw Bluff, and the construction of fortifications was in progress there as well.[30]

Bankhead reported to McCown while the men rested underneath some nearby trees. To these Irish immigrants and urban Memphians, there was a sight before them they could only have imagined. A city of canvas was under construction. Many of the tents were already up, and they could see men putting up more. The area beyond the tents was soon to become the drill field of eight artillery batteries.

When Bankhead returned, he drew the officers and sergeants together and gave them their orders. Half of the men were ordered to go with several sergeants into the woods and bring back firewood, while the other half of the men were to proceed to some nearby wagons, retrieve tents and poles, and make a company street. The street had already been marked out with

---

[30]   Colin A. Strickland and Timothy Huebner, *From Civil War Fort to State Park* (Memphis, Tennessee: Rhodes College, n.d.), 3–6.

sticks and twine, and each company was given a frontage of about twenty yards. Under the direction of the second lieutenants, the tents were erected in two lines facing each other about five yards apart. The tents were of solid-sewn construction with sloping sides that came to a point at the top. They were commonly called wedge tents. The men also erected tents for the officers some twenty yards away from the men's tents. These tents were larger and were called wall tents, as there was a canvas wall about three feet tall before the roof of the tent sloped to a point. The lieutenants would share, with two officers to a tent, and the two tents would be about fourteen yards apart. Bankhead would have his own tent ten yards behind the lieutenants, but placed evenly between them.[31]

An officers' kitchen was placed ten yards behind the captain's tent, and two kitchens were set up for the men on either side of the area between the lieutenants' tents and the soldiers' tents. The area beyond the soldiers' tents would be the drill field. When horses and guns become available, they would be kept on the drill field. The assignment of the men to the tents would come later that day.[32]

Bankhead had raised his company to be a flying artillery battery. The term *flying* indicated that all of the men would be mounted on horses. There were no horses available yet, so the men would be trained in light artillery. Since there was no light artillery available yet, the men would train with the heavy artillery already at Fort Pillow until their guns arrived. Light artillery referred to cannons that fired projectiles of twelve pounds or less. These guns could weigh from 600 to 1,800 pounds and were often called six-pounders or twelve-pounders. Some of the newer light artillery would fire 3-inch or 4.6-inch projectiles and had names like Parrott or Napoleon. Teams of four or six horses could move these guns. Cannons larger than these were called heavy artillery and could not be moved easily. They were too heavy to move with a field army. However, heavy guns would be needed to stop federal boats from descending the river.

After the firewood was neatly stacked at the three kitchen areas and all of the tents were up, First Sergeant Brown read the orders of the day. The men were divided into groups, each under a sergeant, and assigned to

---

[31] *Instructions for Field Artillery*, Prepared by a Board of Artillery Officers, J. B. Lippincott & Co., 1861, 66; Thomas Lawrence Connelly, *Army of the Heartland* (Baton Rouge: Louisiana State University Press, 1967), 36. See Appendix 2.

[32] Ibid.

tents. There would be six men to a tent that measured about nine feet by nine feet and stood about seven feet tall in the center. Then the men were marched to the commissary tent where they would each be issued a tin plate, cup, spoon, knife, and fork. Eight men would be assigned to a mess and would do their own cooking. Each mess received an iron kettle, an oven, a wash pan, a tin bucket, a wooden bucket, and a coffee pot. They would receive their rations at 10:00 a.m. daily and had to do their own washing. The state government also provided a blanket for each man.[33]

Captain Bankhead was responsible for training the men so that they not only knew how to fight in a battle and serve the piece, but also know where they belonged. Each man had a position. The men had to know where they belonged in a formation, on the march, and while firing the guns.

Bankhead also had to continue to recruit more men to fill the ranks. He needed 125 men and barely had half that number. Two more men were quickly added to the roster. Both of them had been at Randolph, Tennessee, just a few miles south of Fort Pillow at the infantry training camp. They had come up to Fort Pillow to join the artillery. Charles Campbell joined the battery on June 5, and John Ragan, on June 6. Bankhead would make several trips back to Memphis to do recruiting, but for now he had to get training under way.[34]

A captain's duties not only involved recruitment and training; he also had to make sure there were enough supplies for the guns as well as the men. The lieutenants supported the captains, and the most senior lieutenant would take the captain's place if he was wounded or absent. The three senior lieutenants would each command a section of guns. Two guns were a section; one gun was a detachment. The most junior lieutenant served as the captain's adjutant and would be in charge of the caissons during battle. In addition to supervising the ammunition wagons, the lieutenants also were in charge of requisitions and keeping the equipment in good order.[35]

First Sergeant Samuel Brown reported directly to the captain and fulfilled an administrative role. He held the roll call each morning, assigned the men their duties, and wrote the daily reports. He was also responsible for posting guards and pickets, repairing equipment, and grooming the

---

[33]   *Memphis Appeal* May 17, 1861.

[34]   CCSR m268 roll 97–98; *Instructions for Field Artillery*, 6.

[35]   Ibid, 69–70.

horses. During battle he had no duty, but remained close to the captain to fulfill any roll necessary. If needed, he could become the chief of caissons to free up that officer for section command. In an emergency, he could fill in as a section commander.[36]

A battery of six guns should have six sergeants. Excluding First Sergeant Brown, there were four who would serve as the detachment leaders. A detachment served one artillery piece and was made up of eight privates. Six additional privates were the drivers of the limber and caisson assigned to their cannon. There were two corporals in each detachment, one of whom would be the gunner. The other would be in charge of the caisson. The men were divided into platoons, and the sergeants began the task of training the men. Since there were no caissons, limbers, or horses, the men practiced on marching and school of the piece (preparing and firing the guns) with some of the heavy artillery pieces nearby.[37]

Until the battery acquired horses, all of the men drilled as gunners. They learned to march in column; that is, two men abreast and four deep with the sergeant to the left and the corporal to the right. This would be the marching position behind the gun as they traveled on the road. At the command "From column into line" the cannoneers formed a double line to the left of the corporal. From this formation, the men served the gun.

By watching the men drill and analyzing their skill, Bankhead and his officers determined which jobs the men should have once horses and guns arrived. Some of the men would become drivers. Six drivers were needed for each gun. Six horses pulled the limber and caisson, and the drivers rode on the left-side horses. Each driver was responsible for the care of the horse he rode as well as the right-side horse. Duties included feeding, watering, and grooming the team. The cannoneers were not allowed to ride on the limber except in extreme cases due to the strain on the horses.

Other privates could be assigned as wagoners or teamsters. They would be under the command of a sergeant. They drove the battery forge, battery wagon, and supply wagons, which were usually pulled by just two horses. At full strength, this involved eight men, but at times could fall under the command of the brigade or battalion. A few other privates were also necessary. Artificers had a skill in blacksmithing. They stayed with the traveling forge to make or repair tools and parts. Nicholas Schriner was

---

[36]   Ibid, 70–71.

[37]   Ibid.

the only artificer recruited, and Bankhead desperately wanted to recruit a few more. A farrier would also be needed. His job was to keep all of the animals shod, and the battery could have as many as one hundred animals. Bankhead was aware that a bugler or two would also be needed. Bugle calls during battle were easier to hear than voice commands, and very important. Buglers announced the daily activities in camp and also served as messengers and clerks. Finally, a few extra privates would provide the battery with replacements that would be necessary due to casualties or sickness. They learned all of the private positions and served with the caissons until ordered to another post by the first sergeant.[38]

As June gave way to July, Bankhead decided to take a trip to Memphis. The drill was coming along well, but the men were getting tired of marching in the heat and learning to tie knots. A few horses had arrived in camp as well as a few pieces of light artillery, but none had been given to Bankhead's Battery. More men were needed, and Bankhead wanted to recruit the specialists he needed. He would also find the orders for the cannons and artillery equipment for the battery.

Arriving at Memphis, Bankhead first went to the law office of L. J. Dupree at the corner of Madison and Bank. Dupree was on the city council and was a good friend of Bankhead's. They had met in 1856 when Bankhead had been the city attorney and Dupree had first won a city council seat. Bankhead explained the need to get artillery equipment and hoped Dupree could help. Dupree had connections in the city, and his son, Lewis J. Dupree, age thirty-one, owned an auction house and knew where to find various articles. Bankhead recruited young Dupree so that he could freely travel between Memphis and Fort Pillow. However, it was agreed that, once Bankhead received his desired equipment, Dupree would drop out of the battery. Bankhead accepted this arrangement, and nothing more was said. Dupree and Bankhead would make several trips between Memphis and Fort Pillow in July.[39]

After stopping at his home to see his wife and daughter, Bankhead began to look for recruits. He specifically wanted to find artificers. He was successful in finding three men throughout the month whom he recruited

---

[38]   Ibid., plate 5.

[39]   John Mark Long, "Memphis Mayors 1827–1866: A Collective Study" (The West Tennessee Historical Society Papers, 1998), 127–128; Seventh U.S. Census; Memphis City Directory 1859; *Instruction for Field Artillery* plate 80.

as artificers. He also recruited one man as farrier (a man who shoes horses). He also recruited five more privates; four of them were Irish immigrants. Thus nine more men were added to the rolls. It still was not enough, but time was running out. Bankhead knew that the battery would be moving to engage the enemy at the end of July.[40]

On July 13, Leonidas Polk, who had been made major general in charge of the Mississippi River defense, moved into the Gayoso Hotel and made it his headquarters. Polk had been appointed by the Confederate government to take over the command of Gideon Pillow, who would now be his second. Polk would command the forces in the Mississippi Valley until his West Point classmate, Albert Sidney Johnston, arrived later in the fall. Polk, after graduation from West Point, became an Episcopal priest with his church at Ashwood near Columbia, Tennessee. Later he became the missionary bishop of the Southwest and moved to Louisiana. As the war progressed, Bankhead would get to know him very well. Knowing of his arrival, Bankhead sent Dupree to see Polk. The following letter dated July 13, 1861, was personally delivered to Polk at the Gayoso House:

Gen. Polk,
Dear Sir,

We marched to the city this morning at 5, o'clock & would state that our orders from Gen. Pillow requires our immediate return. One of us Mr. Johnson is sent here to get four horses for Capt Hamilton's heavy battery, sabers, and the other guns. Mr. Dupree, comes to buy horses & take up the caissons of Bankhead's Flying Artillery. We would be pleased to have an audience with you at the first practicable moment. Mr. Johnson is required to return to New Madrid today.

Very Respectfully,
L. J. Dupree of
Bankheads Artillery
T. M. Johnson of
Southern Guards[41]

---

[40] CCSR m268 rolls 97–98.

[41] Ibid., roll 97.

Through Dupree's efforts, Bankhead was able to acquire the caissons and eighty-four horses for the battery.

July finally saw the arrival of light artillery pieces for Bankhead's Battery. The Quinby & Robinson Company on Poplar Street in Memphis usually made steam engines and saw mills and had a contract to produce six cannon for Byrne's Battery in Kentucky. They had first tried to make a thirty-two-pound seacoast gun, but failing that, concentrated on light artillery, particularly U. S. Model 1841 six-pounders and twelve-pound howitzers. The first gun was completed on May 31, and production increased throughout June. Most of the guns were made of bronze, and the company required large amounts of copper, tin, and zinc. Quinby & Robinson produced a few iron guns as well. Cannon carriages were produced at other locations in the city and delivered to Quinby & Robinson where they would mount the cannon tube. Then they would be delivered either to the railroad or to the wharf for shipping. The Confederate government paid for the guns partly in cash and partly in raw materials. A fire destroyed the foundry and shops on September 30, 1861. Although they would rebuild and start producing cannon again in November, the production records were destroyed that showed which guns went to Bankhead's Battery.[42]

With the arrival of guns, limbers, and caissons the drill of the men began to take on a more serious note. The detachments numbered the men from one to eight and perfected the drill called "school of the piece." The number indicated the position the men served on the gun. Standing in their double ranks with the even numbered men in the front, odd in the rear, either in front of the gun or behind the limber, the sergeant commanded, "Cannoneers, to your posts!" The corporal then commanded, "Detachment, right face, forward march!"[43]

The men proceeded to the gun with the odd numbered men to the right of the gun and the even numbered men to the left. At the command, "Commence firing!" the corporal, also called the gunner, took command of the piece. He commanded, "Load!" Man number one stood even with the hub of the wheel and moved to the front of the muzzle. His equipment was an eight-foot-long pole with a rammer at one end and sponge at the

---

[42] Larry J. Daniel and Riley W. Gunter, *Confederate Cannon Foundries* (Union City, Tennessee: Pioneer Press, 1977), 48–49; Larry J. Daniel, *Cannoneers in Gray* (Tuscaloosa: University of Alabama Press, 2005), 16.

[43] *Instructions for Field Artillery*, 107–117.

other. Number two, also even with the hub, proceeded to the muzzle and inserted a projectile attached to a cloth gunpowder cartridge, and number one rammed it down the tube. The cloth powder bag, which held about a pound of black powder, was attached to the shell with a tin strap. The rounds were solid shot, case shot, or canister.[44]

At the same time, number three held his left thumb over the touchhole. He had a small leather pad over his thumb that would provide a good seal on the vent so air could not escape during the ramming of the round. Number three also had a brass pick about six inches long in his right hand that he would use to puncture the gunpowder cartridge when ordered to do so.[45]

Number four stood fast, taking out the lanyard that was made of stout twine with an iron or brass hook tied to the end. He took out a copper or brass friction primer from his leather tube pouch and attach it to the hook. When the round had been rammed, numbers one and two returned to their positions at the hub of the wheel. The corporal stepped in to aim the gun from behind the tube while number four went to the handspike attached to the end of the trail of the cannon carriage (the part that rests on the ground). The corporal adjusted the elevation with the elevating screw while looking through the pendulum hausse (a free-swinging sighting piece), which had been placed on top of the rear of the cannon barrel. He indicated right or left to number four, who changed the direction of aiming. When finished they resumed their positions, and the gunner cried out, "Ready!" Numbers one and two covered their ear nearest to the muzzle, number three picked the cartridge attached to the round, and number four inserted the primer and stepped back to fire. The primer was a small brass tube about two inches long filled with fine gunpowder. Beeswax kept the powder from falling out the bottom, and a wire was crimped at the top. When the wire was pulled out with a lanyard, the friction caused by its removal ignited the powder in the tube and set the cannon off. At the command "Fire!" the gun recoiled perhaps a dozen feet and had to be repositioned before loading the next round. The crew then continued the same procedure with number one sponging out the

---

[44]   Ibid.

[45]   Ibid.

bore with water to put out any burning embers that might remain in the tube before ramming the next round.[46]

The men numbered five, six, seven, and eight did their duty at the limber, which was positioned about twenty feet behind the gun. Number five brought the round from the limber to number two, who put the round down the tube. Number six set the fuse for an explosion. This type of shell is called case shot. There were several types of fuse. A paper fuse, roughly three inches long, was filled with gunpowder. Marks on the fuse indicated where it should be cut for a time of flight for the case shot to explode—from one to six seconds. The fuse was pounded into a hole in the shell with a wooden fuse mallet. A Bormann fuse was a round metal disk with powder in it. Number six punched a hole in the fuse at the recognized time of flight. He then gave it to number seven who gave it to number five. Number eight read the chart under the limber chest lid that gave the information about elevation and time of flight and shouted it out so the gunner and number six knew the elevation and amount of time to set on the fuse. Number eight got the distance from a lieutenant, who used a stadia to estimate the distance to the target. A stadia is a flat brass plate with distances marked on a sliding scale. Holding the stadia at arm's length toward the target, the officer adjusted the scale to get the approximate distance. Officers and sergeants watched for the explosion of the shell. If it was not on target, they made adjustments verbally to the crew for the next round. Solid shot, a non-exploding shell, and canister (a tin can full of musket balls) did not require any preparation before firing.[47]

The men of each detachment learned all of the positions, and if the command "Load in detail!" was given, they went through each step of loading by the numbers. This command was never given in battle, as it was a slow and very precise process. The sergeant commanding "Change posts march!" rotated the men in a clockwise direction. Number one took the place of three, number three took eight, number eight took six, number six took seven, number seven took five, number five took four, number four took two, and number two took one. Taking the guns to the riverbank and firing them gave the men much delight, and Bankhead and his staff soon learned which men were best at each position.[48]

---

[46] Ibid.

[47] Ibid.

[48] Ibid., 117–119.

Some of the men were deemed to be drivers either because of their horse knowledge or because they were not as adept in the school of the piece. These men were instructed in the care of horses, with a focus on proper fodder, water, and grooming to start. Then they had to learn to drive a team and do the maneuvers. The drivers drilled by driving the caissons down the road from Fort Pillow into the countryside and practicing the maneuvers under the command of a sergeant. They practiced wheeling, right and left about, countermarching, and moving from column to line of battle with empty chests on the caissons so as to not overburden the horses. This was called the school of the battery.[49]

During July, Bankhead pressed Colonel McCown for a bugler. Bankhead was able to borrow a bugler from some of the other batteries at Fort Pillow one once in a while. Bankhead had been unable to locate any musicians while in Memphis, as they had all been taken by the infantry in early May. In battle, the men would need to know a few calls like "Commence firing" and "Cease fire." Other bugle calls could be heard in the other camps. "Boots and saddles" was always the call for the men to prepare for battle or the march. Some of the calls were for the men such as "reveille," "sick call," "fatigue call," "dinner call," and "tattoo." Others were for the drivers, such as "watering call." During the march there were calls like "walk," "trot," "left oblique," and "halt."[50]

On July 29, McCown came through with a bugler for the battery. Frank A. Pfaffenschlager, a forty-seven-year-old music teacher, became a member of the battery. He had enlisted in Memphis on May 15 and had been serving with the infantry at Randolph. He arrived in camp just in time to leave, as orders had been given to board the steamers on the river, and the men were taking down the tents and packing up the equipment. The men had had two months of training and learning the basics of army life and artillery drill. Now they loaded the guns and equipment onto the steamers and headed for New Madrid, Missouri.[51]

---

49   Ibid., 141–173, 274–280.

50   Ibid., plates 81–88.

51   CCRS roll 98.

The Officers

Bankhead's Battery was still officially First Tennessee Artillery Regiment Battery B, but nobody called it that. In fact, the First Tennessee Artillery Regiment existed in name only. Colonel John McCown made no effort to combine the eight companies at Fort Pillow into a cohesive unit. In fact, General Pillow had given no orders in regards to artillery organization. The men, having been told that Bankhead was forming a flying artillery unit, often referred to themselves as Bankhead's Flying Artillery. The reality was that Bankhead would never be able to form a flying artillery battery, because there just were not enough horses available for all of the men to be mounted. Once horses were available, the men were already drilling as light artillery, and it became necessary to begin the training of drivers. Some official records show the unit as Bankhead's Battery B, and sometimes as Battery C. This confusion comes from a lack of organization. McCown was more interested in a promotion and soon would be transferred to the infantry. General Pillow lost his top command spot to Leonidas Polk, and so the artillery continued to train on their own. Neither Pillow nor Polk had given any directions for an artillery organization.[52]

Smith P. Bankhead was one of the few officers at Fort Pillow with any military experience. The other battery commanders often called upon him for advice. While in Memphis, Bankhead heard about the coming of Leonidas Polk to take command of the Provisional Army of Tennessee even before this was published in the *Appeal*. With some of the other commanders in the city, Bankhead signed a letter requesting that Gideon Pillow be retained as army commander:

Memphis, July 5, 1861

Hon. Secretary of War of the Confederate States;

Sir: The undersigned have learned with deep regret, in an unofficial manner, that the forces and military command of this portion of the Confederate States has been tendered by the Government to another than Major-General Pillow. We do not desire to reflect upon the discretion exercised by the Government in placing a distinguished citizen of Louisiana in command of

---

52   CCRS m268 rolls 97–98.

the valley of the Mississippi, but we cannot hesitate to express satisfaction that it would have afforded the citizens and Army of Tennessee that this command should have been given to their own distinguished fellow-citizen Major-General Pillow. His indomitable energy, his sleepless vigilance, his masterly ability, as displayed before our eyes since he took command of our army, has won for him the esteem of all, and we think fairly entitles him to lead the army which he has created. In a few weeks he has brought into the field a force of more than 20,000, armed and equipped, ready to meet the enemy. Taking command without ordnance, commissary, or quartermaster's stores, he is now fully prepared not only to resist but to make invasion. We feel that no eulogium that we could make would do justice to the services that he has rendered the cause, but we simply and respectfully to suggest to the Secretary of War, and through him to the President, that the appointment of Major-General Pillow to the command of the active force on the banks of the Mississippi would be but an act of justice to him, and would give the greatest satisfaction to the force thus placed under his command.

William T. Brown
Smith P. Bankhead
P. Smith
M.C. Gallaway
Jno. D. Martin
Benj. S. Dill[53]

Nothing came of this letter, but Bankhead was not afraid to get involved in politics. He knew full well that the army was not in the condition described, as he was in Memphis to procure the equipment that Pillow had not provided, but was merely sticking up for a fellow Tennessean.[54]

First Lieutenant Humes was beginning to show signs of leadership. He proved himself to be quick to learn and was soon looked upon for advice from the second lieutenants. Bankhead felt comfortable leaving

---

[53] OR XII, vol. 4, 363–4.

[54] *Memphis Appeal* July 7, 1861.

him in charge while he was in Memphis. McDavitt and Scott were likeable men and were seen with the men constantly during drill and training. Greenlaw, on the other hand, although present daily, was showing signs of malaise, as he was struggling with some of the commands. As he was younger than most of the privates, he found it hard to gain the respect of the men, especially when he was officer of the day.[55]

The Enlisted Men

Smith P. Bankhead recruited only two men in June, as training was the foremost activity and required all of his attention. Ten men were recruited in July. Only one of the new men was married, making only six married non-officers. The average age of this group of men was just over twenty-seven, making the average age of all of the men from Memphis just over twenty-eight and a half. The Irish immigrants still dominated the ranks, but more men would be needed, and many captains had recruited Memphis very heavily.[56]

As the men learned the drill, it became apparent that shorter men had difficulty serving as number one and number three, and although every man needed to learn all of the positions, the taller men were usually assigned these positions. There was also a need to promote a few men so that there would be six sergeants and six corporals. This would provide the necessary command structure for six guns. There was a need for three more corporals, and it was decided to promote Edward Cearns, John Hayes, and William O'Donnell to that position. Two additional sergeants were created for Charles Cooley and Albert Sailhorst.[57]

On July 7, 1861, the Shelby County sheriff came into the camp and arrested Private John Rooney. It is not recorded what the charges were, but he never returned and was carried on the rolls until December 31, 1861. That left forty-eight privates, minus the bugler, to drill on the guns, but not enough men to be drivers. All of the men practiced driving the teams, and enough men would be assigned to the vehicles as needed. More men were still needed, and Bankhead knew he still had to do more recruiting.[58]

---

[55]   Ibid., July 21, 1861.

[56]   CCRS m268 roll 97–98.

[57]   Ibid.

[58]   Ibid.

Camp life was often very tedious and was filled with boredom, mischief, fear, and disease. The day started at 5:00 a.m. with roll call. Roll call was required for all of the men except those on picket or guard duty or men on sick call. The first sergeant would read the roll and give any orders of the day. The men then went to their mess area to boil coffee and cook any breakfast they might have. There could be as many as five drill sessions each day lasting about two hours each. On some days, knot tying was taught to the men. Between drills, the men cleaned the camp, collected firewood, dug sinks (latrines), or carried water. Clean water was a major concern in the prevention of disease. A spring at Fort Pillow kept the men healthy, as none went sick in the hot summer sun.[59]

Around 5:30 p.m. the drills ended and the men returned to camp for another roll call. Here the officer of the day gave any needed orders and lectured the men. This could be praise for a job well done, but was probably more likely a rebuke for being lax in the drill, or for back talk, being untidy in line, not saluting properly, or being boisterous in camp. This preaching could be on fifty different topics, all bearing on the characteristics of a good soldier. They would then be dismissed to prepare their evening meal. The food at Fort Pillow was adequate. There was either beef or pork daily, with rations of bread and a vegetable (usually beans). The men also received flour, coffee, salt, and sometimes sugar and vinegar. Dried beans, peas, or corn were also rationed out. The men were not allowed to leave the camp, and alcohol and gambling were forbidden. At around 8:30 p.m., there would be a final roll call. The men would then have thirty minutes to put away their things, tidy their beds, or make a nature call before retiring to sleep.[60]

---

[59] William C. Davis, "Life in Army Camp," *Encyclopedia of the Civil War* (The Civil War Society, 2002), 86; John D Billings, *Hard Tack and Coffee or The Unwritten Story of Army Life* (Williamsburg, Massachusetts: Corner House Publishers, 1984), 164–197; Daniel, *Cannoneers in Gray*, 11.

[60] Ibid.

Chapter 3

New Madrid-Columbus August 1861–March 1862

First Division Western Department	Bankhead's Battery B
Major General Leonidas Polk Brigadier General Gideon Pillow Major Alexander Stewart Bankhead's Battery B	Captain Smith P. Bankhead First Lieutenant W.Y.C. Humes Second Lieutenant James C. McDavitt Second Lieutenant William B. Greenlaw Jr. Second Lieutenant William L. Scott First Sergeant Samuel Brown Second Sergeant Lewis Putney Sergeant Charles Cooley Sergeant Lewis Merchant Sergeant John Purcell Sergeant Albert Sailhorst Sergeant James Welsh Corporal Edward Cearns Corporal John Hayes Corporal Miles Kehoe Corporal James McLaughlin Corporal William O'Donnell Corporal Patrick Talty 50 privates

Orders were given on July 27, 1861, that the forces at Fort Pillow and Fort Wright were to break camp and prepare to board steamers the next day for a movement to New Madrid, Missouri. Eight packet steamers would take the first wave of 6,000 troops under the command of General Pillow. Only two infantry regiments and the heavy artillery gunners would remain at Fort Pillow. Bankhead's Battery would come up with the steamboats in the second wave planned for the following day. This involved the moving of guns, limbers, caissons, as well as the horses and all of the camp equipment onto the transport—and unloading it upon arrival at New Madrid. General Polk, with the approval of Governor Harris, was about to take the offensive.[61]

New Madrid was a sleepy little town founded by the Spanish in 1789. In 1861 it was a hamlet of a few hundred people who eagerly welcomed their Tennessee brothers. A permanent camp was not being planned, so the soldiers moved west or north of the town and set up temporary camps, as they were to move out as soon as everything was ready. Already several local men had come forward to join the expedition. These men were rounded up and sent to the units that needed men the most. Two men were enrolled in the battery on July 30.[62]

On July 31, seven men from the same township joined together. Their story is typical of the local Missouri men. The leader of the group was L. R. Richardson. His name was Lorenzo, but he went by Ranz. He was born in Tennessee but was now living in St. James Township in Mississippi County, Missouri. He and the six others had walked the twelve miles to join the army and were enrolled by Bankhead. The men were all rural farmers with sympathies for the South. Ranz's two best friends, brothers Andrew and Francis Marion Oliver, joined with him as well as brothers John W. and William J. Cooper. When they heard of the troop arrival in New Madrid, they did not hesitate to join the ranks. Throughout the month of August, a total of twenty men would join the battery at New

---

61 Ibid.; Larry J. Daniel and Lynn N. Bock, *Island No. 10* (Tuscaloosa: The University of Alabama Press, 1996), 1.

62 CCSR m268 roll 97–98.

Madrid, along with one man from Sykeston, Missouri, bringing the total number of privates to seventy.[63]

The movement toward St. Louis never happened. Faulty intelligence and lack of transport delayed any rapid advance, and sickness began to plague the army. Polk could gather only 203 wagons when he had planned for 314. Support from Missouri commanders was grossly overinflated, and now measles had broken out in the army. The planned movement was cancelled.

With no activity at New Madrid, Bankhead determined that the men should drill and not to be lax in their duties. Other batteries followed suit. On August 3, Private Joseph Garey of Hudson's Mississippi Battery, recorded in his diary: "The weather is scorching hot. Two or three of Captain Bankhead's Artillery dropped on the ground from excessive heat & our men were not far behind them."[64] Drilling in the heat could take its toll, but Bankhead believed the men must be ready. There were also many false alarms, which found the men in the battery scrambling to get into position. Private Garey also recorded the following in his diary:

> We took up our position on the wharf, unlimbered our guns & prepared for action, when up came our rival company (Capt. Bankhead's) under full headway, but they soon found that we had stolen a march on him by being a little quicker than he was & he had to send three guns of his battery to the rear, about ten miles, & take a position on the edge of the swamp, where they were not very likely to get a chance to show their prowess, which was everything but gratifying to him.[65]

Then on August 9, 1861, the men under Polk's command officially were enrolled into the Confederate Army. On that day, eighty-five officers and

---

[63] Ibid.; Jerry Herd (descendant of L.R. Richardson) personal correspondence with author, April 2004 and March 2013. Richardson married the Olivers' sister Elizabeth in 1869. Francis Marion Oliver died in 1940 at the age of 99. See Appendix 3.

[64] David A. Welker, ed., *A Keystone Rebel* (Gettysburg, Pennsylvania: Thomas Publications, 1996), 17.

[65] Ibid.

men of Bankhead's Battery were officially under Confederate authority. Only Michael Nason was missing on the rolls.[66]

On September 2, 1861, a small force of Federal troops occupied Belmont, Missouri, across the Mississippi from Columbus, Kentucky, and made a demonstration opposite of Paducah. Polk now took the initiative and ordered Pillow to seize Columbus. Pillow moved upon Hickman, Kentucky, that night and Columbus on September 3. The Federals, under Major General U. S. Grant, countered this move by seizing Paducah on September 6. Polk had made a bold move, which Jefferson Davis would defend, but he violated Kentucky's neutrality without anyone's approval and then failed to move on Paducah. Kentucky would turn to the union, and Paducah would become a Federal base for operations on the Tennessee River. Columbus, however, would become a Confederate fortress and effectively block the Mississippi.[67]

Bankhead's Battery had been loaded onto the packet boats and was steaming towards Hickman, Kentucky. The fifteen-mile trip took about four hours, and the men either slept or watched the river on the crowded boats. As they traveled east to the first bend in the river, they passed Island Number Ten where a small work party was building some defensive works. Then they sailed north and arrived at Hickman.

After the packet boats were unloaded and everyone was getting in order to march to Columbus, two Federal gunboats appeared up river. The Confederate gunboat at Hickman opened fire. Soon Captain Bankhead ordered the guns to be in battery. An infantry soldier recorded in his diary, "As soon as the firing opened she [Confederate gunboat] dropped down below us. The enemy came down to within three and one-fourth miles, firing being kept up all the while." Bankhead's Battery fired a few shots but they were all short. About twenty shots were fired before the Federal boats withdrew. This was the first time the men had come under fire. The battery then marched on to Columbus.[68]

---

[66] Daniel and Bock, *Island No. 10*, 3; CCSR m268 roll 97–98.

[67] OR XII pt. 3, 188; Nathaniel Cheairs Hughes, Jr., *The Battle of Belmont* (Chapel Hill: The University of North Carolina Press, 1991), 5.

[68] Lindsley, *The Military Annals of Tennessee*, 790; L. Alex Scarbrough Jr., "Camp Journal of Corporal Lemuel A. Scarbrough, Sr. Company E 'Dixie Rifles' 13th Tennessee Infantry Regiment," *The West Tennessee Historical Society Papers*, vol. LXVI, 2012, 138.

When they boats approached Columbus, the men saw a town of about 150 buildings on the east side of the river nestled low between towering bluffs along the river. South of the town were the Chalk Bluffs, so named because of their bright coffee color. To the north of the town was the Iron Bank, named by Marquette and Joliet because of the hint of iron visible along the bank, which faced north and rose to over one 150 feet above the river.

This position seemed to be perfect. If properly fortified, the location could prevent Union gunboats from moving south. In 1861, Columbus had a population of about 1,000 people and was the terminus of the Memphis and Ohio Railroad. When Bankhead's Battery arrived, they ascended the Iron Bank, which was being fortified for about a mile. The men were instructed to unlimber the guns about three-quarters of a mile from town overlooking the river and to make camp.[69]

The camps at Columbus stretched about a mile long from north to south and 400 to 500 yards from east to west. To make room for this camp, the trees needed to be cleared. This also opened clear firing areas to the east. Already soldiers were clearing the forest, and soon the men began using the wood to put floors in their tents. Other soldiers were placing artillery along the top of Iron Bluff and building embrasures. Guns were being delivered at the wharf and coming up the railroad from Memphis. Polk would soon have 11,000 men and 140 guns, both heavy and light, at Columbus. The men of the battery would be busy for weeks making Columbus into a fortress. However, Bankhead still did not have enough men, but for now, being stationary would require fewer men. A six-gun battery needed 120 to 150 men, and the horses still needed to be kept in shape, fed, and groomed.[70]

Bankhead recruited a few men at Columbus, some being transfers from the infantry. Although Bankhead was responsible for recruiting, the Confederate Army had taken over recruiting throughout the South. The following advertisement appeared in the *Memphis Daily Appeal*:

Light Artillery

I need fifty men to fill vacancies in my command. They are wanted for immediate active service in the field. The Battery is

---

[69]   Hughes, *The Battle of Belmont*, 36.

[70]   Ibid., 36–37.

otherwise well equipped with horse, guns, Ac. Apply at Kendig & Cooks, No. 35 Front Row, where recruits will be sworn in, and furnished with transportation to this place.

Smith N. Bankhead
Captain Comm' Light Battery
Columbus, Ky.

This ad resulted in only three recruits from Memphis. Others came in from recruiters in Nashville and Jackson. By December 8, 1861, thirty-six additional men were added to the battery.[71]

Polk was determined to hold Columbus. He ordered guns to be placed in a three-tiered defense facing the river. Thus boats could be hit horizontally as well as with plunging fire from above. Forts were constructed at various intervals by filling corn sacks with sand and piling them up and covering them with dirt taken from a ditch ten feet deep and eight feet wide in front of them. There were no slave laborers available, so the men did all of the work. The men called the forts "bull pen forts." Overall, the forts, works, and entrenchments extended for four miles. In addition, Polk had a giant chain stretched across the river and buoyed to a series of rafts and secured by huge anchor on each shore. He also placed numerous mines, called torpedoes, in the river as well as placing mines in the woods northeast of the fortifications[72].

Polk also changed the command structure of his force. Pillow was still Polk's second in command, and he commanded the largest brigade. McCown was promoted to brigadier general and commanded the regiments facing the river and the left defenses. He still oversaw the artillery, but Major Alexander Stewart was the overall artillery commander. Stewart was in direct command of the heavy batteries, and Captain S. D. H. Hamilton commanded the Tennessee Siege Battery. Bankhead commanded one of the four light artillery batteries that fired toward the river. Colonel John S. Bowen commanded the third brigade, and Brigadier General Benjamin Franklin Cheatham commanded the other brigade as well as the right wing and the land defenses. Three other batteries were placed in the works facing

---

[71] CCRS m268 rolls 97–98; *Memphis Appeal*, September 18, 1861. See Appendix 4.

[72] Hughes, *The Battle of Belmont*, 36.

east in case of an attack from Paducah. More artillery and infantry were on their way to Columbus.[73]

The men did not have long to wait to see some action. On September 8 the Federal timber-clad *Lexington* made an appearance before Columbus and opened fire upon the works. The *Lexington* was too far away for Bankhead's guns to participate, but the heavy guns at the fortress sent enough shot and shell her way that the *Lexington* withdrew, gaining the knowledge that the Confederates were at Columbus to stay.

These raids by union boats would continue sporadically for the next two months. A reporter from the Memphis *Avalanche* was present during one of these forays, and he published the following story on September 25:

> Three different times at New Madrid, Hickman and now at this place [Columbus], I have witnessed the attacks made upon our troops by Northern gunboats. The effect has been, apparently, only to stimulate the desire of our men to have an actual encounter with the enemy. The shells last thrown towards us were directed to the very spot where I was standing, occupied by Bankhead's battery on a lofty bluff, half a mile or more above the village of Columbus. The Mississippi at this place runs east and west for about two miles, then striking the bluff bank; it makes a right angle running due south. Our battery is so located below the bend, that it is invisible to them on a descending boat till after the point has been passed, which is within a mile and a half of our guns. It may be added that we are one hundred feet above the water's edge, on a perpendicular line, while the Missouri shore is below high water mark, like that on the Arkansas side at Memphis. Our brass pieces have a range of fifteen hundred yards, about the distance to the point, from behind which the gunboat throws forty-two or sixty-four pound shells. One passed far below us, another within one or two hundred yards, both having exploded far above the bluff. The fragments were scattered over the water, some of them went whistling above our heads with a noise like the whirling of a partridge when suddenly frightened … Our men stood quietly by their pieces awaiting the appearance of the gunboat from beyond

---

73   Ibid. 36; OR X pt.4, 699.

the point, but she came not; then they swore vigorously as ever soldiers were want to do when disappointment overtakes them.[74]

During this encounter, Mrs. Bankhead and little Ada were present but did not seek shelter as they observed the fireworks. The men did not like garrison duty and waiting for the enemy to approach them. An anonymous cannoneer from the battery went on to say, "We shall not remain inactive. Idleness costs too much. We should [attack] Paducah, Cairo and Bird's Point. The sooner this is done the more easily will success be achieved and the less costly will be the battle. The strength of our enemy is being constantly augmented." Obviously the spirit of the men in Bankhead's Battery was to attack and end this war. However, Polk was not interested in attacking and continued to fortify Columbus.[75]

On October 24, 1861, Bankhead's Battery had its first casualty of war. Dennis Leary was wounded during drill when a Parrott six-pounder burst. The new Columbus newspaper, *Daily Confederate News*, was the first to carry the story. In Memphis the *Appeal* said, "A Parrott gun belonging to Bankhead's artillery exploded yesterday afternoon, while the company were practicing, breaking the arm and otherwise slightly injuring a private of the company, whose name I have been unable to procure. The arm is broken near the elbow, and it is feared that amputation will be found necessary."[76] The *Appeal* followed up a few days with a story entitled "Irish Humor and Coolness" making fun of the incident:

> Just after the bursting of one of Capt. Bankhead's six-pounder cannon a few days since, several Irishmen were sitting off some distance, and were covered with the dirt thrown up by one of the fragments which had buried itself at their feet. On hearing of the accident one of the number jumped to the place, and removing the rubbish, took out the piece-some ten pounds in weight-and ran to a loose heap of dirt close by and began burying it. Michael, who had not yet uncrossed his legs, exclaimed: 'An' what in the h-ll, Pat, will ye be afther in burying the like o' that, before Misther Bankhead has seen after its mending?' 'Och, an' is it any

---

[74]   *Memphis Avalanche*, September 25, 1861.

[75]   Ibid; Hughes, *The Battle of Belmont*, 5.

[76]   *Memphis Appeal,* October 25, 1861.

yer bissness?' replies Pat, at the same continuing in a soliloquizing tone: 'Ates me that will write this very night to Mary Delone, an' put the piece in my letter and tell her I found the Yankees wid the gun an' took it away from 'em and' broke the same against a tree.[77]

The term *Parrott* was generally used in the South to identify any rifled iron cannon. The cause of the accident was not determined; however, it could have been caused by the use of small-grained rifle powder, as it was known that there was a shortage at this time of the large-grain cannon powder. The small grain burns faster and hotter than the large grain. Also, this was an iron gun, and the iron used may have been inferior in quality. Another iron gun exploded on November 7 during the Battle of Belmont in the Point Coupee Battery, and in Jackson's Battery, three men were killed and one wounded when one of their Parrotts burst after firing just two rounds. They all had received guns from Quinby & Robinson as had Bankhead. Bankhead's Battery soon had a replacement bronze gun and would never use an iron again.[78]

Dennis Leary was sent to Memphis where he was hospitalized, and he did lose his arm. Since he was the first casualty in the battery, and not many men had been killed or wounded in the war yet, Bankhead sponsored a fund-raising event to help with Leary's expenses. The following article appeared in the *Appeal*:

The Wounded Artilleryman.—In response to an appeal of Colonel Bankhead, on behalf of Private Leary of his company, who has lost an arm by the bursting of a cannon at Columbus, the theatrical company that has been performing at Odd Fellows Hall will this evening play the drama of "Retributing" and the farce of "The Secret," the proceeds of the performance to be for the benefit of the unfortunate Leary. Between the pieces, the Inkermann Zouaves will sing some of their best songs. This is an occasion, which particularly appeals to the Memphis public. Mr. Leary being one of our citizens wounded while in his country's

[77] Ibid., November 2, 1861.

[78] *Daily Confederate News*, October 24, 1861; *Louisville Daily Courier*, October 26, 1861; Hughes, *The Battle of Belmont*, 67; Daniel, *Cannoneers in Gray*, 17.

service in a manner to disable him for life. The dramatic company we learn will perform again on Saturday night.[79]

Sympathy like this would be hard to find near the end of the war.

At daybreak on Thursday, November 7, Major Henry Winslow woke up General Polk and informed him that scouts reported gunboats upriver and transports landing troops on the Missouri shore. Polk issued a number of orders and headed up to the forts on the Iron Banks. Drums were heard in the camps, and the cry "Turn out! Turn out!" had men scurrying about gathering ammunition and falling in to formation. Fearing the Missouri move was a diversion and the real attack would be on the Kentucky side, Polk sent out several regiments from the camp to the northeast to check for signs of the enemy. Bankhead's men were already forming up near their guns on the Iron Banks.[80]

Around 8:30 a.m., two timber-clad boats, the *Lexington* and the *Tyler*, rounded Belmont Point about four miles upriver in full few of Bankhead's Battery. They moved toward the fortifications and then began sailing in a tight circle all the while lobbing shells at the fortifications. Bankhead's light guns opened fire but could not achieve the range; all of the shots fell short. The heavy guns of the forts were all overshooting. During the firing, a Parrott gun burst in the Point Coupee Battery killing two and wounding one. These were the only casualties in this engagement. Confederate firepower was impressive, but the accuracy was very poor. All of the drilling had made the crews efficient at their loading and firing skills, but range finding and target plotting were something to be desired.[81]

After about thirty minutes, the boats withdrew behind the bend, but the heavy guns continued to fire. Fearing a lucky shot might hit the transports, all of the boats withdrew out of range of the heavy guns. Then the timber-clads returned, and, using the tight circle maneuver, again began to shell the fortifications. This went on for some time until the *Tyler* was hit by a solid shot that killed one man and injured two. Then the boats broke off the engagement and withdrew out of range.[82]

---

[79] *Memphis Appeal*, November 8, 1861.

[80] Hughes, *The Battle of Belmont*, 60–61, 66.

[81] Ibid., 60–66.

[82] Ibid.

On the Missouri shore, the Battle of Belmont was in progress. U. S. Grant had landed about 3,000 troops and began to engage the Confederate force. Captain Bankhead now directed his guns to shell the woods across the river where Federal troops were believed to be moving. There is no indication that this firing had any effect. Fearing that Confederate troops could also be hit, Bankhead ordered, "Cease fire!"

The battle raged through the morning with Grant capturing the Confederate camp and overrunning a battery of artillery before Confederate reinforcements were ferried over the river and counter attacked. When Polk saw the camp at Belmont being burned and gray-clad soldiers running into the woods, he ordered the Columbus guns to open fire on the old Confederate camp. This firing caused the Federal troops to retire into the woods for safety, and by 2:00 p.m. Grant ordered his troops to return to the transports. This was the end of Bankhead's Battery's participation in the Battle of Belmont.[83]

---

[83]   Ibid., 118.

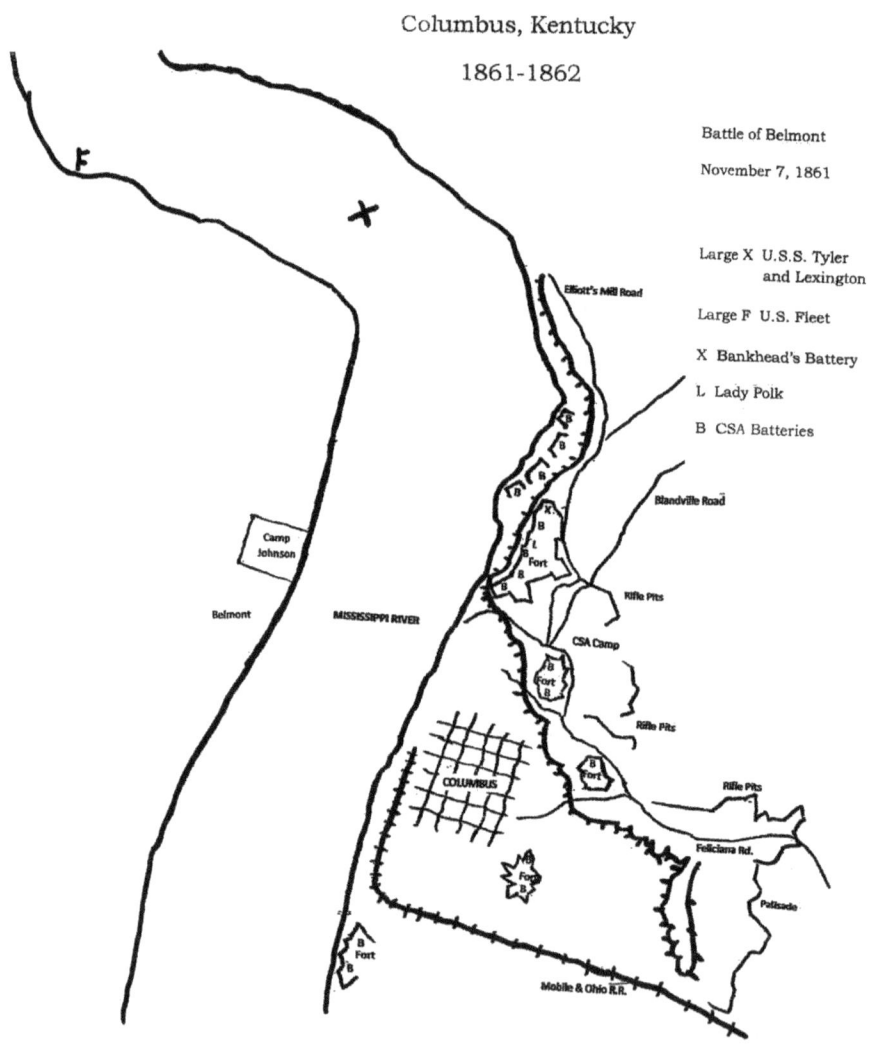

Columbus, Kentucky

1861-1862

Battle of Belmont

November 7, 1861

Large X U.S.S. Tyler
                and Lexington

Large F U.S. Fleet

X Bankhead's Battery

L Lady Polk

B CSA Batteries

The battle raged for the rest of the day. More Confederate reinforcements were sent across the river under the command of General Cheatham. Grant was forced to fight his way back to the transports. The Federals were routed and running for the ships with the commands intermingled. The men scampered onto any boat available and cast off in such haste that many men were left behind. The Confederates fired upon the boats until the timber-clads began firing canister upon the shore. It was now dusk, and the battle was over.

The next day Lieutenant Humes took a party of men from the battery to the battlefield on burial detail. The dead and wounded were everywhere—in the woods, sitting beside trees or fences, or out in the cornfields. Some wounds were ghastly, and some bodies had been torn to pieces by cannon balls. The Confederate dead were taken across the river and buried close to the camps. The wounded were taken to the hospital in Columbus and later shipped to the hospitals in Memphis. A truce had been agreed upon so that the Federals could claim their own dead and wounded. Even so, about one hundred Federal prisoners were taken that morning.[84]

Artillery practice was ordered for November 11. On that day a tragedy occurred in Jackson's Battery. The largest gun at Columbus was a 128-pound columbiad nicknamed the "Lady Polk" in honor of the general's wife. This gun was actually an Anderson rifle manufactured at the Tredegar foundry in Richmond, Virginia, and had been the terror of the fortress during the Battle of Belmont. Apparently the gun had remained loaded since the battle and burst on the first shot killing at least eight men. Among the dead was the captain of the battery, William Keiter, and Lieutenant Snowden of Polk's staff. Polk himself was severely shaken, as he had been standing directly behind the gun; he actually turned over command of Columbus to Pillow for a month until he recovered. With the loss of Keiter, Humes was promoted to captain of Jackson's Battery, which became known as the Belmont Battery.[85]

Bankhead's Battery now needed to adjust its staff. Bankhead requested that his battery have two first lieutenants and two second lieutenants like

[84]   Ibid., 178–179.

[85]   John Kelly Ross Jr., *Confederate Columbus and the Story of the "Lady Polk,"* (Clinton, Kentucky, Hickman County Museum, 2003) 5, 12; *Memphis Appeal*, November 14, 1861; Hughes, *The Battle of Belmont*, 191; Connelly, *Army of the Heartland*, 104.

most of the other batteries. This was approved, and McDavitt and Scott were promoted to first lieutenant. Greenlaw remained at second lieutenant, and Lewis Bond, formerly of Jackson's Battery, came to Bankhead as the other second lieutenant.[86]

The building of more fortifications and more drill were the orders for the coming winter. More guns were arriving, including the floating battery *New Orleans*. Additional recruits also arrived to help fill the ranks of the battery. The men were also permitted to build more comfortable shelters than their tents. The Columbus *Daily Confederate News* recorded the activity:

> We passed yesterday through a greater portion of the encampment at this place [Columbus]. Everywhere we noticed the active preparations for going into winter quarters. The soldiers are busy, some chopping round logs, some hauling, others hewing or notching in, and still others making what in Kentucky parlance are called clapboards. The houses are snug looking shanties, of round logs, well arranged for keeping dry. The wind and rain is kept out by mud, or what is called daubing, and a chimney made in old Kentucky fashion, called cut-in-clay, lets out the smoke.[87]

Some 18,000 men now defended Columbus. The winter passed with the men comfortable as could be, but the war was bypassing Columbus. Grant had decided to flank Columbus rather than attack it. On February 6, 1862, Fort Henry on the Tennessee River had fallen, and Fort Donelson on the Cumberland River fell on February 15. Albert Sidney Johnston was forced to withdraw from central Kentucky, and Nashville fell to the Federals on February 25 without anyone firing a shot. Middle Tennessee had no defense, and the Confederate forces were scattered. General Beauregard had arrived in Tennessee to replace Polk at Columbus. Beauregard took command of the forces and ordered the evacuation of Columbus on February 26. The men were ordered to destroy the works and burn their clapboard shelters.

The effect of this order on the Confederate troops was disheartening and demoralizing. Lieutenant William M. Polk wrote:

---

[86]   CCSR m268 rolls 97–98.

[87]   *Daily Confederate News*, November 22, 1861.

There appeared to be a feeling among the men that if they could not make a successful stand in a position upon which they had spent so much time and labor, and upon which they had come to rely even to the extent of a willingness to withstand a siege in it, there was small chance of their being able to acquit themselves creditably in (new) hastily assumed position.[88]

Whether it was a good or bad idea to hold Columbus, the men believed it would have made a good example to have held the post.

Most of the infantry and cavalry would march into West Tennessee, but the artillery would move by boat with most of the guns going to Island Number Ten. Bankhead's Battery was ordered to prepare to move by river to New Madrid with the Second Brigade, commanded by Colonel William E. Travis of the Fifth Tennessee. General Polk's order number 19 had created this brigade, which was made up of the Fourth and Fifth Tennessee and the Twelfth Louisiana infantry regiments. Bankhead's Battery arrived without incident, unlike the Point Coupee Battery, which lost a gun and its ammunition due to a leaky steamer. Before the battery left, Lieutenant Bond returned to the Belmont Battery, which was going to Island Number Ten under the command of Captain Humes, and General Polk's son, William M. Polk was assigned to take his place.[89]

Island Number Ten was the key defensive position on the Mississippi River in the New Madrid area. It commanded an unobstructed view upriver from a point just south of the Tennessee state line. This part of the river was known as the Seven Mile Reach. Island Number Ten was located in the first curve of an inverted *S*. New Madrid was located to the north of Island Number Ten on the north shore of the second curve. To the west of town, Fort Thompson had been built with two regiments of Arkansas troops and a battery of guns. The New Madrid position was the western flank of the Island Number Ten defenses.[90]

General J. P. McCown was in command of the Island Number Ten defenses. He ordered the Second Brigade to New Madrid. Bankhead's

---

[88] William Mecklenburg Polk, M.D., LL.D. *Leonidas Polk: Bishop and General,* in two volumes (London: Longmans, Green, and Co. and New York: 15 East 16th Street, 1893), vol. 2, 79–80.

[89] Daniel, *Cannoneers in Gray,* 21; CCSR 268 roll 98.

[90] Daniel and Bock, *Island No. 10,* 2.

Battery, and the Fifth Tennessee arrived on February 27 and were ordered to the east of town near the mouth of the St. John's Bayou to construct a defensive position. The men set about digging an earthen breastwork soon to become known as Fort Bankhead.[91]

The fort consisted of a long parapet ditch in an irregular line. In front of the fort was a short area of abates of brush and felled trees. The works were about 300 to 400 yards long extending from the river to the east side of town. A series of trenches connected Fort Bankhead to Fort Thompson, which was a four-sided fortification.[92]

Fort Bankhead was a fort in name only. It was poorly fortified. To make it look stronger, Bankhead ordered a number of wooden "Quaker" guns to be placed on the north face of the fort. Two additional regiments from Fort Pillow soon arrived to fill out this garrison. They were the Fortieth Tennessee and a strangely named regiment, the First Alabama, Tennessee, and Mississippi Regiment. This regiment would later be called the Third Confederate Infantry Regiment. About 3,000 troops held this position, of which 132 men were from Bankhead's Battery.[93]

The artillerymen came with complete baggage and set up camp near their guns. As soon as the men had set up their tents, they went to work building defenses. They constructed wooden platforms for the guns. In addition to the six guns of the battery, four thirty-two-pounders were also manned. There was some concern about a protracted engagement, because Bankhead's Battery was stretched to man ten guns, and there were no relays of men to serve the pieces. The men were not informed about strategy, and even the Confederate commanders were uncertain if offensive or defensive operations were being planned. There would be no more reinforcements, and the forces present were too weak to go on the offensive. This became clear when Federal forces began to arrive.[94]

Federal forces had been moving into the area since February 18. Brigadier General John Pope, with about 18,000 men, began arriving on March 2. A reconnaissance force appeared at the outskirts of the town on Sunday, March 2. Captain Bankhead was ordered to move his battery to a position near the sawmill, while Colonel Walker's Fortieth Tennessee was

---

[91]   Ibid.

[92]   Ibid.

[93]   Ibid.; OR VIII, pt. 2, 162–163.

[94]   Daniel and Bock, *Island No. 10*, 2.

ordered to attack. A few rounds were fired by Bankhead's Battery, and the enemy retired. The troops then retired to their positions in Fort Bankhead. This was the only offensive action taken.[95]

On March 4, the Federals returned with artillery and infantry, and an artillery duel commenced for some time. Bankhead's Battery, with the help of six Confederate gunboats, forced the enemy to withdraw. The engagement appeared to be a Federal test of the Confederate defenses, as no assault was planed. On March 6, General Pope captured Point Pleasant south of New Madrid and began to engage the Confederate gunboats. A renewed attack was made on Fort Bankhead on March 7. This has been described in the official records as a "strong advance," but Bankhead's Battery and the gunboat *Pontchartrain* repulsed it. The Federal commander, Brigadier General D. S. Stanley, considered an attack on Fort Bankhead as utterly impossible and called off the attack. Federal casualties amounted to six wounded.[96]

The Federals brought more guns to Point Pleasant on March 8 and 9 and skirmished with Fort Bankhead on March 10. On March 13, around 9:00 a.m., Fort Bankhead was again attacked, and two of the heavy guns were hit and dismantled. Two men were wounded. More heavy Federal guns were brought up to fire upon Fort Thompson.[97]

Bankhead's Battery directed its fire upon the Federal siege guns about half a mile away, striking two twenty-four-pounders and dismantling them. The Federals soon withdrew. Meanwhile, 2,000 troops of Brigadier General John M. Palmer's Indiana Division had gotten within 800 yards due north of Fort Bankhead with orders to attack the fort. Palmer refused to attack, claiming he could not take the fort with the men he had. By noon the Federals had withdrawn. During this engagement, the Confederate boats had come under fire, and the navy was losing its ability to stay in the area of New Madrid.[98]

---

[95]   Ibid. 57–58. OR VIII pt. 2, 129–130.

[96]   Daniel and Bock, *Island No. 10*, 61–65.

[97]   OR VIII pt. 2, 164.

[98]   Ibid., 172; Daniel and Bock, *Island No. 10*, 61–65.

New Madrid, Missouri

March 13, 1862

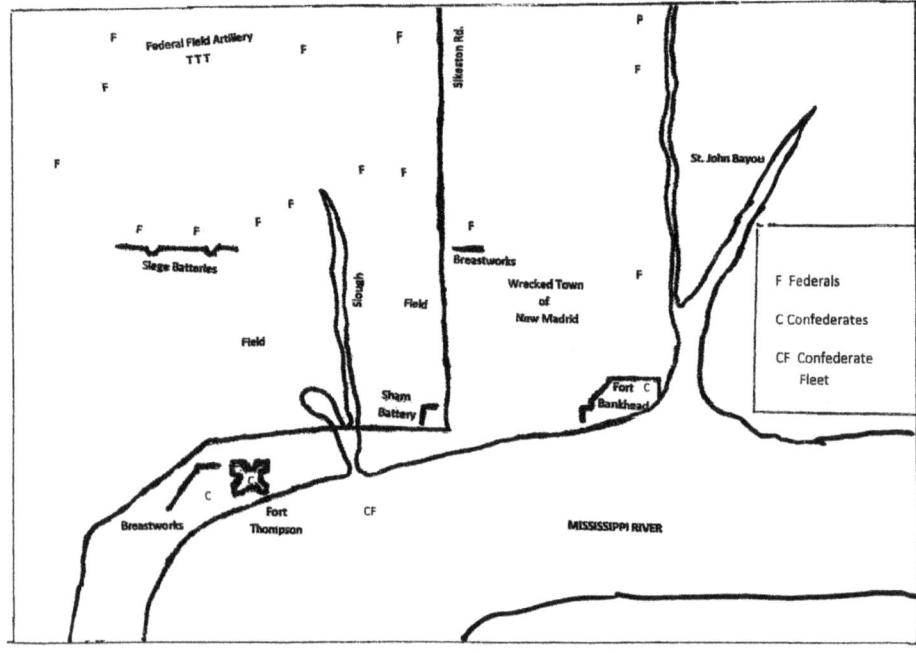

General McCown decided to evacuate New Madrid during the night of March 13. He was criticized by Confederate authorities for giving this order, but the position was untenable. Pope was getting closer and closer to Fort Thompson, and the unarmored Confederate gunboats were under fire. Federal infantry had been massed for an attack, but thanks to Confederate artillery, this force had been dispersed. Very little damage had been done, but the next day did not look good, as no reinforcements were available.[99]

General L.M. Walker was placed in charge of evacuating Fort Bankhead. The steamer *De Soto* was ordered to take Bankhead's Battery with the help of the gunboat *Ohio Belle*. Another gunboat, the *Winchester*, was also ordered to help but did not obey the order and left the area. Guns and equipment were to be loaded first and tents last so as to deceive the enemy.[100]

Panic soon broke out while loading the boats. Lieutenant Polk wrote to his sister: "It was more like a rout than an evacuation. Everyone seemed to be panic struck except a few." It became apparent that there would not be enough room for all the equipment, so the caissons and some limbers with their contents were thrown into the river, and the heavy guns were spiked and some of their carriages damaged. A heavy rainstorm began about 11 p.m., at which time the tents were struck and carried on board wet.[101]

Bankhead's Battery arrived at Fort Pillow the next day. The men had been engaged with the enemy several times and had suffered only two men wounded. General McCown, in his after-action report, commended Captain Bankhead, calling him "a reliable man and a well-instructed soldier." McCown had even considered sending him to Island Number Ten where good artillerymen were needed, but that was not possible now. As the artillery commander of the upper works at New Madrid, Bankhead had worked his men well, and it is very commendable that the position was called Fort Bankhead.[102]

---

[99]   Ibid., 130.

[100]   Ibid., 165.

[101]   William Polk to his sister, March 29, 1862, Polk Letters, University of the South.

[102]   Daniel and Bock, *Island No. 10*, 771.

The Officers

More and more, the name Bankhead's Battery was being used to describe the unit. Bankhead's Battery B was recorded on many company documents. It was becoming the Confederate practice to call an artillery company after the name of the captain. Some organization had finally arrived at Columbus when Polk decided to set up a chain of command and responsibility. While in Columbus, Major Alexander P. Stewart would be the overall artillery commander. Stewart was a very competent commander and would be promoted to brigadier general in the infantry at Shiloh.[103]

Bankhead spent much of his time recruiting and drilling the battery. As more men were recruited, more training was necessary. At Columbus the business of organization settled down, and Bankhead was not able to make trips back to Memphis. Confederate recruiters helped him get the battery almost up to full strength. His wife and daughter came to visit a few times, and that was comforting to him. The battles at Columbus and Fort Bankhead had shown some of his skills. He was cool under pressure and kept the men disciplined. Camp life was easy at Columbus, and the battery was in a static position. Except for an occasion at New Madrid, this was the case for the action in Missouri as well. The artillery had merely been static defenders, and the men itched for some offensive action. Bankhead had received laurels from several superiors and would soon be promoted and placed in charge of an artillery battalion.

The lieutenants of the battery had worked with the men and were developing the skills of gun captains. Much of the paperwork at Columbus fell on the shoulders of the junior officers. The army was a bureaucracy that required these officers to fill out a multitude of forms and reports and submit them to their superiors. Examples of forms were certificate for furlough, certificate for discharge, certificate for disability, requisition for forage, report for duty, requisition for quartermaster stores, and officers pay report. Bankhead's Battery left Fort Pillow in July 1861 with one first lieutenant and three second lieutenants and returned to Fort Pillow eight months later with two first lieutenants and two second lieutenants. Bankhead had asked for this change in structure, but also had some changes that he did not plan on.[104]

---

[103] Ibid., 154; CCSR m268 rolls 97–98.

[104] Ibid.

His good friend Humes had been promoted to captain after the "Lady Polk" explosion and had taken command of Jackson's Heavy Battery. The battery did not go by the name of Humes Company, but instead went by the name Belmont Battery. This was because of the huge 128-pounder gun called the Belmont was in his battery. This gun would burst on the second shot during the upcoming battle. After the evacuation of Columbus, Humes became the artillery commander on Island Number Ten, and after several weeks was forced to surrender unconditionally on April 8, 1862. Humes and the rest of the island defenders became prisoners of war.[105]

James C. McDavitt was promoted to Humes' old position of first lieutenant. McDavitt had already been noticed for promotion in a letter to General Polk from Alexander P. Stewart, the head of artillery at Columbus, dated November 1, 1861. Stewart had recommended McDavitt be promoted to first lieutenant and assigned to a new battery being raised by Captain E. W. Rucker. Nothing had come of this letter before the accident, and Bankhead's immediate need trumped the request. McDavitt was obviously a good officer and well respected.[106]

William L. Scott had also proven to be a good subordinate, and Bankhead offered the other first lieutenant position to this competent officer. This promotion was not without controversy, however, as William B. Greenlaw had seniority over Scott and issued a protest. Polk requested an explanation from Bankhead, and in a three-page letter, Bankhead explained that Greenlaw was the only officer who did not assent to making his enlistment for the duration of the war, and he "stated his determination to seek other occupation on the expiration of his term which was one year." Greenlaw had expressed that he had "fidelity, zeal and sobriety," while Bankhead brought up the "question as to the *competency relationship* of the individuals *and their willingness to serve affecting the men.*" (Emphasis in the original).[107] Bankhead went on to say:

> Mr. Greenlaw had expressed his determination to retire from the service at the expiration of his term … he certainly could not expect to be made second in command, by any organization, which he did not intend or desire to participate in … He is a

---

[105] Daniel and Bock, *Island No. 10*, 123, 146, 148.

[106] Ibid., 97.

[107] CCSR m268 roll 98.

sorry young man—21 years, if that—[who] has seen no service in artillery, except under me; and has not profited by that to the same extent as those who [were] appointed First Lieutenants of my Battery … it is respectfully submitted that the Public interest must not be allowed to suffer in order that individuals may be advanced.[108]

Polk did approve the promotions for both McDavitt and Scott on November 19, and Greenlaw resigned his commission on January 25, 1862, in a letter to Polk in which he stated, "I feel that I cannot serve in a company where I have been superseded and maintain my self-respect." President Davis accepted the resignation on March 8, 1862.[109]

Lewis Bond was serving as a second lieutenant in Jackson's Battery and came over to fill the vacancy in Bankhead's Battery. He served only three months and then returned to his old company while two new second lieutenants joined the unit. The first was Joseph Phillips, who had been one of Polk's recruiters to help fill the artillery ranks at Columbus. Polk had first selected him for recruiting shortly after receiving a letter from N. C. Steverson in Nashville on August 3, 1861. Steverson professed that, "Lieutenant Phillips is one of our most promising young men educated in our military schools … [and] he belongs to one of the best families in Tennessee" Phillips was twenty-two years old and had a young bride back in Nashville. The other was William M. Polk, the son of General Polk, who had been a cadet at VMI. Born in 1844, he was barely eighteen when he got his commission. He had been raised around slaves, and one slave, known as Mammy Betsey, had had a strong influence on his character. General Polk had selected for his son the best artillery captain of all of his batteries. This was the command structure that would lead the men of Bankhead's Battery to their greatest challenge.[110]

The Enlisted Men

Most of the men who joined Bankhead's Battery that summer were farmers. Drill was still the activity that was needed to help the men work

---

[108]   Ibid.

[109]   Daniel and Bock, *Island No. 10*, 123, 146, 148.

[110]   Ibid.; CCSR m231 roll 34; Polk, *Leonidas Polk*, vol. 1, 163–165.

in cohesion. By the time Bankhead's Battery moved to Columbus, a total of twenty-four men had been recruited including Louis Myers, a bugler recruited in Nashville and sent to Bankhead.[111]

On August 10, occurred the execution of one of Bankhead's men. Private Patrick Mathews was charged with desertion and shot that afternoon with the entire company present. The Thirteenth Tennessee Infantry Regiment was given the gruesome task of carrying out the execution. One man from each company was drawn by lots to shoot "at him." It would be nearly two months before anyone deserted again.[112]

Recruitment continued while the battery was at Columbus. Bankhead personally enlisted only seven men at Columbus, the last one being W. P. Bradshaw on February 5, 1862. Bankhead was busy with other things now, and he also knew that recruiting agents were at work for him. First, eight men were transferred from the Fourth Tennessee Infantry Regiment with permission of General Polk. Then there was the recruiting office in Memphis. Sadly, this resulted in only four men. One of them was a bugler, known only as Erlin, who was needed due to the loss of Frank Pfaffenschlager, who was discharged because of chronic bronchitis and diarrhea. Lieutenant Joseph Phillips, recruiting artillerymen specifically for Polk, sent six men from Nashville to Bankhead on November 25. During December, fifteen more recruits came from the Jackson area of West Tennessee recruited by Captain Caruthers.[113]

The biggest addition to the battery was occurring in Arkansas. Thirty-four men were recruited in Camden on December 6, 1861. Captain G. W. McCown specifically recruited for Bankhead. The size of this group led to appointing two sergeants and one corporal, as they would take some time to make their way to Columbus. The makeup of the battery had now changed. There still remained a large number of Irish immigrants and a number of Tennessee city dwellers, but now a large number of farmers had joined the unit. Many of the men owned land. The men were not all Tennesseans anymore; neither did the Memphis men form a majority. Bankhead's Battery was also made up of men from Missouri

---

[111]   CCSR m268 rolls 97–98. See Appendix 3.

[112]   Scarbrough, L. Alex Jr. "Camp Journal of Corporal Lemuel Scarbrough, Sr. Company E 'Dixie Rifles' 13th Tennessee Infantry Regiment" (The West Tennessee Historical Society Papers, vol. LXVI, 2012), 131.

[113]   Ibid. See Appendix 4.

and Kentucky. Later, men from Georgia, Mississippi, and Louisiana would also be members.[114] In March another group of thirty-eight Arkansas men were recruited in Ouachita County by Captain D. W. Harris, but it is not believed that any of these men arrived in the unit before the Battle of Shiloh.[115]

There were a few men who left the army. Emile Huffmeister was a deserter. He turned up missing at roll call on October 14 and was never seen again. On October 25, the surgeon, Colonel Thornton, discharged two men, W. D. Jackson and Charles H. Jones, as they both had consumption. Henry Kraps was discharged on December 31 for the same reason. Dennis Leary lost his arm and never returned, although he was carried on the rolls until June, perhaps so he could still collect army pay. General Polk discharged W. C. Green and Samuel Denton for reasons not found in the records. One of the artificers, James E. Johnson, was reassigned to the ordnance department. One man died at Columbus. J. T. Maroney died on February 6 while sick, and several men were in the Columbus hospital from time to time. Another desertion occurred when the battery returned to New Madrid. Edward G. W. Moon was missing at the March 1, 1862, roll call.[116]

With all of the new men coming in, it was only logical that there would be some changes among the noncommissioned officers. On December 1, Miles Kehoe was reduced to corporal, and William O'Donnell was appointed sergeant. December 13 saw Louis Merchant reduced from sergeant to private, and Daniel O. D. Brennan, who had been made sergeant November 1, was also demoted. On December 21, Frank M. McShane was promoted to corporal, and Alfred T. Watson was appointed sergeant. The new recruits from Camden, Arkansas, arrived with B. R. Harrell and James Kennedy as sergeants. The court-martial of First Sergeant Samuel Brown was conducted on January 25. The charges are not found in the records, but he was stripped of his stripes and continued to serve as a private.[117]

It seems that some sick men may have been furloughed home to recover. The case of J. G. Westbrook illustrates this. Westbrook wrote the

---

[114]   Ibid. See Appendix 5.

[115]   Ibid. See Appendix 6.

[116]   Ibid.

[117]   Ibid.

following letter to General Beauregard on March 15, 1862, just two days after the evacuation of New Madrid, from Medon, Tennessee:

> Sir, I was sick from Gen. McCowns commission at New Madrid about the 7th of this month being sick of Diarrhea & fever & as we were expecting a battle there of the steamer Vicksburg having been snagged and set off land all the rest of the sick were put on without any passes or transportation. I came home & by taking care of myself am well enough to join my command in a short time.
>
> You will oblige me very much by sending me by next mail the necessary pass & transportation & direction to return to my company Capt S B Bankhead Company B Flying Artillery, New Madrid Mo if not moved, [Send] sufficient money & w[h]ere sure & could [?] in by Memphis & would not this trouble you.[118]

It is not known what response was made from this letter, or if he arrived in time for the Battle of Shiloh, but he was marked present on the next pay call.

The men of the battery received pay twice while at Columbus. On November 1, the records indicate that ninety men, including officers, were paid, and three men were marked as absent. On January 1, 1862, there were one 110 men paid, including officers, and nine were absent. Of those absent, one was Dennis Leary, who was in Memphis, and two, Charles Gravitt and James Campbell, were in the Columbus hospital. Gravitt would return to duty but Campbell would not. The official reports of Captain Bankhead record that 132 men reported for duty at Fort Bankhead. However, as Bankhead's Battery prepared to go to Corinth and the Battle of Shiloh, 111 men were recorded as present and nine were absent.[119]

---

[118] Ibid.

[119] OR, X pt. 4, 80; CCSR m268 roll 97–98.

CHAPTER 4

SHILOH
APRIL–JUNE 1862

Army of the Mississippi	Bankhead's Battery B
Lieutenant General Albert S. Johnston	Captain Smith P. Bankhead
Lieutenant General P. G. T. Beauregard	First Lieutenant James C. McDavitt
First Corps	First Lieutenant William L. Scott
	Second Lieutenant Joseph Phillips
Major General Leonidas Polk	Second Lieutenant William M. Polk
First Division	Acting Quartermaster Sergeant Lewis
Brigadier General Charles Clark	Putney
	Sergeant James Canada
First Brigade	Sergeant Edward Cearns
Colonel Robert M. Russell	Sergeant Charles Cooley
11th Louisiana Infantry Regiment	Sergeant B. R. Harrell
Colonel Samuel Marks	Sergeant James Kennedy
12th Tennessee Infantry Regiment	Sergeant William O'Donnell
Lieutenant Colonel Tyree Bell	Sergeant John Purcell
13th Tennessee Infantry Regiment	Sergeant Albert Sailhorst
Colonel Alfred J. Vaughan Jr.	Sergeant Alfred T. Watson
2nd Tennessee Infantry Regiment	Sergeant James Welsh
Colonel Thomas J. Freeman	Corporal Miles Kehoe
Bankhead's Battery	Corporal James McLaughlin
Captain Smith P. Bankhead	Corporal Francis McShane
	Corporal Patrick Talty
	90 privates
	9 absent

There was grumbling in the ranks as Bankhead's Battery left New Madrid and headed for Fort Pillow. The caissons had been thrown into the river, and the men were wet and realized they could have been caught in a trap. Morale had been low since the evacuation of Columbus. They had spent so much time and labor at Columbus only to abandon it for a weak location at New Madrid. And then they had been forced to retreat from there. Bankhead, however, was proud of the men and their performance during the past months, but there was a disheartening feeling among the rank and file. Newspapers had been easy to find while at Columbus, and they knew of the loss at Fort Donelson and Fort Henry and the loss of Nashville without a fight. Now they, too, were retreating for an unknown destination.[120]

Bankhead knew his destination was Corinth, Mississippi, and that he must get there a soon as possible. When they arrived at Fort Pillow, there was no time to tarry. Everyone was packing up and leaving at Fort Pillow. The place did not look like the training camp most of the men knew. It was beginning to look like a ghost town with many abandoned buildings and few tents. The two Alabama regiments that had been stationed there had already left for Corinth. Arrangements were made to continue to Memphis, but the men had to be watched for fear that the Memphians might go home and not return. The sick were taken to Overton Hospital; some of these men never returned to duty. New caissons and limbers were quickly procured, and the battery went to the train station where all of their equipment was loaded onto railroad cars for the trip to Corinth. This was no easy task. The guns had to be dismounted and put on board with the caissons and baggage. Most of the men rode the train, but the drivers and horses traveled overland.[121]

This was a time of confusion and a lack of normal routine. Morale was low. Some men were lost during this transition, but no roll call or records were kept during this time. There would be time later. Of the 14,000 men Polk had at Columbus, only 9,000 made it to Corinth, although some of them were defending Island Number Ten.

The train ride was uneventful. Bankhead's Battery arrived at Corinth on March 27. As they pulled into the Memphis and Charleston railroad station, they saw an amazing sight of activity. Nearly 40,000 troops were

---

[120]   Daniel, *Cannoneers in Gray*, 20–21.

[121]   Connelly, *Army of the Heartland*, 146–147; OR X pt. 1, 15.

busy setting up camps and building entrenchments around the town. Corinth had only been founded in 1854 and already had a population of 1,200 due to the intersecting of the Memphis and Charleston and the Mobile and Ohio Railroads. The town was made up of one-and two-story wooden buildings. Most of the buildings were whitewashed, and many soldiers noticed that the post office was painted pink. Only the courthouse and one church were made of brick. The Tishimingo Hotel was located right next to the depot. There were five churches and a female college, and many shade trees lined the streets. Busy was the word. There had been fifteen troop trains in the past two days, and train whistles could be heard at the Mobile and Ohio Station. The men unloaded the equipment and moved to their designated camp.[122]

Bankhead's Battery set up camp in the First Brigade area described as a grove surrounded by a swamp. The rain-soaked area was described by one soldier as a "slough … full of mud and surrounded by water … [the white tents appeared] to be floating about through the mist and rain."[123] Another Tennessee private said, "I think this is the poorest country I ever saw."[124] It was early spring, and it rained almost daily. In these conditions, it didn't take long for many men to become ill. The horses began to lose their hair, and much effort was made to groom the animals each day. One member of Stanford's Battery exclaimed, "We are suffering very much for water. What little we get is awful and I am afraid it will make us all sick."[125]

On Tuesday, April 1, word was out that General Bowen's Brigade had been ordered to mark the left shoulder of every man with India ink. The men were puzzled and wondered if this order would soon reach everyone in the army. There was much discussion among the men about whether such an order could be given, and if it could, what if someone refused to participate? Eventually word came around that this was nothing but an

---

[122] OR X pt. 1, 396; Larry J. Daniel, *Shiloh: The Battle that Changed the Civil War.* New York, New York: Simon and Shuster, 1997, 68.

[123] William S. Dillon, Diary, March 24, 1862, John Davis Williams Library, University of Mississippi, Oxford.

[124] Earl C. Woods, ed. *The Shiloh Diary of Edmond Enoul Livaudais* (New Orleans, 1992), 20.

[125] George W. Jones, Diary, March 31, 1862, Chickamauga-Chattanooga Military Park.

April fool prank played by the general. Apparently Pettus's Battery was the biggest fool.[126]

Albert Sidney Johnston commanded the largest concentration of Confederate troops west of the Appalachians. The army was divided into four corps with Polk's corps being designated the first corps. Further, Polk divided his corps into two divisions of two brigades each. Bankhead was appointed to be the overall artillery chief for Polk's corps, although his promotion to major would not occur until after the battle. This meant command over four batteries (Bankhead, Stanford, Polk, and Smith) comprising 446 men, 347 horses, 24 guns, and 24 caissons. However, Bankhead chose to serve his battery during the battle and did not move to the staff position, as he felt he would be more productive commanding his own battery. The specific function of artillery chief was not well defined.[127]

Johnston intended to go on the offensive and had stockpiled ammunition and supplies. The infantry would have one hundred rounds per man, and the artillery two hundred rounds per gun. Each man would carry three days' rations and have two days' more in the supply wagons. They would not be able to take their tents, so the men tied their blankets over their shoulders. The wagons were plentiful, and Johnston provided fifty wheelwrights and mechanics to assemble them at the rail yards.[128]

On Thursday, April 3, the men of Bankhead's Battery heard the long roll sounded throughout the camps. It was 4:00 a.m., and the men were being told to be ready to march in two hours. Johnston had only made the decision to move out two and a half hours before. Bankhead had no written orders, but was soon informed by Polk to get everything ready. Of course, no one was ready to move at six, and an officers' meeting was being called for eight o'clock. Still by noon, no one had moved, and the streets of Corinth were cluttered with men and vehicles. Finally the march got started around 3:00 p.m. and made good time down the roads leading to Tennessee.[129]

It was on this day that Bankhead's Battery received its battle flag. Flags had not been standard as the war began, and many units had received flags from their hometowns or from their wives and sweethearts. General Polk

---

126   Welker, *A Keystone Rebel*, 82.

127   OR, X pt. 1, 414.

128   Daniel, *Shiloh*, 21.

129   Ibid. 121–123; Connelly, *Army of the Heartland*, 152–153.

had designed a Christian flag with a dark blue field and a red cross with eleven white stars in the cross. Polk had ordered that this flag be made in Memphis, and he had it distributed to the units at Columbus on January 30. It was made completely of silk and was four feet on the hoist by eight feet on the fly. Bankhead had received one, but it was much too large to be carried by an artillery battery.[130]

General Beauregard had designed a flag based on the eastern battle flags with a blue Saint Andrew's cross (like an *X*) on a red field. It was made of cotton. There were twelve six-pointed white stars in the blue cross, and it was trimmed on three sides with a one-inch pink outline made of silk. Beauregard had hired a New Orleans sail maker to make the flags, and they were passed out to Bragg's Corps with some fanfare. Bankhead's Battery was not in Bragg's Corps, but because there were extra flags, he was presented with a thirty-eight-inch-by-thirty-eight-inch banner. After the Battle of Shiloh, someone in the battery painted, in white, the letter *B* within the top *V* in the cross, and the number *1* within the bottom (upside down) *V*. This flag would be carried on the battlefield to mark the position of the battery.[131]

Special Order No. 8 was designed by Beauregard as the marching and battle plans. Written orders did not arrive until April 4 while the troops were on the march. The artillery would march in column, section front, in the rear of the brigade intervals. The infantry would form line of attack by corps with Hardee's Corps in front of Polk's Corps. Polk's Corps was now

---

[130]   Daniel, *Shiloh*, 95, 122.

[131]   Ibid.

in reserve west of the Corinth-Pittsburg road. Thus Bankhead would find his battery in the rear of the far left of the battle line. His instructions were to "mass their batteries in action and fight them twelve guns on a point." However, the guns of the corps were widely separated by these orders. Stanford's Battery was on the far right of the line, and Polk's and Smith's Batteries were farther to the rear. Thus the batteries would operate on their own, at least in the morning.[132]

The plan of march was not only complicated, but it did not consider the terrain between Corinth and Pittsburg Landing. The area was rough and thickly wooded. It was cut with creeks, ravines, and swamps, and the dirt roads could be confusing, as they were not marked. Once the Federal camp area was reached, there was scattered fields and numerous wagon trails created by the Federals. The movement was march, stop, wait, march, stop wait. Early on Friday morning, it began to rain. A quagmire developed, and several units were lost. Often the guns had to be dragged out of the mud or lifted over obstacles. The attack planned for April 4 had to be postponed. This allowed more time to close up the army, but early on April 5 it rained again.

One soldier described it: "One of the hardest rains fell I ever saw in life and wound up in considerable hail."[133] Another Tennessean described it this way: "We were drawn up at the edge (of the road). As we stood there, troops tramped by in the mud and rain and darkness ... To us we were simply standing in line, but those men who were going by were wading, stumbling, plunging through water a foot deep."[134] During the night, the men huddled under their blankets for whatever rest they could get. By 3:00 a.m. on April 6, Bankhead's limbers were hitched to the teams, and the caissons were ready to go.[135]

Soon after daybreak, Bankhead's men heard shooting ahead. By 7:15 a.m., they could hear cannon fire, and the shooting became continuous. Bankhead's Battery was caught in the rear of the second wave and made very slow progress toward the action. Finally, around 9:00 a.m., Russell's

---

[132] Daniel, *Cannoneers in Gray*, 31.

[133] James Rosser, Diary, April 5, 1862, Gloria Gardner Collection, Jackson, Tennessee.

[134] Beattie, John, *The Citizen Soldier: Or, Memoirs of a Volunteer*, Cincinnati, 1879.

[135] Nathaniel Cheairs Hughes Jr. *The Pride of the Confederate Artillery* (Baton Rouge: Louisiana State University Press, 1997), 21, 24.

Brigade veered to the right side of the Pittsburg-Corinth road and was stopped by Johnston just south of the Rea Field. However, Bankhead ordered the battery to the left of the road on a hill where Major Francis A. Shoup, Hardee's chief of artillery, had assembled twelve guns about 800 yards south of Shiloh Church. Bankhead came into battery on the right side of Shoup's guns. To the left of Shoup was the Fifth Company, Washington Light Artillery from New Orleans. The Fifth Company and two guns of Shoup's left were firing at Battery E, Second Illinois Light Artillery, commanded by Lieutenant George L. Nispel. They had already found the range and had dismantled one of the enemy guns. Calling for case shot, Bankhead joined Shoup's other guns in shelling the Federal camp to the right of the church.[136]

In Bankhead's right front, a very hard fight was taking place with Polk's infantry brigades and Federal brigades of General Sherman's command at the north end of the Rea Field. The Eleventh Louisiana was cut up badly and fell back as did the Twenty-Second Tennessee. Captain Marshall T. Polk's Battery had set up too close to the enemy and was being cut down. Losing twenty-four men and thirty-two horses, they fired double canister until they could stand no longer. Marshall Polk was severely wounded, and only one gun was able to continue for the rest of the battle.[137]

The focal point of the Federal defense was Battery E, First Illinois Light Artillery, commanded by Captain Allen C. Waterhouse. Under heavy pressure and with the collapse of Federal infantry, Waterhouse ordered the withdrawal of his battery about 300 yards to the rear near Shiloh Church. This was a poor location. Bankhead ordered the battery to fire upon this position, but it wasn't long before six companies of the Thirteenth Tennessee, under the command of Colonel Alfred J. Vaughan, attacked the battery in flank, over ran the battery, and pushed on to Shiloh Church. All of the guns of Waterhouse were captured; some of the men escaped.[138]

---

[136] OR X pt.1, 471, 496–497; Hughes, *The Pride of the Confederate Artillery*, 24.

[137] OR X pt 1, 276–277, 414, 444–447; George F. Witham, *Shiloh, Shells and Artillery Units* (Memphis, Tennessee: Riverside Press, 1980), 24–25.

[138] Ibid.

Battle of Shiloh

April 6-7, 1862

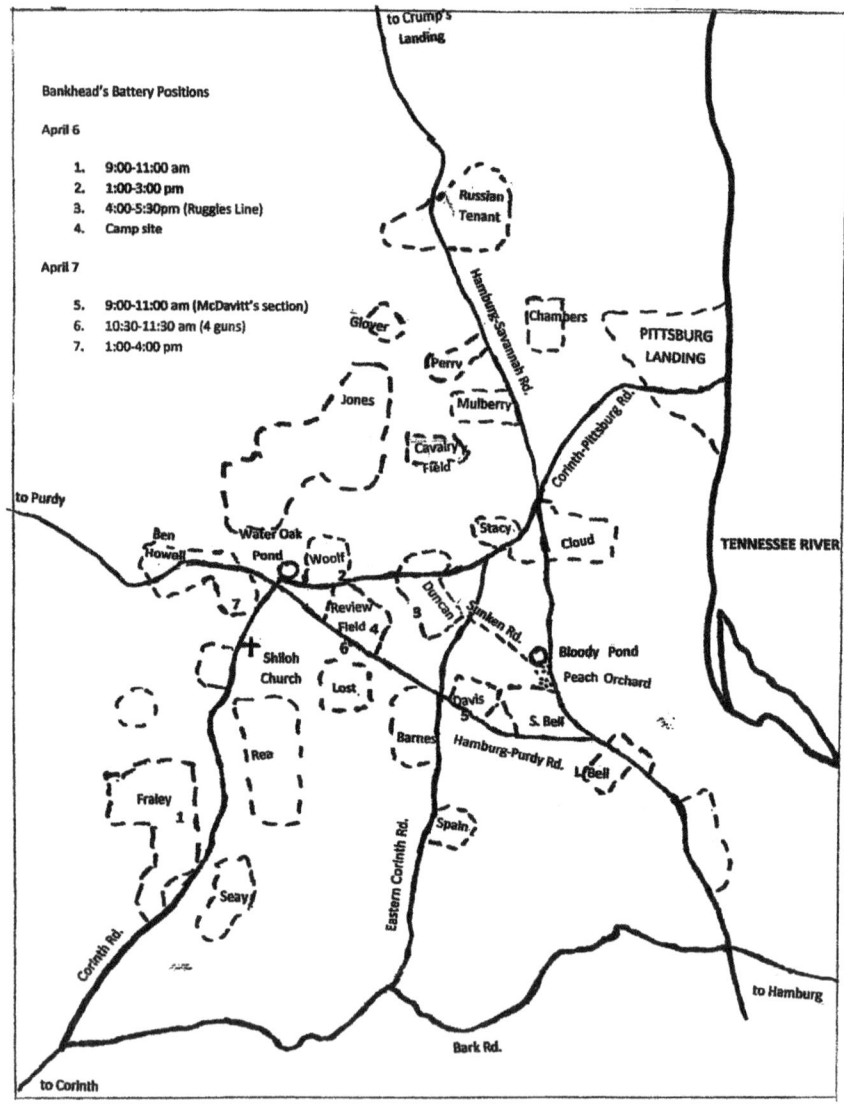

Bankhead's Battery Positions

April 6

1. 9:00-11:00 am
2. 1:00-3:00 pm
3. 4:00-5:30pm (Ruggles Line)
4. Camp site

April 7

5. 9:00-11:00 am (McDavitt's section)
6. 10:30-11:30 am (4 guns)
7. 1:00-4:00 pm

It was now about 10:00 a.m., and there were no more targets as the battle had now gone beyond Shiloh Church. Exploding enemy case shot had wounded some of Bankhead's men. Bankhead ordered up the caissons to replenish the ammunition. After the soldiers changed the ammunition boxes from the caisson to the limber and the depleted box from the limber to the caisson, Bankhead's Battery proceeded north along the Pittsburg-Corinth road. The men observed many Federal tents being pillaged by stragglers as the whole area was covered with enemy camps. As they passed through the intersection with the Purdy-Hamburg Road, the men saw the carnage of the struggle at the crossroads. Dead and wounded men and horses were mixed with five Federal guns, four from Captain Jerome B. Burrows' Fourteenth Ohio, and one from Captain Adolf Schwartz's Battery E, Second Illinois Light Artillery. Then they turned east on the Corinth Road just before the Water Oaks Pond. Around 11:15 a.m. the command "Halt!" "Action Left!" was given. The guns unlimbered on the road and faced north. The limbers and caisson moved into Review Field south of the road where one gun and several dead horses of Battery D, First Illinois Light Artillery, sat abandoned, having recently been captured by the Fourth Tennessee. There were thirty to forty dead men in Review Field. There were also about 160 wounded, mostly from the Fourth Tennessee that the cannoneers helped move to prevent them from being run over by the limbers and caissons.[139]

The crossroads area had been a serious struggle with all of the Federal units retreating some 600 yards to an area called Jones Field. Bankhead's Battery had not been involved in this fighting as Bankhead had been replenishing his ammunition, and the men arrived to see the enemy fleeing. From their position at the north corner of Review Field, Bankhead observed his next target. Two fresh but green regiments, the Fifteenth and Sixteenth Iowa, had just been ordered forward. They had advanced only a few paces when they were hit by Russell's brigade backed by artillery. Thomas Boyd of the Fifteenth Iowa noted, "It was every man for himself. We knew nothing about officers or orders. Indeed the companies now became all mixed up and without organization." Both regiments retreated

[139] OR X pt. 1, 423, 427, 432; Witham, *Shiloh, Shells and Artillery Units*, 2, 6.

to the north end of Jones Field having lost 316 men killed and wounded in just fifteen minutes.[140]

Just as the Iowans fled to the rear, Major Ezra Taylor brought up nine guns from three different Federal batteries and set them up some 200 yards east of the Iowan retreat. In addition, Federal infantry was being sent to this area to support the guns. Bankhead directed the battery to fire at this new threat. In the meantime, Cobb's Kentucky Battery and one gun from Polk's Battery unlimbered directly in front of Taylor's guns about one hundred yards closer than Bankhead's Battery was to the enemy. This artillery duel lasted until noon. One of the Federal cannoneers described his experience thus: "Their shell burst over and around us, killing and wounding many of our horses and some of our men." During the artillery dual, Lieutenant Scott's horse was struck and killed. While Scott was mounting a second horse, another shell burst, and Scott was severely wounded in the neck. He was removed to the rear and was hospitalized for a long time. Lieutenant McDavitt was also wounded when a bullet grazed his head, but he remained at his post. Finally the Federals, running low on ammunition, withdrew, leaving one of their guns behind.[141]

The Federal infantry now made a charge straight toward Cobb's guns. General McClernand himself ordered the charge, and three of his staff officers pushed the men forward. Bankhead continued to fire at the onslaught but to no avail. Cobb's Battery and Polk's gun were overrun. Confederate counterattacks hit the Federal right flank and the Fifth Company, Washington Light Artillery, unlimbered about one hundred yards southwest of Cobb's lost guns. With the Fifth Company firing canister on the left and Bankhead firing case shot from the right and Colonel Robert Trabue's Kentucky brigade counterattacking, the Federals were shaken and withdrew to their start position on the south end of Jones Field. Cobb's Battery was retaken, but with thirty-seven casualties and

---

[140] OR X pt. 1, 104, 105, 287, 289; William W. Belknap. *History of the 15ᵗʰ Regiment Iowa*

Veteran Volunteer Infantry from October 1861 to August 1865 (Keokuk, 1887), 179–181; Daniel, *Shiloh*, 186.

[141] OR X pt. 1, 147, 255, 274, 276; Blaisdell to wife, April 12, 1862, Timothy M. Blaisdell Letters, Civil War Times Collection, Carlisle Barracks, Pennsylvania, United States Military History Institute; Lindsley, *The Military Annals of Tennessee*, 791.

the loss of seventy-eight horses Cobb's Battery was done for the day. Cobb found some mules to pull his guns to the rear, but still left behind two guns and all of his caissons. General Hardee later commented, "but for the artillery the place could never have been taken."[142]

It was now about 2:30 p.m., and the Federals could be seen withdrawing further to the northeast. Bankhead ordered, "Cease Fire!" "Limbers to the Rear!" The limbers came up to the rear of the guns and the cannoneers pushed the guns backward until they could lift the lunette up to the pintle hook. When the gunner said "Driver, drive on!" the limbers retired 200 yards to the rear to the caissons and exchanged the ammunition chests with the limbers. So far, Bankhead's Battery could be considered lucky compared to some of the other units. The men had seen the carnage of several Federal batteries that had been overrun, and had witnessed the destruction of Polk's and Cobb's Batteries. Bankhead had selected good positions, first with Shoup's batteries and then slightly to the right of the heavy fighting when he selected the position at the northern tip of Review Field. In both cases, he had worked with other batteries, but not in overall command. He had selected both locations without any superior officer telling him where to go. His battery was already on their third ammunition chest, and the men at the caissons were combining the ammunition from the used boxes. He had suffered only light casualties, and he had kept his men from looting the Federal camps. A staff officer from General Daniel Ruggles now rode up and ordered Bankhead to move his battery a short distance to the east to Duncan Field.[143]

Bankhead's Battery proceeded about 600 yards to the edge of Duncan Field and turned right to a position that swept the enemy approaches. Several batteries were already there firing into the woods about 500 yards to the northeast. The Fifth Company, Washington Artillery, was already posted at the edge of the field, and Bankhead ordered his company to proceed behind them and then form up on their right. At the same time Stanford's Battery was also arriving and went into battery on Bankhead's right. A short time later, one section of Ketchem's Alabama Battery arrived and set up on the left of the Fifth Company near the road. To the right of Stanford's Battery were Robertson's Battery and Rutledge's Battery. This comprised thirty guns, and Bankhead took nominal command of this *ad*

---

[142]   OR X, pt. 1, 513, 616–617.

[143]   Ibid., 472.

hoc battalion facing what the Federals called the hornet's nest. To the right of this group were thirty-two more guns commanded by Major Shoup.[144]

It was now about 4:30 p.m., and some sixty-two artillery pieces had been gathered to bombard the hornet's nest. Staff officers from General Daniel Ruggles had gathered Bankhead's side of the line, and Major Shoup had put together the right side of the line. Several infantry attacks had been attempted against the Federals throughout the day at this location, and infantry commanders had been calling for artillery support. The Federal commander was Brigadier General Benjamin M. Prentiss, whose division had been swept from the field in the morning but was now hunkered down along an old wagon trail. General Grant had personally told him to hold at all costs, provided him with reinforcements, and expected him to delay the Confederates. Prentiss had done this for hours until the Confederates massed their cannons.[145]

The sixty-two guns fired three or four shots per minute continuously for about an hour; the smoke darkened the field. Bankhead reported in his after-action report that, "The effect of this tremendous concentrated fire was very evident. The reserves, which could be plainly seen going up to Prentiss' relief, fell back in confusion under the shower of shot, shell, and canister that was poured upon them, while our infantry, encouraged by such a heavy artillery support, rushed forward with a shout and carried the position."[146] Many of Bankhead's men were becoming exhausted, and replacements were ordered to take their places, particularly the position of number 1. During the action, Private Patrick Joyce, serving as number 1, was wounded when the cannon fired prematurely while Joyce was ramming a round. Both of his arms were badly mangled, and he was taken to a field hospital in the rear.[147]

The continuous crashing of artillery began to take effect. Some of the Federal artillery began to pull out of the hornet's nest. One Federal officer said the cannonade sounded like "a mighty hurricane sweeping everything before it."[148] Federal infantry hugged the ground, and some

---

[144] Ibid., 472, 475.

[145] Ibid., 476.

[146] Ibid.

[147] CCSR m268 roll 97.

[148] Ibid. 477-478.

of the wounded perished when some of the brush caught fire where they lay. The "shells and shot passed over us terrifically at about the height of a man's head from the ground while sitting down … continued so long that is was a relief when the Rebels began to advance against us," wrote a captain of the Second Iowa. Shoup recalled, "I remember a distinct sense of disappointment, feeling that if they had only stayed a little while we should have punished them handsomely." Many Federals escaped but those who could not began waving white flags of surrender.[149]

Bankhead ordered, "Cease Fire!" around 5:30 p.m. Prentiss surrendered about 2,200 men to avoid useless bloodshed. Confederate infantry rounded up the Federals, some taking the Federal rifles to replace their own, and marched them to the rear. Massed artillery had saved the day for the Confederates, and everyone was in high spirits. The battle would rage on for another two hours. Shoup would order his artillery to push on to capture Pittsburg Landing, but the army was spent, commands were intermingled, and many soldiers were either pillaging Federal tents or going to the rear. Bankhead ordered his men to retire to Review Field where they would camp for the night. The battery was nearly out of ammunition, and the men needed to rest.

There were things that needed to be done, however, before the men were allowed to rest. The horses had been harnessed for fifteen hours and needed to be taken care of, ammunition had to be found to replenish the limbers, as the caissons were nearly empty, and Bankhead needed some instructions from one of the generals. Polk was never found, as he had gone back to his April 5 camp. No orders were given all night. There was talk that Johnston had been killed, which turned out to be true. Some ammunition was found in abandoned caissons on nearby fields. The men slept in Federal tents or camped in the woods nearby. They believed that the battle had been won and the Federals were retreating across the river under the cover of their gunboats. These boats fired all night into the camps. One soldier described it as, "many thunder claps breaking overhead at once." There could also be heard the groans and shrieks of the wounded. Around 10:00 p.m. it began to rain, and by midnight it came in torrents.

---

[149]   Francis A. Shoup. "How We Went to Shiloh," *Confederate Veteran*, vol. 2, 1894, 139.

At sunrise, April 7, 1862, the clouds had cleared, and Bankhead's men could hear gunfire to the north.[150]

Grant had been reinforced through the night and now began a general attack. The Confederate forces were being driven back across the fields they had won the day before. Having no orders, Bankhead moved to the sound of the guns. The battery headed east along the Hamburg-Purdy road, then turned south on the Eastern Corinth road. The guns were placed in battery across the road from Barnes Field. Here the battery was placed in reserve under General Breckenridge. To their front was Davis Field, which could not be seen because of the trees. A Confederate counterattack had pushed the Federals out of the field. The infantry commander was their old friend Alexander P. Stewart, who had ordered a battery to come and support his infantry.[151]

Jefferson's Flying Artillery was already on its way with its four guns, so Bankhead went with one section to support them. When he arrived, he found the infantry, who were replenishing their ammunition in a nearby ravine, being hit by artillery fire. The guns responded to the artillery fire, and the infantry resumed the defensive. The Fifth Company, Washington Artillery, was also engaged, and together the twelve guns dueled the Federal guns. Bankhead then returned to the rest of his battery leaving Lieutenant McDavitt in charge of the section.[152]

At about 1:00 p.m., the infantry was nearly out of ammunition again and pulled back. Jefferson's Artillery, commanded by Lieutenant Putnam Darden, had taken many casualties and had only six men on each gun. The Confederate artillery held out for another thirty minutes under extreme pressure when they were commanded to retreat. The Jefferson Flying Artillery left one gun behind due to the loss of men and horses. McDavitt retired to Barnes Field, but Bankhead was gone. He had received orders earlier to return to Review Field.[153]

On the eastern edge of Review Field, Stanford's Battery, after a gallant stand, was being overrun. Bankhead immediately went into battery with two sections and commenced to fire upon the Federals around Stanford's

---

[150] Daniel, *Shiloh*, 263; Connelly, *Army of the Heartland*, 172.

[151] OR X pt. 1, 609–611

[152] Ibid.

[153] Ibid; Witham, *Shiloh, Shells and Artillery Units*, 72; Sam Davis Elliot, *Soldier of Tennessee* (Baton Rouge: Louisiana State University Press, 1999), 44.

guns. Bankhead reported, "Coming upon the scene of this disaster, shortly after its occurrence … the enemy was driven back and these guns recaptured, and orders were immediately sent by me to Captain Stanford to haul off his guns." His failure to obey this order resulted, as he reports, "from an inability to get horses enough to execute it, as most of his horses were killed or disabled." Stanford's Battery was wrecked, having lost twenty men, four guns, and all six caissons.[154]

Bankhead's Battery now came under a withering fire of shot and shell. Bankhead ordered, "Limber to the rear!" and the guns were pulled back towards Shiloh Church. The battery had now lost enough horses that two empty caissons had to be left on the field. Arriving on a hill to the east of the Shiloh Church, the battery unlimbered next to several batteries that Bragg had ordered to make a stand. McDavitt arrived only moments later, having seen Bankhead to his front and followed him. It was about 2:00 p.m., and there were fifteen guns under the command of Shoup with about 2,000 infantry. At 2:30 p.m., Beauregard ordered a retreat from the field and ordered Shoup to cover the retreat.[155]

The artillery fired for another hour and then were ordered to attach prolonge. The prolonge is a rope about thirty feet long wrapped on top of the cannon's trail. On one end of the prolonge is an iron bar, about seven inches long; at the other end is an iron ring, about four and a half inches in diameter. The limbers were turned around, and the iron ring was placed over the pintle hook. The iron bar went through the lunette of the cannon. Attaching the prolonge allowed the guns to withdraw more quickly while firing.

The order was given "Withdraw by prolong!" and "Withdraw in echelon!" The guns would fire and recoil, and the limber would pull them back about fifty yards. While one section reloaded, another section would do the same. With this maneuver, the guns continued to fire while they withdrew. Shoup later recalled, "We were very much absorbed in a movement we never before had had a chance to practice on the field." By 4:00 p.m. there was no further Federal pressure, and the guns were limbered and withdrawn from the field.[156]

---

154   OR X pt. 1, 479; Daniel, *Shiloh*, 284; Daniel, *Cannoneers in Gray*, 42.

155   Ibid.

156   Ibid. 35–36; Shoup, "How We Went to Shiloh," vol. 2, 140; *Instructions for Field Artillery*, 332–334.

The Confederacy had lost the Battle of Shiloh, but the return to Corinth was another disaster. The roads had become a quagmire, and it was almost impossible to move the guns at a steady pace. Many wounded were left along the road, and some hospitals were abandoned with the patients left to their own devises. Patrick Joyce was one of them. He would be captured and sent to Camp Denison Hospital in Ohio. Bankhead's Battery did not arrive back in Corinth until April 10. Two men had been killed and eighteen had been wounded; thirty-seven horses had been lost. Bankhead was requested to write a report on the condition of the artillery in Polk's Corps. On April 17 he wrote:

> The large loss of caissons is attributable to the extraordinary mortality of (139 out of 347) horses; the disabling of six on the field; using teams of some to haul off captured guns, and the abandonment of others on the road. Many of these last, however, have been recovered and turned over to the ordnance department at this place. I conclude, from all of the information before me, that not more than six or eight of these caissons were left on the field, and that the ammunition in all of them had been expended before they were abandoned.[157]

He explained that Stanford's Battery had lost all of its guns, as had Polk's Battery. Smith's Battery had lost three guns, but took three captured James Rifles back to Corinth. Only Bankhead's Battery returned to Corinth with all of its guns, having lost only two caissons.[158]

Reinforcements and replacements were arriving at Corinth almost daily. General Earl Van Dorn arrived with his corps of 14,000 men from Arkansas, and an arc of fortifications faced north towards the oncoming Federal attack. All of the batteries at Corinth were in need of reorganization including Bankhead's. Beauregard ordered that all six-gun batteries would be reduced to four, and any excess lieutenants would fill in for any casualties. Also there should be a uniformity of calibers in each battery. Bankhead would retain two six-pounders and two twelve-pound howitzers and turned the other six-pounders into the ordnance department. It had

---

[157] OR X pt. 1, 479.

[158] Ibid; Hughes, *The Pride of the Confederate Artillery*, 43; Daniel, *Cannoneers in Gray*, 43; CCSR m268 roll 97.

been difficult to operate a six-gun battery without more men, and a full account of the men would need to take place. Bankhead's promotion to major had now come through, and as Polk's chief of artillery, he gave up command of his battery on May 20, 1862.[159]

The battery remained at Corinth awaiting the Federal attack that never came. There were many false alarms and a few skirmishes in the woods. Henry W. Halleck, who was advancing slowly toward Corinth, had replaced Grant. Beauregard, who had replaced Johnston, knew he could not go on the offensive against this foe. On May 25, a council of corps commanders was held. It was decided to withdraw from Corinth, because a siege would be too costly and Corinth could easily be flanked. There was also the problem of sanitary conditions that had put many men on sick call; and there was a lack of clean water. Trains were arranged to take the army south on the Ohio & Mobile to Baldwyn, Mississippi, but when they failed to find adequate water there, the final destination became Tupelo, fifty-two miles from Corinth. The Federals were completely fooled by this move, and the entire army successfully arrived in Tupelo by June 9. Beauregard then turned over the command of the army to Bragg on June 15, and the reorganization was completed in the next two weeks.[160]

The Officers

Captain Smith P. Bankhead had shown himself to be a valuable officer. During the Battle of Shiloh, he skillfully commanded his battery on five separate occasions, combining with other batteries on three of them. On April 7, at Review Field, his battery single-handedly recaptured Stanford's Battery, but Captain Stanford, due to a lack of horses, was unable to retrieve his guns. Throughout the battle, he remained with his men and kept them from pillaging or otherwise deserting. There had often been a breakdown in the upper command, but Bankhead kept his battery together and showed a great skill in its operation.

At Corinth, it was time to reorganize the battery. All of the officers would retain their positions, but Bankhead knew he would soon be promoted and was already doing the paperwork of a chief of artillery. Polk required several reports, and the lieutenants were already doing much

---

159 OR X pt. 2, 642; Welker, *A Keystone Rebel*, 90; CCSR m268 roll 97.

160 Connelly, *Army of the Heartland*, 176–181.

of the paperwork for the battery. When Bankhead reported to his new position of chief of artillery on May 20, it was not known who would replace him as captain.

James C. McDavitt was the ranking lieutenant in the battery. On May 8, he sent form No. 38 to the quartermaster. This was a request for fifty envelopes, twelve steel pens, and a pint of ink. Obviously there were reports and requisitions to write. Form No. 2 was sent to the quartermaster on May 10 for 125 canteens and canteen straps. McDavitt was taking care of the business of Bankhead's Battery, but was surprised on May 17 when he received a transfer to the ordnance department. He became the assistant chief of ordnance for Polk's Corps with no promotion of rank. Polk knew he was a superb officer who would do his duty. Already, on May 21, McDavitt wrote to the army ordnance officer, Colonel Oladouski, about the difficulties of his job,

> I herewith submit a return of the small arms, ammunition, etc. of this Corps as called for by you in your order of 12th May. No report of the surplus arms has been received, though the various regiments have been turning them over to the Ord. Item Keeper.
> The report is ... [the responsibility of] the Ordnance Officer not having yet begun to act for the Division and Brigades.
> I am Very Respectly, Colonel,
> Your Obedient Servant
> J. C. McDavitt
> First Lieutenant Arty.& Asst. Chief Ord.
> First Corps, Army Miss.

McDavitt would be missed in Bankhead's Battery, as he was an able officer.[161]

William L. Scott remained in the hospital until May as a result of the wound he received at Shiloh. The exact date of his release is unknown, but he went on to become the ranking officer in the battery with the transfer of Bankhead and McDavitt. He was not made captain right away. He did step in and take command and would be responsible for the reorganization of the men in June. He still received lieutenant's pay for May and June and signed his pay record, "inspector and mustering officer of Bankhead's Battery." Pay records indicated that his promotion to captain occurred on

---

161   CCSR m268 roll 97.

July 1, 1862, by order of General Polk. Bankhead's Battery at this point became Scott's Battery, or as the official records report, "Captain Scott's Company Tennessee Light Artillery."[162]

With Scott's promotion to captain, Phillips and W. M. Polk were promoted to first lieutenant. Alfred T. Watson then filled one of the positions of second lieutenant. Watson had joined the battery as a private and had been promoted to sergeant while at Columbus, Kentucky. He was a promising NCO and won the approval of Scott, who recommended him to be commissioned. The other second lieutenant position was left vacant until a replacement could be found.[163]

The Enlisted Men

While there was a change in the leadership of the battery, the men continued to take care of the horses and equipment. Some men had been lost due to battle, sickness, and even desertion. Some men grumbled about the war and the fact that they had lost at Shiloh. The reorganization of the men was necessary, and discipline needed improvement. On April 12, all of the Tennessee units in the army were formed up to witness the execution of a deserter. He was from Tennessee and was to be made an example. He was shot at 2:00 p.m. On April 16, all men were ordered not to be more than one mile from their own camp "at a penalty of courts-martial for the liberty." After Bragg became the army commander in June, punishments for lack of discipline increased.[164]

New recruits were also arriving to join the ranks. From Oauchita County, Arkansas, came thirty-eight additional men specifically recruited for the artillery. They arrived with the name Harris' Company and were turned over to Bankhead. One more man from Harris' Company, James B. Watt, arrived in early June. News had also spread about a Conscription Act passed by the Confederate Congress. Many men's enlistments would be up after the expiration of their twelve-month enlistment, and now the law would extend enlistments for two more years. The new law also could draft anyone between eighteen and thirty-five. One cannoneer recorded in his diary, "I suppose we will have to put up with it no matter how much

---

[162]   Ibid, roll 98.

[163]   Ibid.; Lindsley, *The Military Annals of Tennessee*, 792.

[164]   Welker, *A Keystone Rebel*, 86–87, 88.

we dislike it. It is very unjust & I fear will cause many to desert the army who would have been free volunteers for the war."[165]

On May 25, 1862, Girardey's Georgia Battery was disbanded after losing all of its guns at Shiloh. The men were transferred to other batteries. Bankhead's Battery received twenty-one additional men who already had artillery training. With the battery reduced to four guns and the addition of new men, it was necessary to determine the actual number of men in the battery. Several men were sick and would not be able to return to duty. Some of the men were over the age of thirty-five and were going to use the new Conscription Law to get out of the army. Also the actual number of desertions needed to be determined.[166]

A total of 232 men enlisted or transferred into Bankhead's Battery. Although the men were raised in Memphis, only 33 percent of them were from Memphis. There were fifty-two Irish immigrants that made up two-thirds of that number. There were only five German immigrants, and four of them were musicians or artificers. When the West Tennessee recruits were added to form a total in the battery, it was found that 43 percent of the men came from Tennessee. Arkansas accounted for 32 percent; Georgia, 9.6 percent; Missouri, 9 percent; Kentucky, 3 percent; Louisiana, 0.9 percent; and Mississippi, 0.4 percent. Only men recruited from Memphis and Nashville came from urban locations; most men were from rural areas, and 61 percent proclaimed to be farmers.[167]

Many of the men were illiterate. A check of discharge papers, paroles, and pay records reveals that 52 percent of the men could read and write. Only 23 percent of the men from Memphis were literate, with the Irish immigrants the least likely to be able to read. In contrast, 75 percent of the men from Arkansas were literate, an interesting fact that demonstrates the contribution of rural schools. None of the men from Missouri was literate, and half of the men from Georgia were literate.[168]

The average age of the battery was 28.79, but that would soon change. According to the Conscription Act, any man over the age of thirty-five could voluntarily leave the army. Sixteen men elected to leave, and only sixteen remained who were over the age of thirty-five. Four of these men, James

---

[165] Ibid. 95; CCRS m268 roll 97–98. See Appendix 6.

[166] Ibid. See Appendix 7; Witham, *Shiloh, Shells and Artillery Units*, 70.

[167] CCSR m268 roll 97–98.

[168] Ibid.

Roach, John King, William B. Thompson, and James Hill, stayed on as teamsters. They received extra pay for the duty of driving the supply wagons and were exempt from drills or other military activities. Some men received medical discharges, including Sergeants William O'Donnell and Lewis Putney. Former First Sergeant Samuel Brown was discharged as well. A total of twelve men left due to illness or wounds. Miles McCullom was wounded at Shiloh and was not released from the hospital in Meridian, Mississippi, until August 29. Other sick men were forgotten or unable to return to duty.[169]

The case of Lorenzo R. Richardson shows how some men were later listed as deserters. Ranz had been placed in Overton Hospital on March 19. He returned to duty, but was placed in the hospital in Corinth. It is unknown if he was in the hospital before or after the Battle of Shiloh, but family lore says he was wounded. However, when the army retreated to Tupelo in late May, Ranz was still in the hospital and was captured by the Federals when they arrived. He spent time in Alton prison, and when he was released he return home.[170]

Patrick Joyce, with his badly wounded arms, was left behind at a field hospital and was captured by the Federals. Joyce was taken to Camp Denison Hospital in Ohio on April 18. His wounds were cared for, but his left hand was amputated, and he was then transferred to Camp Chase prison stockade on May 12, where he remained until exchanged on August 25. Records show that Captain Scott wrote him a furlough on July 2, but he did not want to go home. He wanted to get back to the battery, but the battery was currently involved in the Kentucky campaign, and he was not allowed to leave Chattanooga. He was granted detached duty status, and he regularly drew a clothing allowance of twenty-five cents per day and a food allowance of sixty cents per day. By November, his wounds were not healing properly, and he was sent to a Richmond hospital. Here his other hand was amputated, and he made a good recovery. Joyce refused to be discharged and did not want to go to Federal occupied Memphis, and so he returned to Scott's Battery on May 5, 1863, and served as a messenger.[171]

Prior to the Battle of Shiloh, a total of twelve men had left the battery. James T. Maroney had died in the hospital, and five were discharged for

---

[169] Ibid.

[170] Jerry Herd (descendant of L.R. Richardson), personal correspondence with the author, March 10, 2013. See Appendix 9.

[171] CCSR m268 roll 97–98.

illness. Dennis Leary had been wounded and sent home. One man had been arrested, two had been dismissed by General Polk, one had been transferred, and one had deserted. It is hard to tell when men deserted, as there were many opportunities. A man could have walked off while loading the boats at Columbus, or easily left while in Memphis. The train to Corinth or the train from Corinth to Tupelo offered opportunities. Of course a man could have walked off before, during, or after the Battle of Shiloh.[172]

Regardless of when the men deserted, the seriousness of the situation was revealed in June when sixty-seven men were marked as deserters. Just two weeks of June saw the battery lose thirty-seven men. Many of them had been known for some time, but a June 24 order from General Polk asked for an official accounting. Taking into consideration desertions, discharges, and other reasons for leaving, a final accounting can be made. Of the seventy-six men from Memphis, fifty-one of them were gone. That included thirty-eight of the fifty-two Irish immigrants. Fifteen of the twenty men recruited in Missouri had gone home, plus all of the men from the Fourth Tennessee Infantry Regiment who had joined at Columbus. However, not a single man of the seventy-five men from Arkansas deserted. F.M. Adams went home because he was thirty-nine, and four others were discharged from the hospital.[173]

Many men left the army. For one thing, army life was no longer a fun campout. Harsh conditions due to the weather and living in tents were a factor. The rations of food were unacceptable to some men. The gruesomeness of the battlefield was also a factor, and the sight of soldiers' own messmates being killed or wounded took its toll. The army had also retreated and now had lost a major battle. Historian Larry J. Daniel asserts that, "Clearly, loyalty of home was stronger for many men than loyalty to the Richmond government." Weak Southern nationalism was the real issue. These deserters were not strong supporters of the cause. Returning home dominated the thoughts of many.[174]

A typical example might be made with the Talty brothers' story. Simon Talty had been sick at Columbus and was discharged from the army. He

---

[172] Ibid.

[173] Ibid. See Appendix 10; Larry J. Daniel, *Soldiering in the Army of Tennessee* (Chapel Hill and London: The University of North Carolina Press, 1991), 128.

[174] Ibid.,136.

went home to Memphis to recover. While in Memphis in March, his brothers joined him. They had had enough of the war and knew that something big was going to take place at Corinth. After the Federals occupied Memphis on June 6, river traffic with the north was again possible. The Taltys left Memphis and went upriver to Davenport, Iowa, where their parents lived. In 1863 they lived in the west end of Davenport where George and John got married. Patrick became a stonemason, and Simon took up farming. They all moved west after the war and settled in Atlantic, Iowa.[175]

The battery had lost all of it artificers except Edward Ford. He was a private and now worked as an artificer for extra duty pay. The buglers and the farrier, Isaac Harrison, were also gone. Harrison was actually in the hospital and would return to the ranks. His position would be private with extra duty pay to be the farrier. Sergeants and corporals needed to be reassigned. Scott decided that there should be fewer sergeants, and there were several men worthy of promotion. Four men were kept as sergeant— James Kennedy, Charles Cooley, John Purcell and Albert Sailhorst. B. R. Harrell was reduced to private. A fifth sergeant, Gabriel M. Crabtree, was appointed on July 23; he had just made corporal on June 13. L. A. Ellis became the ordnance sergeant, replacing A. T. Watson, who became second lieutenant on August 18. T. E. Watts was appointed quartermaster sergeant. The new corporals were W. L. Dail and Joseph Hardin, who were added from Girardey's Battery. Hardin, however, was sick and would be in the hospital for months. Also promoted were Thomas Smart, A. L. Townsend, H. F. Allen, Edward P. Burnett, John Halbert, J. G. Westbrook, and Gabriel M. Crabtree. William Fowler made corporal on August 1.

In Scott's Battery there were 110 men present and 12 absent for pay call on June 30, 1862. Those who remained were from Tennessee, 18 percent; Arkansas, 57 percent; Georgia, 16.7 percent; Missouri, 4 percent; Kentucky, 1.6 percent; Louisiana, 1.6 percent; and Mississippi, 0.8 percent. This group of men, now known as Scott's Battery, would continue to fight for the liberty of the South. Orders were already being issued for an offensive.[176]

---

[175] Phil Talty (descendant of the Talty brothers), interview with the author, March 6, 2003; James Carey (descendant of the Talty brothers), personal correspondence with author, March 2003.

[176] CCSR m268 roll 97–98.

CHAPTER 5

———⊰●⊱———

PERRYVILLE
JULY–NOVEMBER 1862

Army of Mississippi	Scott's Battery
	Captain William L. Scott
Lieutenant General Braxton Bragg	First Lieutenant William M. Polk
Right Wing	First Lieutenant (vacant)
Major General Leonidas Polk	Second Lieutenant Joseph Phillips
First Division	Second Lieutenant Alfred T. Watson
Bgdr. Gen. Benjamin F. Cheatham	Quartermaster Sergeant T. E. Watts
Fourth Brigade	Ordnance Sergeant L. A. Ellis
Brigadier General Preston Smith	Sergeant Charles Cooley
12th Tennessee Infantry Regiment	Sergeant Gabriel Crabtree
Lieutenant Colonel Tyree Bell	Sergeant John Purcell
13th Tennessee Infantry Regiment	Sergeant Albert Sailhorst
Colonel Alfred J. Vaughan Jr.	Corporal H. F. Allen
47th Tennessee Infantry Regiment	Corporal Edward P. Burnett
Colonel Munson R. Hill	Corporal W. L. Dail
154th Tennessee Infantry Regiment	Corporal John Halbert
Colonel Michael Magevney Jr.	Corporal Joseph Hardin
9th Texas Infantry Regiment	Corporal A. L. Townsend
Colonel William H. Young	Corporal J. G. Westbrook
Scott's Battery	87 privates
Captain William L. Scott	13 absent

Tupelo, Mississippi, was far enough from the Federal forces at Corinth to be safe from attack. It was hot and dry in June and July of 1862. There was a summer draught, and the creeks were dried up. Bragg's army had to be supplied with water by wagon, as there was no railroad connection as he had at Corinth. One army clerk wrote, "When he took command at Corinth, the army was little better than a mob. The din of firearms could be heard at all hours of the day. Now a gun is never fired without orders."[177]

"Genl. Bragg is strict in enforcing discipline throughout the army now," noted one private. Several men had been shot for being deserters, none of whom were in Scott's Battery. The artillery division chiefs got together and decided to camp all of the artillery together. A large field east of town was selected with all of the guns parked together, and the horses' and men's quarters were separated.[178]

The time at Tupelo was spent getting equipment and horses ready for a renewed campaign. Many horses had been lost, and replacements were soon arriving. Some batteries needed horses desperately. The Fifth Company, Washington Artillery, was down to twenty-five horses, and almost all of the replacements were white. Batteries needed about a hundred horses, and Scott's Battery received thirty. One cannoneer remarked, "The horses get full rations here now, besides grazing every day."[179]

Artificers were also busy repairing limbers and caissons. Units that had lost equipment were given replacements from the artillery ordnance depot in Grenada where a small stockpile of guns (mostly six-pounders and twelve-pound howitzers), carriages, limbers, and caissons were stored. Scott's Battery did not need any equipment, but several other batteries did. Soon everyone had enough horses, all their equipment was cleaned up, and drill was begun in earnest.[180]

Daily drills took place about half a mile from camp in a wheat field. This was the first time serious drilling had taken place since winter. A competition was held between Scott's, Carnes', Stanford's, and Smith's

---

[177] Connelly, *Army of the Heartland*, 198; Daniel, *Cannoneers in Gray*, 42; John Bluie to his father, September 30, 1862, John Bluie Papers, Duke University.

[178] James Searcy letter to his father, June 20, 1862, Searcy Letters, Alabama Department of Archives and History.

[179] Hughes, *The Pride of the Confederate Artillery*, 54; James Searcy to his mother June 24, 1862, Searcy Letters.

[180] Daniel, *Cannoneers in Gray*, 43.

Batteries. Lieutenant Colonel James Hallonquist, who had just been promoted to army artillery chief, and the two division artillery chiefs, Bankhead and Shoup, were the judges.

The competition involved the checking of the condition of the guns, limbers, and caissons. All of the implements were checked and the ammunition chest was checked for cleanliness and order. The battery wagons, forge, and tool chests were checked to see if they were well supplied and in order. The horses were inspected, and here Scott's Battery may have faltered, since they still had many original animals from Shiloh.

The men also went through the drills of bringing up the guns, going into battery, and serving the pieces. Stanford's "battery had the praise of the best kept horses," but the winner of the competition was Carnes' Battery. William W. Carnes, only twenty-one years old, an 1861 graduate of the Naval Academy, had only recently been promoted to be captain of Jackson's Battery and was well liked by his men.[181]

With all of the artillerymen in parade formation, General William Hardee called Captain Carnes front and center. Hardee said, "I am pleased to say to you, that the decision of the judges is that you have the best equipped and best handled battery on the field today." The men of Scott's Battery were certainly unhappy and knew that they could do better.[182]

There was a lot of talk in the ranks about where they would meet the Federals in the next confrontation. Bragg, after discussions with officials in Richmond as well as with department commanders, had decided to join Major General Edmund Kirby Smith in Chattanooga to combine forces and drive Federal General Don Carlos Buell out of Middle Tennessee. There was much discussion about recapturing Nashville and driving into Kentucky to get new recruits into Confederate service. To move his army would require good planning. His chief ordnance officer, Colonel Hypolite Oladowski, was sent to Dalton Georgia, twenty-three miles south of Chattanooga, to set up a supply depot. Oladowski had accumulated supplies for 60,000 men, along with a hundred pieces of field artillery.[183]

Bragg intended to move 31,000 troops to Chattanooga, and there was no easy route to get there. He temporarily gave Hardee command of

---

[181] James Searcy to Stella, July 16, 1862, Searcy Letters.

[182] James Searcy to Stella, July 16, 1862, Searcy Letters; Hughes, *The Pride of the Confederate Artillery*, 56–57; Daniel, *Cannoneers in Gray*, 42.

[183] OR XVI pt. 2, 740–741; Connelly, *Army of the Heartland*, 187–194.

the Army of Mississippi with Polk his second in command. Once they arrived in Chattanooga, the army would be divided into two wings with Hardee in command of the left wing and Polk the right. Scott's Battery would be in Polk's fourth brigade commanded by Preston Smith with some familiar infantry regiments, the Twelfth, Thirteenth, Forty-Seventh and One Hundred and Fifty-Fourth Tennessee, and the Ninth Texas Infantry. Bragg continued the usual one battery attached to one brigade even after the Battle of Shiloh had demonstrated the power of massed batteries.[184]

Looking back at this operation, Lieutenant Polk wrote, "Thus was inaugurated the most extensive, and, had it been successful, far-reaching campaign ever attempted by any Confederate commander." The soldiers were enthusiastic about the operation, and it met with high appeal to the public.[185]

Orders were given to move the army beginning on July 23. Two hundred rounds per gun were issued to the artillery, and an additional fifty rounds per gun would be waiting at Dalton. The infantry would travel by train on a long 776-mile route from Tupelo to Mobile, Alabama, then cross the bay and get another train to Dalton. This involved six railroads for overland travel, as well as a ferry for transport across Mobile Bay. About 5,000 men per day set off on this journey.[186]

The cannoneers and the guns of Scott's Battery also traveled by train. However, the drivers took an overland route of 432 miles, driving the limbers and caissons to Aberdeen and Columbus, Mississippi, to Tuscaloosa and Gadsden, Alabama, then to Rome, Georgia, where they would finish the journey by rail. A cavalry escort went with the batteries on the road to provide security. The trains ran in relays with the last troops leaving Tupelo on July 27. Although the trip was long and hard, morale improved as the men anticipated an action that would reverse their misfortunes.[187]

Those traveling by rail had the easiest journey. At times it seemed like a picnic as people came out to cheer them and give them fruits and flowers. The most difficult time was unloading the guns at Mobile, putting them on boats, and then unloading the boats and putting the guns on another rail car. The trains then traveled north to Montgomery where the men

[184]   Ibid., 197; Kenneth W. Noe, *Perryville* (University of Kentucky Press), 369–370.

[185]   Polk, *Leonidas Polk*, vol. 2, 124–125.

[186]   Connelly, *Army of the Heartland*, 204.

[187]   Ibid., 30; OR XVI pt. 2, 741.

were given some free time in the city before continuing on to Atlanta. The final leg of the trip took them over the Chickamauga bridges and then through the tunnel on the north end of Missionary Ridge to the Chattanooga station. One member of the One Hundred and Fifty-Forth Tennessee wrote:

> Old Georgia beat all … [there] was a perfect ovation, and the men were almost wild with delight, and some, I'm sorry to say, with Georgia peach brandy … [we are] eager to meet the Yankees, and I have no fears of the result … they all say that they will never forget the people of Georgia and will fight as cheerfully to defend them, as they would their own homes.[188]

The overland journey was more difficult, as most of the roads were nothing but dirt trails. On the second day of the journey, Carnes' horses refused to cross a stream. This held up the entire battalion, and his horses were so worn out that Carnes took his vehicles to the railroad at Artesia and loaded them on flatcars. Scott's drivers snickered at Carnes' misfortune and couldn't wait to tell the others what had happened to the winners of the artillery competition.[189]

Generally the trip was orderly. At Aberdeen a "rich and varied banquet set by the citizens awaited the column." A gunner in Stanford's Battery wrote a letter to the Memphis *Appeal,* in which he said:

> But let me not forget to mention the invariable kindness and hospitality of the good citizens along the way. We had plenty of fruit, milk, honey, vegetables, chicken etc. At nearly every place where we camped, we were visited by the citizens, and especially the ladies. The boys were frequently invited to dinner or supper, and in one or two instances a public dinner was given to all of the soldiers present.

---

[188]   Ibid; Benedict Semmes to his wife, August 8, 1862, Semmes Papers, University of North Carolina.

[189]   Lindsley, *The Military Annals of Tennessee,* 811.

The column made fifteen to thirty miles per day and arrived at Rome, Georgia, on August 15. The horses would continue to Chattanooga by road, but all of the baggage and equipment would now move by rail.[190]

Kirby Smith was ready to move against the Federals at Cumberland Gap, but Bragg was still waiting for his artillery to come up. So Bragg provided him with two additional brigades to add to his force. He was given Cleburne and Smith's brigades, and on August 16 they departed by train for Knoxville. Scott's Battery belonged to Smith's Brigade but was unable to go along, as the unit had not fully arrived yet. Douglas' Texas Battery would serve temporarily with Smith's Brigade. When Bragg did move forward on August 28, Scott's Battery was assigned to Stewart's Brigade. Thus Scott's Brigade and Stanford's Battery would work together in the move into Kentucky. The battery would rejoin Smith's Brigade before the Battle of Perryville.[191]

Kirby Smith was already in Kentucky when Bragg crossed the Tennessee River on August 28. The journey through the Cumberland Plateau was difficult for artillery. On the southern slope of Walden's Ridge it was necessary to attach ten horses to each gun and assign infantry to help them up the road. Havis's Georgia Battery lost a caisson when it fell into a ravine—horses and men too—on the way down the ridge. It was not only difficult going but it was also oppressively hot.[192]

On September 3, the army had reached Sparta, Tennessee, where Bragg rested the men for three days. Here they heard of Kirby Smith's victory at Richmond, Kentucky. Army morale blossomed even more. It was two weeks of difficult going, but finally they arrived at Glasgow, Kentucky, on September 13.[193]

Here the men rested. On Sunday, September 14, many men attended church services for the first time in a long time, although a few found some whiskey and got into trouble. News arrived that a Federal force at Munfordville had repulsed a Confederate attack by General Chalmers. Bragg ordered a forced march of twenty-five miles through the night. Polk ordered the men to take three days' rations, and at 3:00 p.m. they marched out leaving the supply wagons behind. Polk's troops and Scott's Battery

---

[190] Ibid; *Memphis Appeal* August 26, 1862.

[191] Noe, *Perryvill*, 64, 67.

[192] Ibid.

[193] Ibid; Daniel, *Cannoneers in Gray*, 46–47.

went east around Munfordville, crossed the Green River, and came up behind the enemy. Bragg, with Hardee, arrived south of town and arrayed his troops on the hills south of town. By noon the town was surrounded by seventy-six artillery pieces. A reconnaissance revealed extensive defensive works, and the Federals opened fire with their artillery. Polk received orders to attack at dawn on the next day. Bragg then sent a note and demanded the Federal commander to surrender.[194]

The Federals delayed an answer all day, but after a show of force, the Federal garrison of 4,000 surrendered without another shot being fired. The Federals laid down their arms at 6:00 a.m. and were paroled. They were allowed to march to Louisville with the promise not to re-enter the war without being exchanged for other Confederate parolees. One of the members of the Fifth Company wrote, "[even] with all of their fortifications [they] would have been blown to atoms in half an hour." The men of Scott's Battery came into the town to celebrate. Men enjoyed coffee, hardtack, beef, clothing, and shoes from the surrendered Federals.[195]

Bragg now moved his army to Bardstown. Polk would be left there while Bragg continued on to Frankfort to install Richard Hawes as the Confederate governor. Preston Smith and Cleburne were located forty-five miles north of Bardstown at Shelbyville, having been returned to Bragg's command. The men of Scott's Battery were ordered to prepare some defensive positions. The weather was at times unbearably hot, and the men were complaining about having no tents, as the supply wagons had not come up. Bragg was so incensed with the inauguration that he paid no heed of Buell's advance. On October 2, pressure from advancing Federals drove Cleburne out of Shelbyville, and Polk ordered the withdrawal from Bardstown the same day.[196]

Scott's Battery limbered their guns and proceeded east on the road to Perryville and then to Harrodsburg, where Bragg had ordered the army to concentrate. It was hot, and the men were thirsty. The morale of the men began to wane as they felt they were retreating again. That very day, Hawes was inaugurated governor to jubilation only to flee Frankfort in despair.

---

194 Ibid., 70–73; Connelly, *Army of the Heartland*, 228–30.

195 Ibid; Hughes, *The Pride of the Confederate Artillery*, 61; OR XVI pt.1, 968–971; OR XVI pt. 2, 825–828, 837.

196 Ibid., 892, 896–897, 900–903.

Water was necessary for the thirsty men, and the town of Perryville offered what marching men needed.[197]

The men traveled along the terrain that would be the next day's battlefield. It was hilly ground, but well developed. There were only a few groves of trees and plenty of open space. There were also several deep ravines and shallow or dry creek beds. One Texas soldier recalled, "A beauty ful village ... in one of the finest country's I ever saw ... all the country is fences up & is nearly as open as the prairies of Tex all the timber nearly being cut away."[198]

The town of Perryville had been named to honor Oliver Hazard Perry, a War of 1812 hero, and had grown to become a typical Southern market town. Merchants Row consisted of six buildings on Main Street, which ran along the west bank of the Chaplain River. The area farmers raised hemp, wheat, corn, and potatoes on modest farms of one hundred to five hundred acres. There were several churches in town, and the Presbyterian Harmonia College boasted 700 students. As the people watched the battery pass through town, no one realized that the next day they would be fleeing town to avoid the battle.[199]

Scott's Battery finally arrived in Harrodsburg on the evening of October 6 and hastily made camp. Here the men found "more Southern sympathy ... than any other place on our march thus far." Cheatham's men also arrived, and Scott's Battery was reunited with its brigade. Hardee's wing lagged behind with troops camping by the water sources at Perryville and Salt River east of town. Hardee was concerned about the Federal column following him and, thinking it was a small force, requested that Polk send him Anderson's Division and Cleburne's Brigade. Bragg also ordered Polk to send Cheatham's Division back to Perryville to dispose of this Federal pest. Polk was to rout the enemy immediately, and "then move to our support at Versailles." On the morning of October 7, Captain Scott ordered the men to hitch the horses and be ready to move out at 6:00 a.m. The battery was on its way back to Perryville.[200]

---

[197]   Noe, *Perryvill*, 107–108.

[198]   Street to his wife, October 10, 1862, Street Correspondence, University of North Carolina.

[199]   Noe, *Perryvill*, 107–108.

[200]   OR XVI pt. 1, 660, 1024, 1096; James Iredell Hall, Diary, Southern Historical Collection, University of North Carolina, Chapel Hill, 58.

October 7 saw Hardee and Polk deploying their men in battle lines. Fearing the enemy would come from the northeast, they deployed to cover the Mackville Road. Only one brigade, under Colonel Samuel Powell, would watch the Springfield Pike. Lack of water was the key, as the Confederates controlled the water sources and the Federals would be arriving hot and thirsty. Around midnight, Cheatham's Division arrived at Perryville without the Fourth Brigade. Preston Smith apparently had received orders to return to Harrodsburg after marching only five miles.[201]

The battle began on October 8 with a Federal push against Powell, who was guarding a water source along Doctor's Creek. Hearing the guns, Chaplain Charles Quintard remarked, "They are fighting for the water now. I am informed that they have had none for two days."[202]

Being overpowered, Powell withdrew, but the Federals, under Major General Phil Sheridan, did not pursue. For the rest of the morning, no more action took place on this left flank of the Confederate line. Polk decided to set in motion a plan to overwhelm the Federals when they appeared on the Mackville Pike. He would move Cheatham's Division from the left, go behind Hardee's line, and mass on the far right. Bragg arrived, but leaving Polk in command, he made his headquarters at the Crawford House on a hill north of town.[203]

Around noon gunfire erupted in front of Buckner's line in the Confederate center. Bragg arrived and ordered an advance to the nearby hill. Polk then ordered Carnes' Battery to open upon the Federals. An artillery duel lasted for about an hour with the Jefferson Flying Artillery and Lumsden's Battery joining Carnes' soldiers. Later Stanford's Battery relieved Carnes' men, when Carnes withdrew his battery to safety in the rear. Apparently Major Bankhead was responsible for the gathering of artillery to duel with the Federal batteries. One of Stanford's caissons was hit and destroyed; a caisson of the Fifth Indiana Battery was also lost. Some men and horses were killed. This artillery duel ended about 1:30 p.m., and thirty minutes later came the Confederate attack.[204]

---

201   Noe, *Perryvill*, 132, 136, 140.

202   Reverend Joseph Cross, *Camp and Field* (Macon, GA: Burke, Boykin & Company, 1864), 61.

203   Ibid., 170.

204   Noe, *Perryvill*, 175–176; Daniel, *Cannoneers in Gray*, 48.

Hardee attacked the Federal position in his front, and Cheatham launched his attack on the far right. Three batteries massed near the Bottom House to support Cheatham. By nightfall the Confederate's had advanced over a mile and captured several enemy guns as well as small arms. The men were elated with victory. However, Scott's Battery was not present. Preston Smith had finally ordered his brigade to Perryville that morning. Arriving after the battle had already begun, the brigade was placed in reserve and spent the entire afternoon in the town.[205]

The Federals, under Colonel William Carlin, had advanced against Powell in the afternoon and pushed him into the town, capturing the Fifth Company's ammunition wagons. With Preston Smith's help, the Federals were chased out of town. The Fourth Brigade suffered only four casualties, all in the Thirteenth Tennessee. A sharpshooter shot one man in the Ninth Texas the next morning, giving Preston Smith's Brigade a total of five casualties. Scott's Battery had not fired a shot, and the Fourth Brigade hardly accounted for any of the 3,996 casualties suffered in Bragg's Army.[206]

Sporadic gunfire indicated that the Federals had not fled the field and might continue the battle the next day. Some captured papers of Federal General Alexander McCook indicated that Buell's entire army was at Perryville. Bragg's decision to leave the battlefield to preserve his army and to combine with Kirby Smith was a sound military decision. Powell's retreat into Perryville indicated that Bragg's own forces might be outflanked.

For the men on the battlefield who had poured out their blood to win a victory, Bragg's order made no sense. At midnight the order was given to retreat. Turner's Battery hauled away several Federal cannons, keeping two nice Napoleons for themselves. As many wounded as possible were carried out, but there was a shortage of wagons, and about 900 wounded were left behind. Preston Smith's brigade formed a defensive position east of town as the army retreated to Harrodsburg, but the Federals did not pursue. General Joe Wheeler's cavalry took over the rear guard as Scott's Battery limbered up and headed for Harrodsburg in the late afternoon.[207]

---

[205]   Ibid.

[206]   Polk, *Leonidas Polk*, vol. 2, 156; Noe, *Perryvill*, 313, 315, 340. One of the men in the 13th Tennessee was listed as missing and may have deserted.

[207]   Ibid., 313–314.

On October 10, Scott's Battery had already passed through Harrodsburg and was four miles west of Bryantsville when a messenger arrived from Bragg. They were to turn around and, with Preston Smith's infantry, return to Harrodsburg. Kirby Smith had met with Bragg at Harrodsburg, and they were setting up a defensive line two miles west of the town.[208]

Returning to Harrodsburg, Preston Smith set up his brigade in a battle line, but the Federals never showed up. Reports through the night indicated that Buell was coming from several roads, and to avoid a trap, Bragg ordered Preston Smith to withdraw and join up with the rest of Cheatham's Division. News had also arrived that Van Dorn had been repulsed at Corinth, and that John C. Breckenridge's reinforcements from Tennessee were not coming to Kentucky. There would be no grand battle for Kentucky. The Army of Mississippi would return to Tennessee.[209]

Disappointed soldiers were told to prepare four days' rations and form in march column to head away from the enemy. Wagons were loaded with everything they could carry, and Bragg's supply depot was set on fire.[210]

It took six days to march to the Cumberland Gap, averaging fifteen to twenty miles per day. Colonel Vaughan of the Thirteenth Tennessee wrote, "The retreat out of Kentucky was one of a greater trial and hardship than any march during the war. Over a rough and barren country, without shoes and thinly clad, with scarcely anything to eat, the suffering was great, yet it was borne with fortitude and without a murmur."[211]

From the heat of Perryville to the frost of Wildcat Mountain, the men endured. They ate half rations of biscuits, pickled pork, and parched corn, and for the first time they were hungry. Anger and rage was simmering in the ranks as well. It was Bragg's fault that victory had been turned into defeat, and now the men must suffer. Historian Kenneth Noe put it this way: "Going all the way back to his refusal to confront Buell at Munfordville, many soldiers censured Bragg as a blundering coward. The failure of the campaign, they vehemently maintained, was his."[212]

---

[208] Ibid., 330, 334.

[209] Ibid.

[210] Ibid.

[211] A. J. Vaughan, *Personal Record of the Thirteenth Regiment Tennessee Infantry C.S.A.*, Memphis, 1897, 23.

[212] Noe, *Perryvill*, 337–338.

Many wanted Bragg to be replaced. John Magee of Stanford's Battery wrote on October 16, "The troops up all night—some cursing such times and some 'Old Bragg'."[213]

By October 20, the army began to arrive at Morristown, Tennessee, where the railroad ran to Knoxville. It was snowing when Scott's Battery arrived on the twenty-fifth to find plenty of food and soap. The men were also given new uniforms, as so much of their clothing was worn out. One of Stanford's men remarked, "Weather rather winterish we have no tents, and but few flys. A great many are sick and others are getting sick. The last 2 weeks have been the hardest two I have ever experienced … Great dissatisfaction exists in regards to Genl. Bragg's course for the last two months."[214]

Within days, orders were received that the army would be moving into Middle Tennessee. The infantry was boarding trains at Knoxville for Chattanooga and Bridgeport, Alabama. The artillery, however, would march into Middle Tennessee. Scott's Battery had just returned from sixty days of marching and counter marching with very little time to rest. They were ordered to Kingston, Tennessee, about forty miles west of Knoxville, to prepare for the journey. Bragg thought that his army was in condition to go on the offensive after the return from Kentucky. Historian Thomas Connelly remarked, "Probably never had a Confederate offensive been so hastily planned and an invading army so unready for a new campaign."[215]

On November 1, when orders were given to move out, six inches of snow covered the ground in Kingston. Scott's Battery marched through the Sequatchie Valley to Pikeville and Jasper. Then they traveled over Monteagle Mountain and finally arrived, on November 18, a few miles north of Winchester. Meanwhile, Bragg had been summoned to Richmond and met with President Davis. Leonidas Polk was also summoned to Richmond. Nothing came out of the meetings, as both commanders

---

[213] John Euclid Magee, Diary, October 16, 1862, Duke University.

[214] Ibid., October 25, 1862.

[215] Thomas Lawrence Connelly, *Autumn of Glory* (Baton Rouge and London: Louisiana State University Press, 1971), 13; Hughes, *The Pride of the Confederate Artillery*, 75.

returned to the army. By Christmas Day, Scott's Battery and the bulk of the Army of Tennessee were at Mufreesboro, Tennessee.[216]

The Officers

There was no change in the officers of Scott's Battery during the campaign in Kentucky. Captain Scott had not distinguished himself on the battlefield, because the unit did not fight any battles in Kentucky. He did show the leadership to organize the battery for travel as well as encampment. He did have good support from the lieutenants. William M. Polk, as the ranking first lieutenant, served in the capacity of commander when Scott was absent. This was the case when he signed the muster roll on August 31, 1862. Few records exist from the time the battery was on the Kentucky campaign, and Scott was never asked to prepare an after-action report.[217]

After Perryville, Major Smith P. Bankhead made a decision that would change the staff of Scott's Battery. Bankhead had accompanied Polk's wing as the chief of artillery. He had organized the movement of the artillery from Tupelo to Chattanooga. Knowing the men of his old unit, he often used them as part of his staff. For instance, Lieutenant Phillips went to Columbus, Mississippi, on July 3, 1862, at the request of Bankhead. Phillips was to return with some special five-spoke wheels of "unusual" size, which Bankhead had found for some other unit. On another occasion, McDavitt, serving in the ordnance department, was sent to Calhoun, Georgia, on August 26 to pick up one hundred horses needed for the Kentucky campaign. His close connection with Scott may have smoothed out any rough edges of his new command, but it also had some privileges.[218]

After the Kentucky campaign, Bankhead did not return with the army to Chattanooga, but went on to Jackson, Mississippi, to help procure supplies for Bragg's army. He found there a letter written on October 30, 1862, by his cousin, Major General John Bankhead Magruder, who had recently served in Virginia, but had been reassigned to Texas, where

---

[216] Ibid., 75–79; The Army of Mississippi officially became the Army of Tennessee on November 1, 1862.

[217] CCSR m268 roll 98.

[218] Ibid.

he became the district commander. He offered Bankhead a chance for promotion and command. Magruder's letter urged him to get Polk's recommendation and "go with it to Richmond & urge your claims & say to Mr. Randolph that I want you with me—I will write to him today." Bankhead wrote to Magruder at Vicksburg where he would be going before crossing into Arkansas and then on to Texas.[219]

Bankhead did receive the recommendation from Polk and was approved to report to his new post in Texas. He arrived in April 1863 and commanded the sub district of San Antonio. Bankhead was promoted to colonel and took a few people with him to serve on his staff. Scott's Battery lost Second Lieutenant Phillips, who received detached service from Scott's Battery, and reported to Texas. Phillips was promoted to first lieutenant and served as Bankhead's adjutant. Bankhead also took with him Privates James Fitzpatrick and John Connell. These men did not leave Scott's Battery until after the Battle of Murfreesboro.[220]

The Enlisted Men

The number of men available in Scott's Battery was always in flux. On July 1, 1862, there were 104 men including those who were absent. At Perryville, on October 8, there were eighty-five men present with no accounting of those absent. On December 1, there were ninety-three men, including the absent ones. Most of those listed as absent were sick, although some were on detached duty and were continued on the rolls. Patrick Joyce is an example of this, as he was in and out of hospitals during this time and did not return to the battery until later. He was not marked on the rolls. Neil Finney, on the other hand, had also been wounded at Shiloh, losing his big toe on his right foot and the sight of his right eye. He was marked absent at every roll call. Although he was released from the hospital on September 1, he remained at the hospital on detached duty serving as a nurse. Joseph M. Hardin was furloughed home to recuperate

---

[219]   Paul Casdorph, *Prince John Magruder* (New York: Wiley and Sons, 1996), 219; J. B. Magruder to Smith P. Bankhead, October 30, 1862, Ada Bankhead Collection, University of Virginia, Charlottesville; OR XV 1066.

[220]   CCSR m268 roll 97–98.

from his wound at Shiloh and returned to the battery on November 28, 1862.[221]

Scott's Battery did not have any battle casualties, although there were sickness casualties in Kentucky. Marcus P. Maxwell was too sick to travel after the capture of Munfordsville and was captured there in the hospital. J. W. Horton had to be left behind at Harrodsburg and died there on November 5. William Brown died on November 12 and was buried at Winchester, Tennessee. Albert Sailhorst was sick on the way back from Kentucky with chronic diarrhea and was sent to the hospital in Chattanooga. He died there in December, and the record of his death was later sent to Selma, Alabama. John W. Cooper died of pneumonia on December 8 in the hospital at Murfreesboro.[222]

Some men were discharged. Miles McCollum never healed from his wounds at Shiloh and was given a medical discharge on August 29. Also discharged was Thomas Smart for being over the conscription age. Smart then became a teamster and remained in the unit. Others were also teamsters on extra-pay duty to help drive the many wagons. William Tatum, D. H. Wink, B. R. Harrel, John King, A. Maxey, and J. R. Brinkley served as teamsters. W. W. Weems became a teamster on the journey out of Kentucky in October. S. D. Irvin rejoined the battery on October 31 after being released from the Chattanooga hospital. He became a teamster. Some of the men returned to their regular duties in December. Edward Ford was the only man serving on extra duty as artificer, and he was overworked. Other men—Wiley Smith, B. R. Harrel (September), A. Maxey (late September), and J. Kreiter (October)—helped Ford with his duties for extra pay.[223]

There were two men recruited by Captain Scott during this period. Eighteen-year-old Lewis A. Davis was recruited to be the guidon. The battle flag of the battery had first flown at Shiloh and now Davis was in charge of its keeping. Davis was from Tupelo, Mississippi, and had joined the unit on July 23 just as the men were leaving on the Kentucky campaign. Scott had also recruited E. W. Blease at Rome, Georgia, on August 14 as the unit passed through on their way to Chattanooga.[224]

---

221 CCSR m268 roll 97–98.

222 Ibid.

223 Ibid.

224 Ibid.

Some men were demoted during this time from sergeant to private. This happened to Daniel O. D. Brennan (August 10), Charles Cooley (September 29), and Gabriel M. Crabtree (December 17). Reasons for demotion are not found in the surviving records. Promotions were in order as some of the men had lost their stripes or had gone sick. James Collins was promoted to sergeant on November 1. As Scott's Battery approached Murfreesboro, there were several promotions made on December 17, 1862. Promoted to corporal were Thomas Cluin, J. D. Echols, Hines Holt, and John B. Watts. W. M. Fowler and A. L. Townsend were promoted to sergeant.[225]

The men arrived at Murfreesboro tired; their equipment was worn. They had been on the move since July 23, much of it over steep hills, and sometimes they had been hungry. They held a resentment for General Bragg for throwing away victory in Kentucky. Now they hoped to settle down for the winter back in Tennessee. Captain Scott had proved to be an able administrator; it was hoped that, maybe in the spring, Scott's Battery would prove itself to be a worthy defender of the Confederacy.

---

[225] Ibid.

CHAPTER 6

———◆———

MURFREESBORO
DECEMBER 1862–JANUARY 1863

Army of Tennessee	Scott's Battery
	Captain William L. Scott
General Braxton Bragg	First Lieutenant William M. Polk
Polk's Corps	Second Lieutenant Joseph Phillips
Lieutenant General Leonidas Polk	Second Lieutenant Alfred T. Watson
First Division	Quartermaster Sergeant T. E. Watts
Major Gen. B. F. Cheatham	Ordnance Sergeant L. A. Ellis
Fourth Brigade	Sergeant James Collins
Colonel Alfred J. Vaughan Jr.	Sergeant William Fowler
12th Tennessee Infantry Regiment	Sergeant John Purcell
Major J.N. Wyatt	Sergeant A. L. Townsend
13th Tennessee Infantry Regiment	Corporal H. F. Allen
Lieutenant Colonel W. E. Morgan	Corporal Edward P. Burnett
29th Tennessee Infantry Regiment	Corporal Thomas Cluin
Major J. B. Johnson	Corporal J. D. Echols
47th Tennessee Infantry Regiment	Corporal John Halbert
Captain W. M. Watkins	Corporal Hines Holt
154th Tennessee Infantry Regiment	Corporal John Watts
Colonel Michael Magevney	Corporal J. G. Westbrook
9th Texas Infantry Regiment	76 privates
Colonel W. H. Young	16 absent
Allin's Sharpshooters	
Lieutenant J. R. J. Creighton	
Scott's Battery	
Captain William L. Scott	

Middle Tennessee in December of 1862 was cold and wet. Some days it would rain; some days it would snow. There had been promotions made in the Army of Tennessee. Polk, Hardee, and Kirby Smith had all been promoted to lieutenant general following their individual trips to Richmond. The promotions may have been a consolation for retaining Bragg as the overall commander, as all three of the men had told Jefferson Davis that they preferred Joseph Johnston to be the new commander. Historian Larry J. Daniels explained, "it smacked more at a pitiful bribe for their cooperation."[226]

During the Kentucky campaign, the Federals had pulled out of Middle Tennessee with the exception of Nashville, which had become their primary base of operations. As early as October 20, Murfreesboro had been retaken by Confederate troops under Major General John C. Breckenridge. The area of Middle Tennessee was a valuable source of food and fodder, which Bragg's army was in need of.

Scott's Battery had only recently arrived at Tullahoma when they received orders on November 18 to move to Murfreesboro. As the men arrived, they found a quaint town of 4,000 people that was only thirty-five miles from Nashville. The town had been named for Revolutionary War hero Colonel Hardee Murfree, who had settled in the area. This railroad town seemed to have a large proportion of upper-class citizens with no middle-class citizens evident. The railroad had only been finished since 1854. The men were ordered into camp south of town with the idea that this would be a good place to spend the winter. The men pitched their tents and began to get them ready. Not having as much wood available as they had at Columbus, Kentucky, they began to put wooden floors in their tents and build chimneys out of brick to help keep their tents warm.[227]

The men began routines of fatigue duties and drill at their camp outside of Murfreesboro. General John C. Breckenridge, who had been at Murfreesboro for several weeks, noted that the artillerymen "are very poorly and thinly clad, and much in need of blankets." Orders were given that drills would commence on a daily basis. Breckenridge also noted, "The cannoneers of the different batteries are required to drill two and a half hours each day at the foot battery; the drivers one and half hours in

---

[226] Larry J. Daniel. *The Battle of Stones River* (Baton Rouge: Louisiana State University Press, 2012), 6.

[227] Ibid. 16, 19.

harnessing and unharnessing, besides a battery drill of three hours. The officers are required to attend recitation in tactics two hours each day."[228]

It snowed on December 5 when Joseph Johnston came to Murfreesboro for a visit. He had been given command of all of the armies between the Appalachians and the Mississippi River on November 12. Private James Hall recalled that the men were drawn up near the train station and there was "wild enthusiasm" and "cheer after cheer rang out in the cold air." Many of the men thought that the new theatre commander had come to replace Bragg. They soon found out that was not the case.[229]

On December 12, President Jefferson Davis arrived by train at Murfreesboro for a meeting with the generals. The next day at sunrise, Polk ordered his corps into parade formation for an inspection by the president. The president rode before each division finding the troops "in fine spirits." Private Private Hall commented, "you could not tell him from any other old citizen." He continued, "some of them [soldiers] hardly believe yet that it was the real Simon pure Jeff. They had been deceived so often by reports that Jeff Davis was in camp that they would not really believe it when it did come." Following a pass and review, Davis passed out promotions to several more generals, including Patrick Cleburne to major general.[230]

Christmas Day was very somber. The weather had been unusually balmy the previous week. Some of the men had gotten drunk, but the most remembered thing was that "we did not have to drill," recalled John Magee. The men expected to stay in camp for the winter but the day after Christmas, at 9:00 a.m., Polk ordered the men to cook three days' rations and be ready to move at a moment's notice. The weather had turned cold, and by night it began to rain. The tents had been struck, and baggage wagons had removed them farther south. On December 27, Hardee's Corps began to arrive at Murfreesboro and set up camp west of Stone's River. One artilleryman remarked, "the whole Army stirring … Everything in a state of excitement; everybody expects a battle."[231]

---

[228] OR X pt.2, 399–400.

[229] Iredell Diary, December 14, 1862.

[230] Ibid., 24–25; Connelly, *Autumn of Glory*, 40; *Memphis Appeal*, December 13, 1862; Iredell Diary, December 14, 1862.

[231] Daniel, *The Battle of Stones River*, 41, 45; John Euclid Magee Diary, December 27, 1862.

On Sunday, December 28, Polk ordered his corps to cross to the west side of Stone's River. The river was named after Uriah Stone, who had discovered it in 1766, and it was the chief feature of the terrain around Murfreesboro. It flowed through low banks of limestone and could be forded almost anywhere. The river was high from all the rain, but still was only waist deep. The road to Nashville had been macadamized in the 1830s and was thirty feet wide with ditches on each side. There were many open fields west of town and a few groves of cedars and some limestone outcrops. Polk deployed his corps from the Nashville Pike southward almost two miles to the Franklin pike. Cheatham's Division was ordered to stay in town and thus became Polk's reserve. Scott's Battery thus remained in town and observed that many of the town's people were preparing to leave. There had been no church bells that Sunday morning, and the soldiers' camps looked like a "city had been destroyed."[232]

Monday morning, December 29, was frosty but clear. Cheatham had been ordered to bring his division to the west side of Stone's River. Captain Alfred Fielder of the Twelfth Tennessee described the movement:

> We marched out on the RR towards Nashville and crossed Stone's River on the RR bridge upon which plank had been laid for the purpose. We then filed left and marched up the meanderings of the River for a mile or two—and were marched back and forth for some time getting a suitable position and finally formed in line of battle in a clear thicket and were ordered to stack arms and rest in place at 10 o'clk … [A]t this writing [10:30] all is quiet and there fore this is one of the prettiest winter days I ever saw.[233]

This position stretched about 1,700 yards between the Franklin Pike and the Wilkinson Pike. Vaughan's Brigade held the left of the line, and Scott's Battery was ordered to the rear of Vaughan to cover the Triune Bridge into Murfreesboro. The infantry built some breastworks, and many took naps. Scott's Battery unlimbered and stayed in battery through the

---

[232]   Daniel, *The Battle of Stones River*, 46–48.

[233]   Ann York Franklin, *The Civil War Diaries of Capt. Alfred Tyler Fielder 12ᵗʰ Tennessee Regiment Infantry, Company B 1861–1865* (Louisville, Kentucky), 1996, 56.

night. No campfires were allowed. Around midnight, a cold drizzle began to blanket the battery as the men spent a peaceful night under the guns.[234]

As the men awoke on Tuesday morning, a mist obscured their vision all around the battery. It was December 30, and the Federals were forming in the nearby woods. A prebattle directive to the chiefs of artillery had stated to "pay attention to posting of batteries and supervise their work, seeing they do not carelessly waste ammunition."[235] The chiefs of artillery had also received orders from Bragg the night before. They were to "mass their batteries in action and fight twelve guns on a point."[236] In spite of the orders, the batteries of Cheatham's Division were assigned individually to their brigades. Captain Scott had not received any orders overnight, and he and his men heard cannon fire at around 9:00 a.m. to the north. It was Cobb's Battery dueling with the Tenth Indiana and Sixth Ohio Batteries. They heard skirmishers in the distance all day as each side felt out the other. By nightfall, still no orders had been received, and the men prepared to sleep under the guns another night.[237]

Bragg planned to attack the next day. Hardee's Corps, minus Breckenridge's Division, would form up on Cheatham's left. Bragg planned for a morning attack that would sweep like a door moving from left to right. This movement could sever the Federal supply line to Nashville and push them up against Stone's River in their rear.

Throughout the night, troops crossed the Triune Bridge near Scott's Battery's position. Off in the distance, bands played music through the evening. Federal bands played "Yankee Doodle" and "Hail Columbia," while Confederate bands played "Dixie" and "Bonnie Blue Flag." At one point, a Federal band played "Home Sweet Home" and was soon joined by a Confederate band, creating a weird harmony.[238]

All night it continued to rain lightly. One Confederate soldier wrote in his diary, "I have never suffered so from cold in any one day of my life." The men did not sleep much that night.[239]

---

234   Ibid., 50–51, 55; Connelly, *Autumn of Glory*, 51.

235   OR XX pt. 2, 672

236   Ibid.

237   Daniel, *The Battle of Stones River*, 59.

238   Ibid., 64, 68;

239   Squire N. Bush Diary (Louisville, Kentucky: Filsen Club), December 30, 1862.

The morning of December 31 was overcast. There was a cold drizzle, and a mist covered the river area. Many of the Federals had been given permission to start fires and cook breakfast. Confederate orders were to be quiet with no talking or laughing. When Cleburne began the attack shortly after 6:00 a.m., he caught the Federals completely off guard, as many were cooking breakfast. Some of the Federal drivers had even taken the horses to Stone's River for water, leaving many batteries without the ability to move. Over 1,500 prisoners were taken before 8:30 a.m., and many of them came past the battery as they were taken into the town. The men of Scott's Battery remained at their guns and could hear the sound of battle to their front. Early reports indicated shattered Federal units and a victory in progress.[240]

---

[240] Daniel, *The Battle of Stones River*, 72–75, 95; Connelly, *Autumn of Glory*, 54.

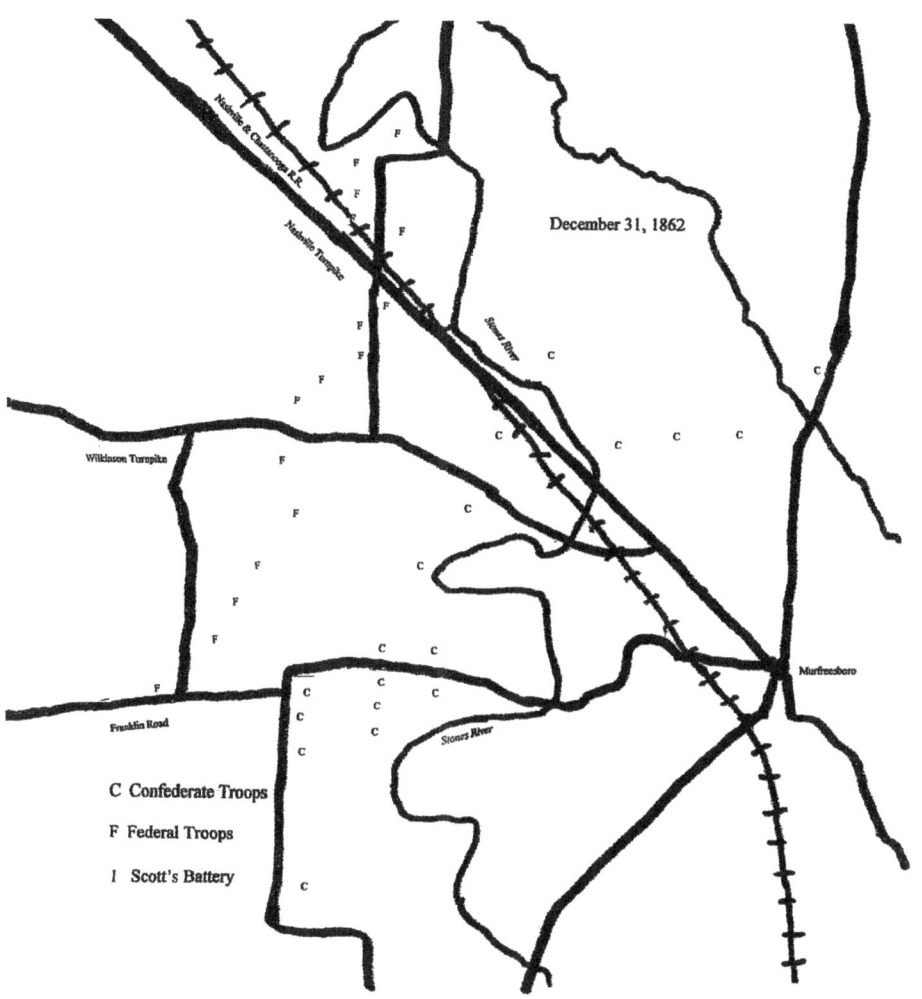

December 31, 1862

C Confederate Troops

F Federal Troops

1 Scott's Battery

At 7:30 a.m., Cheatham ordered Vaughan's Brigade, which had been held in reserve, to advance 300 yards to the front. By now the sun was beginning to burn off the fog. The men dropped their knapsacks into piles and advanced to a cotton field near the Widow Smith's House where their attack failed, and they fell back with heavy losses to the Triune Road. Scott's Battery, which was another 500 yards behind Vaughan's Brigade, never received an order to support Vaughan. Neither Cheatham nor Vaughan sent any messages to Scott. Perhaps they each thought the other had done so. Scott's Battery was not easily seen from their position, and perhaps they did not know where it was. Cheatham was using his staff officers to scout for enemy weaknesses. Lieutenant Fred R. James was killed on one of these missions, and Lieutenant John H. Marsh "narrowly averted being shot."[241] In any case, Scott's Battery remained where they were in a fog of inactivity.

Vaughan's Brigade replenished their ammunition and eventually captured the Federal position without artillery support. The Battle raged on, and at about 10:30 a.m., ten Confederate and ten Federal guns engaged in a ferocious duel along Harding Lane. After a thirty-minute dual and repeated infantry attacks, the Federals were pushed back to their final defensive position called the Round Forest. Those who fought there would call it "Hell's Half Acre." Here the Federal defense held firm, and the Confederate sweep from left to right stalled. Attacks continued until nightfall, and still Scott's Battery had received no orders.[242]

As darkness overcame New Year's Eve, the wounded were gathered up and taken to the rear. Fires were started between groups of wounded men to keep them warm, as the night was getting very cold. Reports from men crossing the Triune Bridge told of terrible horrors and high casualties. Cheatham's Division had suffered nearly 36 per cent casualties. There was good news too. The Confederates had achieved a great victory, and the Federals were in retreat to Nashville. Captain Fielder of the Twelfth Tennessee wrote in his diary, "Thanks to God who gave us the victory and enabled us to drive the boasting foe before us in Wild confusion." Bragg

---

[241] Daniel, *The Battle of Stones River*, 104–5, 109, 116.

[242] Ibid. 120, 154, 157; Polk, *Leonidas Polk*, vol. 2, 181.

even telegraphed Richmond boasting, "God has granted us a happy New Year," and promised to pursue the enemy in the morning.[243]

On New Year's Day, reconnaissance patrols discovered that Rosecrans had not retreated. In fact, he had pulled back some of his lines to make his defensive position even stronger. A hard rain began that morning and later turned to sleet. Cavalry reports confirmed that the Federals were not retreating. Instead, they had received supplies, ammunition, and some reinforcements overnight. Not much action took place that day, as both armies rested and watched what the other would do. That night, at 2:00 a.m., Captain Scott received orders from General Polk to prepare for battle the next day.[244]

The four batteries of Cheatham's Division were ordered to take up positions about 400 or 500 yards in front of the Confederate breastworks between the railroad and the Nashville Pike. Scott's Battery was posted on the right of the Nashville Pike "in an open field opposite the large burnt house."[245] To the right were the batteries of Smith, Carnes, and Stanford. To the left of Scott's Battery was Robertson's Battery, and further to the left were two guns of Lumsden's Battery. Four hundred yards to the front was the Round Forest, which had been occupied by Confederate skirmishers the day before. The guns went into battery about 7:45 a.m., and fifteen minutes later Federal infantry advanced upon the skirmishers driving them from the woods. Robertson's Battery was the first to open fire upon them, followed by Scott's Battery and then the rest. Scott's Battery was firing spherical case and shell with three-second fuses. The Federal infantry was driven back, and the range was increased until they were out of range.[246]

Federal artillery had also moved up with their infantry and, as Captain Scott recalled:

> Two batteries of the enemy to my front and one to my left poured a heavy fire upon me, getting my range with great accuracy. I responded to their fire, and in this engagement lost 1 man instantly killed—Sergeant A. L. Townsend, a brave soldier and

---

[243] Connelly, *Autumn of Glory*, 61–62; Franklin, *The Civil War Diaries of Capt. Alfred Tyler Fielder*, 98; Daniel, *The Battle of Stones River*, 174.

[244] Ibid. 174, 178; Connelly, *Autumn of Glory*, 62.

[245] OR XX pt. 1, 751–753.

[246] Daniel, *The Battle of Stones River*, 178.

good officer. I could not see the effect of my shot upon the enemy batteries, as they were concealed from view by the field immediately in front of me, but have since learned from our skirmishers, in the cedar glade on my left, that I drove one battery from its position, doubling one piece, which had to be left on the field.

Scott's opponents in this dual were the Sixth Ohio Battery and the Eighth Indiana Battery. An officer of the Eighth Indiana Battery remarked, "They had our range perfectly." Many horses had been killed, and two guns were abandoned, one of which was disabled by a direct hit. Other Federal batteries, with rifled guns, continued to fire at Scott's Battery, and since they were out of range, Captain Scott ordered "Cease fire! Limbers to the rear!" and withdrew fifty yards. Soon all of the guns on both side ceased fire.[247]

Lieutenant Polk recalled that, "About 2 o'clock we shelled the enemy skirmishers out of a skirt of timber about 250 yards in our front, from which they had driven out our skirmishers. Their batteries replied, but did us no harm." Although this section of the battlefield had settled down to skirmishing, the main action of the day was taking place on the east side of Stones River. The guns of Cheatham's Division were to create diversionary fire at 3:45 p.m. while Breckenridge's Division made an attack at 4:00 p.m. The orders were late in arriving, and Scott's Battery did not open fire until 4:00 p.m. All of the shells fell short, and Scott ordered, "Cease fire!" Federal guns had returned fire, and with their longer range; one man, Washington McRea, was wounded in the head by a shell fragment and was taken to the rear. The Battery then retired behind the entrenchments for the night. Scott's Battery had fired between 200 and 250 rounds.[248]

---

247   Ibid., 722, 742, 751–753.

248   Ibid; Connelly, *Autumn of Glory*, 63.

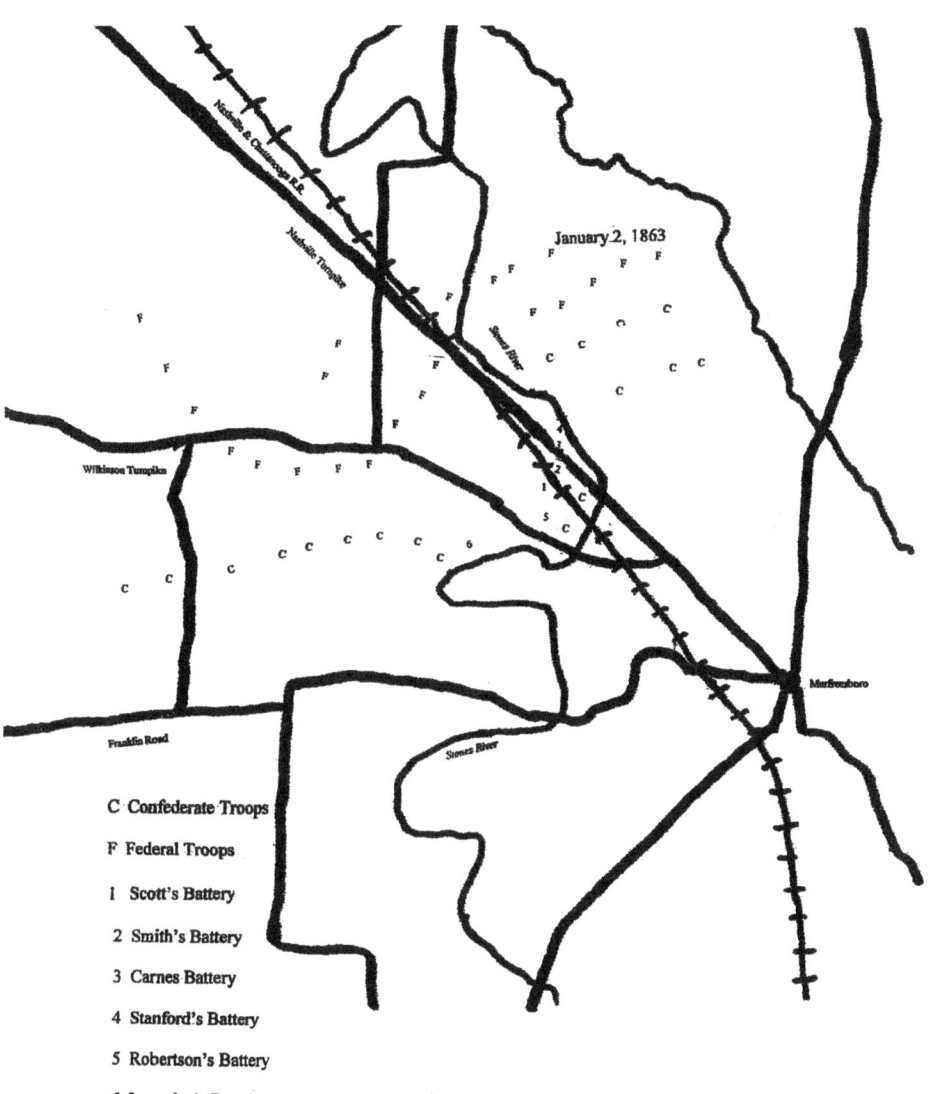

C Confederate Troops

F Federal Troops

1 Scott's Battery

2 Smith's Battery

3 Carnes Battery

4 Stanford's Battery

5 Robertson's Battery

6 Lumsden's Battery

Breckenridge's attack of the Federal left had not gone well. His division was a wreck, and Bragg didn't seem to know what to do. While the generals discussed the situation, the Federal skirmishers had again taken the woods in front of Cheatham's Division. Scott was ordered to return in the morning to his previous position and drive the skirmishers out of the woods. That night it began to sleet, but in the morning, as the sleet changed to rain, Scott's Battery returned to their previous position and drove out the Federal skirmishers. While placing the guns, an accident occurred when Private Patrick Jordan broke his leg when a cannon wheel rolled over him. After a few shots, Scott ordered, "Cease fire! Limbers to the rear!" As the battery returned to the breastworks, Scott was handed a message from General Polk to cease fire. General Bragg had decided to retreat from Murfreesboro.[249]

Fearing heavy Federal reinforcements and that the rising Stones River might isolate the left wing of his army, Bragg had made a controversial decision. A Confederate victory was being given away to the Federals. The retreat from Murfreesboro would not begin until 11:00 p.m. It rained all day, January 3, sometimes in torrents. There were no military actions that day. Murfreesboro was full of wounded, and trains were taking as many as they could to Chattanooga, but many would have to be left behind. Polk's corps withdrew down the Shelbyville Pike. Scott's Battery took its position behind Smith's Brigade of Cheatham's Division. Preston Smith had been absent on the first day of battle and had just returned to relieve Vaughan, who returned to command the Thirteenth Tennessee. One artilleryman described the march in his diary: "My God, what suffering. Wet through—cold and chilly—no sleep for four or five nights, and march through mud and water, some without any shoes, and some sick, and some with fingers and toes frozen, while behind on the bloody field were thousands moaning out the little life left them. The rain still poured down."[250]

At sunrise, January 4, 1863, the clouds began to break and the rain stopped. A rainbow appeared in the eastern sky, but the men were exhausted. Scott's Battery rested five miles north of Shelbyville. Bragg had ordered Polk to take his corps to Tullahoma where he would join with Hardee. Colonel George Brent, a member of Bragg's staff, remarked in

---

[249]   OR XX pt. 1, 751-753.

[250]   Daniel, *The Battle of Stones River*, 200; John Euclid Magee Diary, January 2, 1863.

his diary, "The movement so far to the rear has had a bad effect upon the troops & the public mind." The next day he wrote, "Spirits bad. Matters look gloomy." On January 9, Bragg ordered Polk, who was now a dozen miles south of Shelbyville, to return to Shelbyville while Hardee would remain at Tullahoma. So the men of Scott's Battery had to return on the road they had just traveled reminding many of the countermarching at Perryville, which increased the complaining in the ranks. Some of the men thought Bragg was incompetent; most thought he should be replaced. But in spite of these hard feelings against Bragg, some artillery commanders thought Scott's Battery was Bragg's pet. By sundown on January 9, Scott's Battery was making camp near Shelbyville, Tennessee.[251]

The Officers

Captain William L. Scott had proven himself to be a competent leader. He had diligently obeyed orders and became heavily engaged on January 2, earning the respect of his men. The battery was credited with driving back two Federal batteries and disabling one gun, albeit other batteries were firing into the same area. One man was killed, and two were wounded. No horses were lost, and no carriages were damaged. Scott also received a high honor from the officers of Preston Smith's Brigade. In Smith's absence, Colonel Alfred J. Vaughan of the Thirteenth Tennessee was in command of the brigade on December 31, and Lieutenant Colonel W. E. Morgan was in command of the regiment. Vaughan explained what happened:

> In the battle a battery of four beautiful Napoleon guns was captured from the Federals. Four divisions of our army claimed to have participated in the capture, and each division laid claims to the battery. A conference of the officers of the divisions was called, and after a full discussion and careful consideration of the claims of each division, it was decided that one of the guns should be given to each division, and that upon it should be inscribed the name of the most gallant and meritorious soldier who fell on that battlefield. One of the guns was given to Cheatham's Division and assigned to Preston Smith's Brigade ... Lieutenant-Colonel Morgan ...

---

[251] Daniel, *The Battle of Stones River*, 200, 203; George Brent, Diary, January 7–8, 1863, Bragg Papers, William Palmer Collection, Western Reserve Historical Society, Cleveland.

fell in the first day's fight, and by unanimous consent his name was inscribed upon the gun, and read as follows: "Lieutenant-Colonel W. E. Morgan, Thirteenth Tennessee Regiment, Pres. Smith's Brigade, Cheatham's Division, Polk's Corps." The gun was assigned to Scott's Battery and at the Battle of Chickamauga the gun was skillfully handled and did effective work ... [252]

---

[252] Vaughan, *Personal Record of the Thirteenth Regiment Tennessee Infantry C.S.A.*, 25–26.

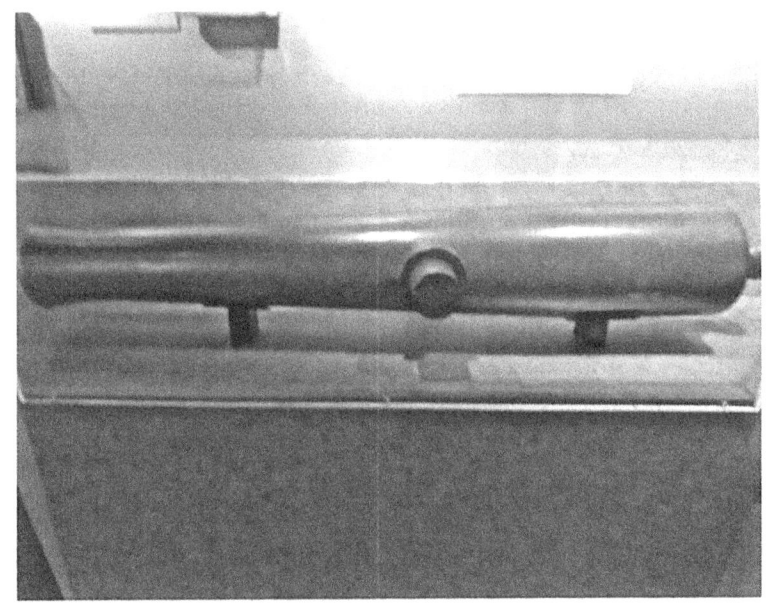

"THE NAPOLEON CAPTURED ON DECEMBER 31, 1862 BY THE THIRTEENTH TENNESSEE INFANTRY REGIMENT ON DISPLAY AT STONE'S RIVER NATIONAL MILITARY PARK PHOTOGRAPHED IN 2014, INSCRIPTION READS: 'LIEUTENANT-COLONEL W. E. MORGAN, THIRTEENTH TENNESSEE REGIMENT, PRES. SMITH'S BRIGADE, CHEATHAM'S DIVISION, POLK'S CORPS,"

Official records never showed Scott's Battery having a Napoleon, but the Thirteenth Tennessee fought beside the battery at Chickamauga and would have known if the gun was present. The gun was later captured by the Federals and was taken to Gettysburg Military Park when it first opened in 1895. In the later twentieth century, it was on display at the Stone's River Military Park and is still on display today. This gun was truly an honor to Scott and his battery.[253]

Scott also was a man of few words but was very punctual. General Preston Smith asked Scott, on the morning of January 9, as the battery was marching to Shelbyville, to write an after-action report of Scott's Battery in the recent battle. Scott wrote a one-page report that very night in his tent while his men were busy making camp, and filed it with Smith. No other report was written as quickly as Scott's. Other commanders wrote theirs on January 10, but many were not written until February. His report was used in writing this chapter and was a tribute to his diligence. Scott received a furlough in late January for some needed rest. He went home to Knoxville and returned to duty in March.[254]

First Lieutenant William M. Polk commanded the battery during Scott's absence. One report Polk wrote described the operation of the battery during battle. Polk wrote:

> The battery remained on the Triune road until Thursday morning, when we received an order to take position at the breastworks between the Wilkinson and Nashville pikes, where we remained until Friday morning, not having fired a shot up to that time. The battery was then ordered to take a position about 400 or 500 yards in front of the breastworks between the railroad and Nashville pike, Capt.'s Stanford's and Carnes' and Lieut. Turner's batteries being on our right beyond the railroad, and Capt. Robertson's battery being on our left beyond the pike. After being in that position about fifteen minutes, the enemy's infantry commenced an advance, when we opened on them with spherical case and shell at three seconds time. The enemy, after a little, fell back, upon which we increased our range and time, and continued the firing until they were beyond our range. Two of the enemy's

---

[253] Ibid.; OR XX pt. 1, 753.

[254] OR XX pt. 1, 670–790.

batteries were advancing with their line of infantry, both of which returned our fire, but both ceased firing when their line of infantry retired. One of the batteries fell back with the line, the other remained in its position, having, as we afterward learned from our skirmishers, one of its pieces disabled. It however, fell back after we ceased firing. As soon as the enemy's line commenced falling back, they opened fire on us with two rifle batteries, which were beyond our range. Having received an order to cease firing, we did so, and fell back about 50 yards, under cover of a little rise in the ground. The batteries of the enemy ceased firing soon after we did. In this engagement we lost 1 man killed. About 2 o'clock we shelled the enemy's skirmishers out of a skirt of timber about 250 yards in our front, from which they had driven our skirmishers. Their batteries replied, but did us no harm. That evening we fired a few spherical case at the enemy's line, all of which burst short, they being beyond our range. We then retired to the breastworks for the night. The next morning we took the position we had occupied the day previous, and shelled the enemy's skirmishers out of the skirt of woods I mentioned before. The enemy's batteries did not reply. From that time until late that evening we occupied the position quietly. About 4 o'clock Saturday evening the enemy opened a well-directed fire upon us with three batteries, all of which were beyond our range. The battery fell back inside of our intrenchments and Capt. Scott reported to Gen. Cheatham, when he ordered him to bring the battery to his headquarters, where we remained until 2 o'clock that night, when Capt. Scott was ordered to cross the river and join the rest of the division, which was on its way to this point. During the various engagements of the battery we used the pendulum hausses with tolerable satisfaction. The most of our shrapnel and shell did very well. Our friction-primers also did very well. My experience in regard to the table of ranges used by us, which is found in the instruction for field artillery, is that it does not answer as well as it should, from the fact that the powder for which it was prepared is so much superior to ours.

During the various engagement of the battery we had 1 man killed, 1 slightly wounded, and 1 man's leg broken by being run over by one of the guns. No horses were lost and the carriages were not damaged. We fired between 200 and 250 rounds, principally spherical case.[255]

Polk preferred to use Bormann fuses in the shells, as the paper fuses were not as reliable

Polk was responsible for supplies for the company. On January 9, he sent in a requisition for jackets, pants, and shirts. A few days later he sent a requisition for more shirts and pants and five pairs of shoes. On the twentieth he requested 250 horseshoes and sixty pounds of horseshoe nails. He also turned in nine horses as unfit for service. As he worked to provide the battery with some of its needs, his father, General Leonidas Polk, was planning to transfer him to his staff as inspector of artillery for the entire corps. On February 17, the nineteen-year-old first lieutenant left Scott's Battery for his staff assignment. Lieutenant John H. Marsh of Bolivar, Tennessee, replaced him.[256]

Twenty-four-year-old John H. Marsh came from a rural family in Hardeman County. The family had about fifty slaves on their cotton farm. Marsh had dropped out of West Point Military Academy in 1861 without even finishing his first year to volunteer in Polk's Tennessee Battery, which was then forming in the county. When the battery was disbanded after Shiloh, Marsh had been transferred to Cheatham's staff. He had two years of experience during the war when he arrived with Scott's Battery.

First Lieutenant Joseph Phillips left Scott's Battery on detached service shortly after the Battle at Murfreesboro. He joined Smith P. Bankhead in Texas, arriving on March 3 in San Antonio. Twenty-one-year-old Second Lieutenant Thomas Peters, who arrived on February 17, the same day as Marsh, replaced him. Peters and Marsh both came from Bolivar, and both had volunteered for Polk's Battery. Peters' father was a respected surgeon who owned a large plantation in Arkansas. Peters had attended the University of Mississippi before joining Polk's Battery as the First Sergeant. He was promoted to Second Lieutenant on September 1, 1861. After Shiloh, he served with his uncle, Thomas Hill Peters, who was the quartermaster on General Polk's staff.[257]

---

[255] Ibid., 753; OR XXXII. pt. 1, 751.

[256] CCSR m268 roll 98.

[257] Ibid; David Wake, personal correspondence with author, May 2013.

Alfred T. Watson continued as a reliable second lieutenant. Technically, the staff of Scott's Battery was full, but Phillips was on detached service in Texas and was still carried on the rolls. These were the men that carried on the duties of the battery in 1863.

The Enlisted Men

The official report for Cheatham's Division showed that seventy-seven enlisted men were at the Battle of Murfreesboro, but Scott reported ninety-eight men present at the end of December. The difference in the numbers is explained by the fact that some of the sick and those on detached service were still kept on the rolls. The traveling from Kentucky and the cold winter weather had taken its toll on the men. There had been no new recruits added to the roster as the Conscription law had intended. Instead, the conscript men were placed in new units. The Army of Tennessee received few of these as the government in Richmond felt that they were needed in Mississippi more than in Tennessee.[258]

Sergeant A. L. Townsend was killed by a cannon shot as the only loss to Scott's Battery at the Battle of Murfreesboro. Townsend had $33 in his pocket and various sundries in his haversack, all of which were sent home. Washington McRae was wounded in the head with a shell fragment. It was only a flesh wound, and he was not sent to the hospital. Patrick Jordan, on the other hand, had been run over by a cannon wheel. He is not listed as wounded on any reports, but was considered wounded by his comrades. He was left behind at the hospital in Murfreesboro and captured by the Federals. He was taken to Camp Morton, Indiana, and exchanged on April 13. He went to Farmington Hospital in Virginia where he was finally given a thirty-day furlough to go home to recover on May 9. As a former Girardy's Battery member, he went home to Augusta, Georgia. In August he was in Atlanta, and his leg had still not healed properly. He drew an issue of new pants, a shirt, and shoes from the quartermaster. He placed his X on a special requisition form No. 40 and never returned to the battery.[259]

There were other men lost at Murfreesboro. James Kennedy had been sick in the hospital and was captured by the Federals. Federal records show that he was paroled on January 22. He came walking into the camp

---

[258]   CCRS m268 roll 97–98; OR XX pt. 1, 709.

[259]   CCRS m268 roll 97–98.

at Shelbyville and told a story about escaping from the Federals, but something wasn't right. He was arrested by the inspector general and taken to Tullahoma. He was not heard from again and was removed from the rolls. The same story was told by Sergeant James Canada when he walked into camp. There are no Federal records of his parole, and the inspector general also arrested him. He did not return to the battery; however, he was carried on the rolls as absent throughout the year.[260]

Other men left Scott's Battery legally. James H. Roach left on January 12 after serving as a teamster for reason of the Conscription Act. Others would follow. January 19 saw six more who had been serving as teamsters receive their discharge. They were John W. King, William Green Lea, James Hill, Thomas B. Wood, William B. Thompson, and Thomas Smart. Records indicate that Sergeant James Welsh was court-martialed on January 25, 1863. Welsh had been listed as a deserter back in June 22, 1862. The records do not show the result of this trial. James Owens was discharged due to disability on February 9. D. L. Vining died of heart disease at the hospital in Tullahoma on February 14.[261]

Neil Finney, who had been wounded at Shiloh, remained a member of Scott's Battery for the rest of the war; but he did not return to the ranks. Drawing his pay and clothing allowance and always signing his name with Scott's Battery as his unit, Finney was assigned as a nurse at St. Mary's Hospital in LaGrange, Georgia, on February 18, 1863. He had lost the sight of his right eye and received extra-duty pay. General Bragg approved this situation on September 1, 1863. W. E. Humphreys also went on detached duty. On February 20 he left for Atlanta where he received extra-duty pay working for the quartermaster department as a shoemaker.[262]

Only one change was made in regards to the NCOs. Daniel McKenzie was reduced to the rank of private because he was in the hospital very sick. John B. Watts replaced him as sergeant. William H. Martin then became corporal. This change was made on February 20.[263]

One man, Michael Nason, did not return from Murfreesboro and was listed as a deserter; he had joined the battery on the very first day Bankhead began enlistments. Desertion was not a big problem after the campaigns of

---

[260]   Ibid.

[261]   Ibid.

[262]   Ibid.

[263]   Ibid.

late 1862. In fact, a few men returned to the ranks in 1863 after recovering from their time in the hospital.[264]

The arrival at Shelbyville provided the men with some much-needed rest. Resentment of Bragg persisted in the ranks and would soon come to a head. New officers, under Captain Scott's leadership, would perfect the skills of the battery into one of the most admired units in the Army of Tennessee.

---

[264]   Ibid.

CHAPTER 7

SHELBYVILLE
FEBRUARY–JULY 1863

Army of Tennessee	Scott's Battery
General Braxton Bragg	Captain William L. Scott
	First Lieutenant John Marsh
Polk's Corps	Second Lieutenant Thomas Peters
Lieutenant General Leonidas Polk	Second Lieutenant Alfred T. Watson
First Division	Quartermaster Sergeant T. E. Watts
Major General Benjamin F. Cheatham	Ordnance Sergeant L.A. Ellis
Fourth Brigade	Sergeant James Collins
Brigadier General Preston Smith	Sergeant William Fowler
Eleventh Tennessee Infantry Regiment	Sergeant John Purcell
Lieutenant Colonel William Thedford	Sergeant John Watts
12th & 47th Tennessee Infantry Regiment	Corporal E. P. Burnett
Colonel T. H. Bell	Corporal Thomas Cluin
13th & 154th Tennessee Infantry Regiment	Corporal J. D. Echol
Colonel A. J. Vaughan Jr.	Corporal Hines Holt
29th Tennessee Infantry Regiment	Corporal John Halbert
Colonel Horace Rice	Corporal William Martin
Scott's Battery	Corporal J.G. Westbrook
Captain William L. Scott	73 privates
	14 Absent

After Murfreesboro, Bragg decided to make a defensive stand along the Duck River, behind the ridges of the Highland Rim. Polk's corps would be camping at Shelbyville, a town incorporated in 1819 on a limestone bluff on the north side of the Duck River. The town was named after Revolutionary War hero Isaac Shelby, who also became a Kentucky governor. Shelbyville had long been known as 'Little Boston," as the people were strong unionists and anti-secessionists and did not like the idea of a Confederate army camping in their town. Scott's Battery would spend the next six months at Shelbyville. It was a time of quarrels in the high command, intensive drilling, and a renewed discipline in army life.[265]

As soon as camps been be set up, the newspapers began to report on the conduct of General Bragg at Murfreesboro. There were still the simmering complaints about Bragg at Perryville as well. The *Daily Richmond Examiner* wrote, "General Bragg has certainly retreated ... from his victory at Murfreesboro, as he did last fall from his victory at Perryville." The *Daily Richmond Examiner* also said that Bragg had no "exercise of military genius." The *Chattanooga Daily Rebel* editorial of January 6, 1863, hit the nail on the head when it criticized that he was not popular in the army, the troops had no confidence in him, and his own generals did not support him.[266]

In response to the newspaper articles, Bragg sent out a letter to all of his corps and division officers informing them that he would resign if he had lost their confidence. Polk was on leave in North Carolina when this came out, but nearly all of Hardee and Breckenridge's officers gave Bragg a no-confidence vote. When Polk returned, he refused to commit himself, and he let Hardee do the dirty work. Polk would not let his division commanders respond either. It was well known that Polk and Cheatham were not well liked by Bragg, but they kept out of this quarrel. Cheatham's brigadiers, however, appear to have been mostly pro-Bragg. This left the impression that Captain Scott was a Bragg supporter. There is no evidence of this, as Scott was not consulted, and being a company commander, he was not involved.[267]

---

[265] Connelly, *Autumn of Glory*, 69.

[266] *Daily Richmond Examiner*, January 6 and February 23, 1863; *Chattanooga Daily Rebel*, January 6, 1863.

[267] Connelly, *Autumn of Glory*, 75; Daniel, *The Battle of Stones River*, 207.

Bragg did not resign, but instead began a vendetta to purge those against him. John C. McCown was suspended from his command, which was given to Stewart, a supporter of Bragg. Breckenridge was transferred to Mississippi after Felix Robertson wrote a strong denunciation of him at Murfreesboro. This was actually a re-written report at Bragg's request. Robertson was rewarded with time off in Richmond and a promotion to major upon his return. Cheatham was attacked by Bragg's official report, but because he was tremendously popular among the Tennessee soldiers, no charges were filed. Polk was also under scrutiny and had begun to gather evidence he could use if Bragg attacked him. Ultimately, the high command was fractured with no outcome in sight.[268]

However, this quarrel did have an effect upon Scott's Battery. Artillery promotions were given to officers who favored Bragg. Major James H. Hallonquist was the artillery chief of Bragg's old corps at Shiloh. He was promoted to lieutenant colonel and appointed as chief of artillery of the Army of Tennessee. According to historian Larry Daniel, "Little in his record suggested that he was ready to handle the new responsibilities that had been thrust upon him."[269] He spent the spring of 1863 supervising test firings and squabbled with ordnance officers. He shunned his administrative office and failed to organize the artillery in the better battalion organization.

Also promoted was Felix Robertson, a harsh disciplinarian who was hated by his men. At the age of twenty-three, he was appointed to the new artillery reserve, which reported directly to army headquarters. The reserve artillery would be getting the new Napoleon cannons being produced in Augusta, Georgia. Captain J. R. B. Burtwell was another Bragg favorite moving up the ladder. He was promoted to major and appointed chief of artillery of Wither's Division in Polk's corps.[270]

Scott and the other battery commanders in Cheatham's Division personally petitioned the War Department requesting the promotion of Major Melancthon Smith as their battalion commander. The request was denied. All of these promotions were done without regard to seniority. Other changes and promotions were made in the artillery branch in other

---

[268] Ibid., 208–210; Connelly, *Autumn of Glory*, 81–85, 90; Daniel, *Cannoneers in Gray*, 82; Elliot, *Soldier of Tennessee,* 77.

[269] Daniel, *Cannoneers in Gray*, 82.

[270] Elliot, *Soldier of Tennessee,* 77.

commands as well. This created jealousies and friction among the various battery commanders. Although Scott did not strive for a promotion, these were the people he would have to work with. Officers who lacked experience or did not improve the performance of their own battery often did not receive the respect for their office. William L. Scott earned the respect of his men as well as the respect of the superior officers.[271]

The Confederate War Department issued General Order No. 7 on January 7, 1863. This made the artillery a separate branch of the army based on the model of Robert E. Lee's artillery. In April it was put into effect in the Army of Tennessee. Division artillery chiefs were given more authority, and thus promotions occurred as mentioned above. Batteries still marched with their brigade and took orders from the brigadier while on outpost, but they now camped together under the command of their division chief. Bragg also created an artillery reserve under Major Robertson. The reserve was made up of Barret's, Havis's, Lumsden's, and Massenburg's Batteries. They received all of the newest guns and more ammunition than other batteries. They had plenty of horses and mules and battery equipment and camped separately at Estelle Springs. The reserve was eventually broken up, as individual batteries were needed somewhere. Even the battalion organization did not last. Major Melancthon Smith's adjutant wrote to his mother on June 22, 1863, "About three weeks ago the batteries were dispersed to their brigades." In the upcoming campaign the old command system continued.[272]

When Scott's Battery initially arrived at Shelbyville, they camped with Preston Smith's Brigade. Areas were marked off and the tents were pitched. The men then began to winterize them by building wooden floors and making chimneys as they had done at Columbus and at Murfreesboro. One soldier wrote, "We have got tents and some durt houses and some bordy shelters and so we all make out the best we can." It rained a lot in January and February. The camps needed to be trenched to keep the water out of the tents and to drain the water out of the camps. Drill was cancelled on many days. The men were often confined to their tents, and the routine was idleness. One cannoneer wrote, "Camp is dull nothing but Eat sleep and drill with an occasional review by some General that wishes to show

---

[271] Ibid., 84.

[272] Ibid. 87; Ed Goelet letter to mother and sister, June 22, 1863, Southern Historical Collection. University of North Carolina, Chapel Hill.

himself in his military glory." Camp hygiene was strictly enforced, and the sinks (latrines) were placed outside of the camps. Guards were even posted to make sure the men used the sinks.[273]

Originally the men had been given uniforms of gray with red cuffs and collars. Few of the men still wore these, as they had become worn out and torn; many had simply been thrown away. Even though new uniforms had been given prior to the Battle of Murfreesboro, the men of Scott's Battery were not outfitted with uniformity of color or cut. Many of the men preferred coarse homespun coats or pants. The men wore brown or gray colors, and many of them preferred felt hats. The discipline of uniformity of clothing was not enforced. Only the officers wore uniforms of gray and kept them very tidy.[274]

Very little active campaigning occurred in the spring of 1863. Cavalry patrols continued to monitor the Federals in Murfreesboro and occasionally clashed with enemy cavalry. In camp the men, when they weren't drilling, amused themselves with foot races and other athletic contests. Gambling also occurred. They played games like faro, seven up, draw poker, and three-card monte. Sometimes they played dice games, like chuck-a-luck. In the nearby infantry camp cock fighting was a big time sport. Mail call was the most important time of the day, although the mail was not regular. Many of the men of Scott's Battery had families behind enemy lines, and so little mail was received for them.[275]

Music was another favorite pastime. Cheatham's Division had three regiments (Fourth, Fifth, and Thirteenth Tennessee) that had wonderful musicians. These were combined and often played "Bonnie Blue Flag," "Kelly Mae," and other favorite songs. Banjo playing and fiddling were also popular. It is not known if anyone in Scott's Battery had any musical talent, but the men often drifted off toward the music.[276]

---

[273] Daniel, *Soldiering in the Army of Tennessee: A Portrait of Life in a Confederate Army*, 72–73; D. Coleman, Diary, February 15, 16, 17, 18, 20, 21, 1863, Southern Historical Collection, University of North Carolina, Chapel Hill; Thomas Warrick Letters, Alabama Department of Archives and History; Belser L. Wyman Letters to father, Alabama Department of Archives and History.

[274] Daniel, *Soldiering in the Army of Tennessee*, 32.

[275] Ibid., 89, 97.

[276] Ibid., 91.

Civilians and women often visited the camps. Of course most of the families of the men of Scott's Battery were behind enemy lines, and so few ever visited the camps. One soldier wrote, "The army is all the time surrounded by debased women—and I believe they are the cause of so much wickedness." He told his wife not to come and visit the camps. Lewd women were known to frequent the camps as indicated in the reports of venereal disease. Historian Larry J. Daniel states, "Bragg's army averaged one case of venereal disease per 183 mean strength." This was higher than both Pemberton or Lee's army, and the camps weren't even close to any large cities.[277]

On the other side of the spectrum was a religious revival, for many men expressed a desire for religion. Historian Bell Wiley has examined this activity and summarizes it as something in "the Southern culture, and growing national and personal insecurity in the form of military reversals and fear of death." How many men from the battery went to revivals is unknown. However, there were large crowds at several revivals held at many camps. Even poor weather and a shortage of chaplains did not prevent the gatherings. One soldier of the Thirteenth Tennessee went to a revival meeting and recorded that it was "the most ignorant sermon I have ever heard in my life." Obviously the revival movement was not for everyone.[278]

On March 30, 1863, Polk's corps assembled for an inspection on behalf of President Davis by his aide-de-camp, Colonel Preston Johnston. General Polk described the assembly with pride,

> The troops looked very well, and I never saw them march so well. My corps was never in better condition, and is now about 20,000 strong. I confess I felt proud of the fellows as they marched by me today. In their hearts is embodied as large and as intense an amount of rebellion as was ever concentrated in the same number of men. It is a pleasure to command such men. Johnston was highly pleased and very complimentary.[279]

---

[277] Ibid., 98–99; John A. Harris to wife, May 16, 1863, John A. Harris Letters, Baton Rouge, Louisiana State University, Department of Archives and History.

[278] Bell I. Wiley, *The Story of Johnny Reb* (Indianapolis, 1962), 183–184; Searcy Letters, June 24, 1863; Daniel, *Soldiering in the Army of Tennessee*, 116–119.

[279] Polk, *Leonidas Polk*, vol. 2, 212–213.

The men felt good too. They had plenty of clothing and all had descent shoes. Rations were more than adequate as well. Also, all of the horses and mules were in great shape.

In April, all of the batteries of Polk's corps were camped together. "We have a beautiful camp four miles west of Shelbyville. We have twelve batteries which are present and a very imposing appearance on drill," wrote Captain James Douglas in his diary. Scott was fortunate to have the skills of John Marsh when it came to drill. Marsh had fought with Polk's Battery at Shiloh and was skilled at the school of the piece. Drill was ordered for every day for four or five hours. Sometimes the drill was held in the evenings as well. Besides the school of the piece the men practiced dismounting the guns from the carriages and remounting them. They practiced at firing at the rate of five times per minute.[280]

There was also practice with the horses and mules. Because of a shortage of horses, mules now made up about 25 percent of the battery's livestock. The men were timed at hitching the teams to the carriages and limbers. Fifteen minutes was considered the maximum time needed, which included six minutes for the men to gather their personal effects and fall in. Times for hitching alone ranged from four to nine minutes, making Scott and Marsh very pleased indeed. At times there was a shortage of forage and also a shortage of currycombs.[281]

Finally a contest was held amongst the twelve batteries of Polk's corps to see who was the best drilled. The division and battalion commanders would judge the contest in regard to school of the piece, school of the battery, and firing at targets of 1,000 yards. The prize would be a banner, and it was highly coveted. On April 21, Captain James Douglas wrote in his diary, "All hands agree that the contest will be between my battery and Scott's." Two weeks later Douglas wrote, "I rather think Scott will win the prize, as he is a pet with Bragg's army."[282]

This remark shows the importance of winning the banner and an excuse by Douglas if Scott's Battery did win. Scott had no antagonism toward other battery commanders but may have been friendly with the

---

[280] Lucia R. Douglas, *Douglas' Texas Battery, CSA* (Waco, Texas, 1966), 64; CCSR m268 roll 97; Jones Diary, April 27–May 11, 1863; Daniel, *Cannoneers in Gray*, 70–72.

[281] Ibid., 73; Hughes, *The Pride of the Confederate Artillery*, 94.

[282] Douglas, *Douglas' Texas Battery*, 115.

judges. It also shows that battery commanders were being affected by their feelings toward Bragg. Remember, others thought Scott was a favorite of Bragg, although there is no evidence to support that. In the end, Stanford's Battery won the contest. One member of Stanford's Battery recorded in his diary that they had drilled four or five hours every day in an open field, and the men were "always glad when it is over in order to get a rest." Obviously the long hours of drill paid off.[283]

The artillery camp was broken up in late May, and Scott's Battery returned to Shelbyville where it passed an inspection by Major Melancthon Smith. The battery had a caisson for every gun as well as a traveling forge and a battery wagon. There was also a complete set of blacksmith tools as well as carpentry tools and harness makers. With the exception of the Napoleon gun, the battery still had all of its original equipment. While other batteries were getting new carriages or guns, Scott's Battery continued to maintain its equipment. Smith's inspection did show that the battery did not have its required 200 rounds of ammunition per gun. Friction primers, however, were more than adequate.[284]

On June 23, Rosecrans' army began to move against the Confederate outposts. These outposts were located at three gaps in the plateau: Guy's Gap, Liberty Gap, and Hoover's Gap. At Liberty and Hoover's Gaps, Federal forces were engaging Confederate defenders on June 24 and 25. Orders were given to General Polk to move out on June 26 and take his corps through Guy's Gap and flank the Federals. Polk opposed this move as very complicated and dangerous. Orders were given to Scott's Battery to prepare to move. It took all day to get ready, and by 5:00 p.m. news arrived that Guy's Gap was already in Federal hands. At 11:00 p.m., Bragg cancelled the planned move and ordered Polk to fall back to Tullahoma. The entrenchments at Shelbyville were abandoned without a fight.[285]

The need for retreat was caused by Rosecrans' left hook march to Manchester, which threatened the supply base at Tullahoma. The road to Tullahoma quickly became a quagmire as rain fell. Cheatham's column got so bogged down by wagons getting stuck or breaking down that Cleburne's

[283] Daniel, *Soldiering in the Army of Tennessee*, 25; George W. Jones Diary, May 8, 1863.

[284] Daniel, *Cannoneers in Gray*, 75.

[285] David A. Powell. *The Maps of Chickamauga* (New York: Savas Beattie LLC, 2009), 10.

men coming from behind tried passing through Cheatham's men. This led to confusion. The Federals were having the same problems behind them, so no pursuit was possible. It took two days for Scott's Battery to travel the seventeen miles to Tullahoma.[286]

Tullahoma was a small village of only a dozen buildings. It had been founded as a construction camp for the Nashville and Chattanooga Railroad just fifteen years before. There were prepared field fortifications, and Bragg was determined to defend his supply base. These field works were slight and incomplete. Cheatham's division was ordered to fill in the gaps in the works. Scott's Battery began to build small lunettes for the guns, but the ground was muddy and the work almost impossible. The position at Tullahoma was a poor choice for making a stand. Meanwhile, Rosecrans moved further around Bragg's right threatening the railroad, so Bragg ordered another retreat.[287]

Bragg had been totally fooled by the Federal movements in June. His command was in disarray, and he had asked only once for a council of war during the previous week. Scott's Battery passed over the bridge at Derchard on June 30. On July 2, orders were received to retreat all the way to Chattanooga. Rosecrans was threatening Bragg's right again, and Bragg had no plan. Scott's Battery entered Chattanooga on July 4, 1863, not having fired a shot at the enemy in six months.[288]

The Officers

William L. Scott returned from his furlough to visit family in Knoxville about March 5. He had drawn his $140 monthly pay the previous month before the scheduled payday of March 1. It is not clear, but he may have met his future wife, Susan Elder, at this time, as they were married the next year. He signed a number of requisitions for clothing that was needed by the men and for additional stationery. There was also a need for horseshoes and mule shoes.[289]

---

[286] Ibid., 12.

[287] Ibid.; Michael R. Bradley. *Tullahoma* (Shippensburg, PA: Burd Street Press, 2000), 82–84.

[288] Ibid. 87; Powell, *The Maps of Chickamauga*, 14.

[289] CCSR m268 roll 98.

The primary activity of the officers at this time was the drilling of the men. Although on campaign for six months, Scott's Battery had been engaged with the enemy only one day at Murfreesboro. While marching or on outpost, the men had drilled only infrequently. Scott set the pace and ordered drill on a regular basis. As other batteries discovered the pace of Scott's drill, they became concerned about the skills of their own batteries, particularly after the announcement of a contest to award a banner to the best-drilled battery. Scott was respected as an able commander by the other batteries, and the men were proud of this distinction they had in Cheatham's division.[290]

Scott was fortunate to have First Lieutenant John Marsh as his second in command. Marsh took on the responsibility of working the men on the guns. It was on the guns that the men would find the camaraderie that made them a highly respected battery, and it was John Marsh who forged this pride. Marsh was high spirited and well known by the staffs of Preston Smith and Benjamin Cheatham. At Perryville and also at Murfreesboro he was known for his gallantry. As the temperatures warmed in the spring and the men moved out to the artillery camp, this pride was instilled in the men. John Marsh, like Scott, was not politically minded and did not take sides in the Bragg controversy. Duty was more important than family. There would be time for family when the war was won. Marsh believed in the patriotism of the Confederacy and was an example for the South.[291]

Thomas Peters was the senior second lieutenant in Scott's Battery and a friend of John Marsh. Peters assisted Marsh in the duties of the drill until March 13 when he asked for a thirty-day furlough. Apparently Peters was ill and needed some time to recuperate. Federal forces occupied his home in Bolivar, Tennessee, at the time, so it is unclear where he went. He returned to his duties in April.[292]

On May 7, a jealous husband shot and killed General Earl Van Dorn in Spring Hill. The killer was Peters' father, Dr. George B. Peters. The victim had been having an affair with Dr. Peters' third wife, Jessie Helen McKissick, who was not the mother of Thomas Peters. Following the shooting, Dr. Peters fled to Shelbyville intending to turn himself in to

---

[290]   Daniel, *Cannoneers in Gray*, 71.

[291]   C. T. Quintard, "Tribute to Lieut. John Marsh," *Confederate Veteran*, vol. 5, December 1897, 599.

[292]   CCSR m268 roll 97.

General Polk. Fearing that he would be incarcerated, Dr. Peters, through his brother and Major J. J. Murphy of the commissary, received a pass through Federal lines. He thereby escaped to Nashville out of the reach of Confederate authorities. It is not known if Thomas met with his father at this time, but the event may have had an effect upon him. On June 8, Lieutenant Peters was granted a sixty-day furlough. He had a surgeon's certificate of disability. He never returned to Scott's Battery.[293]

Second Lieutenant Alfred T. Watson was the mainstay of the officers of the battery. Haven risen through the ranks, he was well liked by the men. He was the obvious go-between if someone had a problem. Marsh and Peters took care of the papers and forms, and Watson was in charge of the equipment. Through his authority, horses were well cared for, and the equipment was cleaned and repaired. The thoroughness of his duty helped make Scott's Battery a respected unit.[294]

The officers of Scott's Battery made the unit into a well-drilled machine. As they were already one staff member short, the loss of Peters to illness put more burdens upon Scott, Marsh, and Watson. Because Phillips was on detached duty and Peters on furlough, there would not be any replacements. Still, the finest men with few scruples led Scott's Battery.

The Enlisted Men

While the men were at Shelbyville, they were paid twice, at the end of February and the end of April. Records indicate that in the first pay call there were ninety-nine men present and eleven absent. At the second pay call there were ninety present and fourteen absent. Captain Scott had enough men for the battery and had not lost many men due to combat or desertion. Other batteries were not as fortunate. Captain Charles Swett went home to Vicksburg to recruit for his battery, but returned empty handed. Conscripts were collected for others, or infantry were transferred to fill the ranks. Scott's Battery added only one man. That was William E. McRae, who volunteered for Scott's Battery specifically because he had three older brothers in the unit. He joined on April 14, when he turned eighteen, but did not arrive from Arkansas until early June.[295]

---

293   Ibid.; David Wake, Peters family notebook.

294   CCSR m268 roll 98.

295   Ibid. roll 97–98; Daniel, *Cannoneers in Gray*, 72.

Illness was the biggest problem for soldiers. The concept of germs was not known at this time, and sanitary conditions were very primitive. Some of the men sent to the hospital were T. L. Rickerson, Oliver M. Bigbee, L. A. Ellis, Edward Martin, William Martin, Lawrence Gilfoil, William Saunders, R. G. McRae, T. Thomas, Patrick Jourdan, and Thomas Goins. Some returned to the ranks, while others, like Rickerson and William Martin, were still in the hospital six months later. Edward Martin died in a Chattanooga hospital on March 8 with $1.25 to his name. T. Thomas died on June 4, and Goins died on July 18. On March 4, Corporal Hines Holt died in camp of pneumonia. Some of the men in the hospital did not return to the ranks and were given detached service. Gilfoil spent two months guarding prisoners in Atlanta. R. G. McRae was kept as a hospital attendant.[296]

Three men were discharged from the army for being over the conscription age. They were Oliver H. Edwards, Phillip B. Land, and G. W. Long. They were all from Arkansas and were discharged in May. Edward Cearns was the only man to desert from the battery, and did so in the spring of 1863. Other units had a problem with desertion, but Scott's was becoming a home for many of the men. The men had pride in and devotion to their company.[297]

The unity of Scott's Battery was based on a grassroots nature. The men had shared the hardships of camp life and campaign. An esprit de corps had developed through sacrifice and shared suffering and the witnessing of death on the battlefield as well as through sickness. This esprit de corps was related directly Scott's Battery, but not so much to the Army of Tennessee. The men had melded into a pride of themselves as a unit and a bonding of the men around their camp life.

Historian Thomas Connolly says that this spirit was derived from "the immense faith of the common soldier in himself."[298] After two years of encampments and campaigning, the hardships of continuous drill and the hardships on the march, there had developed a cohesiveness as strong as family. Unit morale was high due to competition with other batteries in which the men themselves wanted to be regarded as the best unit in the army. Bragg was responsible for any military setbacks, and the men

---

[296] CCSR m268 roll 97–98.

[297] Ibid.

[298] Connolly, *Army of the Heartland*, xiii.

knew they could win on the battlefield. According to historian Larry J. Daniel, "If any unit symbolized the backbone of the Army of Tennessee, it was Cheatham's Tennesseans." Scott's Battery was at the center of this backbone. In a letter written on June 1, 1863, John Cookson wrote, "I have good officers who treat me well & am a private in one of the best batterys in Braggs army."[299]

---

[299]   Daniel, *Soldiering in the Army of Tennessee*, 3, 21–24; CCSR m268 roll 97.

CHAPTER 8

———◦◦⟨◉⟩◦◦———

CHICKAMAUGA
JULY–SEPTEMBER 1863

Army of Tennessee	Scott's Battery
General Braxton Bragg	Captain William L. Scott
	First Lieutenant John Marsh
Polk's Corps	Second Lieutenant Thomas Peters (absent)
Lieutenant General Leonidas Polk	Second Lieutenant Alfred T. Watson
First Division	Quartermaster Sergeant T.E. Watts
Major Gen. Benjamin F. Cheatham	Ordnance Sergeant L.A. Ellis
Fourth Brigade	Sergeant James Collins
Brigadier General Preston Smith	Sergeant William Fowler
11th Tennessee Infantry Regiment	Sergeant John Purcell
Lieutenant Colonel G.W. Gordon	Sergeant John Watts
12th & 47th Tennessee Infantry Regiment	Corporal Edward P. Burnett
Colonel W.M. Watkins	Corporal Thomas Cluin
13th & 154th Tennessee Infantry Regiment	Corporal J.D. Echols
Colonel A.J. Vaughan Jr.	Corporal John Halbert
29th Tennessee Infantry Regiment	Corporal William Martin (absent)
Colonel Horace Rice	Corporal J.G. Westbrook
Dawson's Sharpshooters	73 privates
Maj. J.W. Dawson	14 absent
Scott's Battery	
Captain William L. Scott	

In the summer of 1863, Scott's Battery was stationed in Chattanooga. It was now the army's base and a vital stronghold. Here the railroads converged from East Tennessee, Memphis, and Atlanta. Ordnance depots had been established here and in the rear at Atlanta. There was also a complex of hospitals at Chattanooga, and more of them extended down the railroad toward Atlanta. Chattanooga was the doorway to the South and to the minerals found in the nearby hills. The town had been founded in the late 1830s and boasted a population of about 5,000 citizens. It was not significant in size, but was still a center for industry. At Ninth and Broad Streets was the three-story Crutchfield House. This was the largest building in town, and from the top of the building flew the stars and bars of the Confederacy.[300]

Scott's Battery had arrived at Chattanooga in early July and set up camp south of town with Cheatham's division. The men were put to work building earthworks, but the hot weather of July and August were idled away. During this time, there was a shortage of rations, but food could be found for high prices in town. Historian Peter Cozzens remarks that, "The pall of the army deepened." The continuous retreating demoralized some men, and only if drill was ordered did the men have anything to do.[301]

Reports were coming in that, during the retreat from Tullahoma, several batteries had abandoned equipment along the road. Major Smith found ten sets of harness abandoned, and Major Burtwell found twelve. Burtwell also found a traveling forge and a battery wagon. On July 14, Smith took an inventory of his batteries, and Scott's Battery passed with flying colors. None of the losses along the road had been caused by Scott's Battery.[302]

To keep the artillery occupied, Polk ordered that all of his batteries should do some target practice. A firing range was found east of Chattanooga near Cleveland, Tennessee. One or two batteries would go there each day and shoot at targets. The shooting began on August 5.[303]

---

[300] Connelly, *Autumn of Glory*, 137–139; Peter Cozzens, *This Terrible Sound: The Battle of Chickamauga* (Urbana and Chicago: University of Illinois Press, 1992), 21; McDonough, James Lee, *Chattanooga—Death Grip on the Confederacy* (Knoxville: The University of Tennessee Press, 1984), 73–74.

[301] Ibid., 27; Cozzens, *This Terrible Sound*, 21.

[302] Daniel, *Cannoneers in Gray*, 91.

[303] John Euclid Magee Diary, August 5, 1863.

Stanford's Battery, which had won the coveted banner only three months before, fired on August 6 and had a dismal showing. Regarding firing at targets, one private wrote in his diary, "commenced firing at 10 o'clock with first piece—very unsatisfactory. Each gun had four shots allowed to it. The second piece followed us. Neither one hit the target of 1400 yards. Will not fire the third and fourth pieces—are unfit." Stanford's Battery was given another chance the next day. The diarist continued, "Resumed firing at 10 o'clock—no better success. Our battery condemned." There must have been some glee in the ranks of Scott's Battery when they heard this news.[304]

Swett's and Douglas's Batteries had no hits on their targets either. Fowler's Battery and Turner's Battery, firing on August 8, were able to score two hits each. All of the shooting was considered very bad. Scott's Battery fired on August 11, but the diarist was not present to record the results. Apparently Scott's Battery did well, as the diarist wrote on August 12, "all of the batteries except Fowler's and Scott's very bad."[305] This made the men of Scott's Battery very proud, and in their eyes redeemed them from their performance in the earlier contest. Stanford and several of the batteries would be receiving some of the new Napoleon tubes. Scott's Battery would not. Polk then held a grand review of his artillery and concluded the training.[306]

Bragg had been ill most of July and had taken residence at Cherokee Springs south of Chattanooga to recuperate. Things were changing in the command structure, and rumors were rampant amongst the men that Bragg was being replaced. This might have been wishful thinking, as it was untrue. Bragg had gotten rid of General Hardee and transferred him to Mississippi. His replacement, Lieutenant General Daniel H. Hill, had been in Lee's Army of Northern Virginia. Bragg had decided to promote Major Melancthon Smith to lieutenant colonel and send him to be Hill's chief of artillery. Smith reluctantly left Cheatham's division and traveled eleven miles to his new post only to find that Hill had brought his own chief of artillery from Virginia. Thirty-two-year-old James Bondurant

---

[304]   Ibid. August 6–7, 1863.

[305]   Ibid. August 8–12, 1863

[306]   Daniel, *Cannoneers in Gray*, 92.

already held the position. Embarrassed and crestfallen, Smith returned to his duties with Cheatham.[307]

August 21 was a bright sunny day in Chattanooga. President Davis had proclaimed a day of prayer and fasting, and a group of officers and civilians were attending services at the local Presbyterian Church when an artillery shell exploded in the street. General Cheatham informed the congregation that was just the artillery practicing when another shot sailed over the rooftop. Most of the congregation fled the church as it became apparent that a Federal battery was shelling the town from across the river. Colonel John Wilder with the Eighteenth Indiana Battery had caught the Army of Tennessee completely off guard. Two steamboats were sunk at the wharf, and the shelling continued for days. Bragg soon ordered the civilians to leave town, but many did not need to be told. Soon most civilians were gone, and the bombardment continued. Rosecrans was on the move, but Bragg did not know where he was headed.[308]

The hot days of August soon gave way to a hot, dry September. The men knew that something was in the air. None of Preston Smith's brigade had been given any picket duty until now. This was not normal. Breckenridge's old division had returned from Mississippi, and rumors had it that Robert E. Lee was coming to Chattanooga. Actually, two divisions of Longstreet's Corps were being organized for a long train ride from Virginia. The Federals captured Knoxville on September 3, and the East Tennessee command was added to Bragg's army. The problems of the anti-Bragg faction had never been solved. With more troops and new commands coming to the Army of Tennessee, disorganization appeared on the horizon.[309]

Bragg finally realized that the Federals had crossed the Tennessee River west of Chattanooga and were moving in his rear trying to cut off his supply lines to Atlanta. Orders were given on September 6 to abandon Chattanooga in an effort to "meet" and "strike" the Federals south of Chattanooga. Scott's Battery received orders to break camp that

---

[307] Ibid.; Connelly, *Autumn of Glory*, 137.

[308] Cozzens, *This Terrible Sound*, 35–36, 39; Elliot, *Soldier of Tennessee*, 113.

[309] Connelly, *Autumn of Glory*, 146, 148, 150.

morning. All of the tents were loaded onto wagons, and by nightfall the men marched out the La Fayette Road to Rossville.[310]

The roads were dry and very dusty. The marching kicked up clouds of dust, and the men were covered in dirt. This would be the situation for the next two weeks. Sweaty uniforms from the ninety-degree heat collected the dust, and the dust also got into the soldiers' eyes. The men grumbled about another retreat. With the recent fall of Vicksburg, things looked very gloomy, as many men feared they would retreat all the way to Atlanta. As one diarist exclaimed:

> The idea of our army giving up the city of Chattanooga, the gate to the center of the Confederacy, was trying on our confidence in General Bragg and all others in authority over us, and the saying of all the boys was: "If we can't check them and whip them with advantages of the river and the mountain-locked passes on the right and left of Chattanooga, where is the place we can?"[311]

As the state of Tennessee was being abandoned, there was the fear of the loss of Tennesseans to desertion. General Stewart addressed his men on September 7 about "meet[ing] the enemy in deadly conflict" and returning triumphantly to Tennessee. There were reports that some Tennesseans had even deserted from Nathan Bedford Forrest's command. In fact, two men, J. Lightner and Joseph D. Hardin, had already deserted from Scott's Battery on August 31. Both of them were from Georgia, so the loss of Tennessee was not their issue. There were no other deserters from the battery.[312]

Cheatham's division marched twelve miles that first day and camped at Crawfish Valley along Chickamauga Creek. The next day they camped at Lee and Gordon's Mill while the baggage wagons continued on to Lafayette. The men would not see their baggage for weeks, and on September 17 all of the baggage wagons would withdraw to Rome, Georgia. On September 10 Cheatham's division withdrew six miles southeast of Lee and Gordon's Mill to Anderson's crossroads where the Rock Spring and Pea Vine Roads intersected. The next day they were ordered to Lafayette. After arriving

---

[310] Elliot, *Soldier of Tennessee,* 115; Cozzens, *This Terrible Sound,* 55–57; OR XXX pt.2, 610–611.

[311] Cozzens, *This Terrible Sound,* 64; D. Coleman Diary, 101–102.

[312] Cozzens, *This Terrible Sound,* 57; CCSR m268 roll 97.

at Lafayette they were ordered to countermarch back to Rock Springs Church. What was behind all of these marches?[313]

Bragg was still trying to find Rosecrans. The Confederate forces were scattered, and he was trying to trap some Federals in the nearby hills. According to Thomas Connelly, "command confusion plagued this ... attempt to strike the Federals while they were scattered." Polk was not cooperating with Bragg, and the men paid the price of marching in the heat and dust. Connelly concluded that "high command was afraid to take the initiative. Bragg's officers also had no confidence in his abilities ... [and] Bragg no longer trusting his officers to independent operations."[314]

By September 17, Rosecrans had avoided any Confederate trap and had concentrated his forces along Chickamauga Creek from Lee and Gordon's Mill to McLemore's Cove. Bragg had concentrated his forces to the east of the Federals and planned an attack upon them a little to the north of Lee and Gordon's Mill in the hope of cutting Rosecrans off from Chattanooga and trapping him against the mountains. Polk's corps occupied the center of this line near Lee and Gordon's Mill. The attack would begin about seven miles northeast at Reed's Bridge with Polk ready to reinforce it.[315]

Final orders for the attack were not given until September 18, as troops from Virginia were rushed forward from the Ringgold station. Major General John Bell Hood arrived with the lead brigades of Longstreet's corps while Bragg reorganized his army in the face of the enemy. He would now have two wings, the right commanded by Polk and the left commanded by Lieutenant General James Longstreet. This led to further confusion in the command structure. Already Polk's corps was drawn up in battle lines and would have to wait another day. Two things affected the men that night. First, Captain Scott had become ill and had gone to Lafayette. Therefore, Marsh and Watson were commanding the battery. Second, that night the weather turned cold. It was near freezing, and a hard wind blew through the forest. Men who had perspired for weeks now looked for blankets, and no campfires were allowed as the men shivered in the ranks. Few would get much sleep that night.[316]

---

[313] Cozzens, *This Terrible Sound*, 81, 85; Connelly, *Autumn of Glory*, 173, 179, 186.

[314] Ibid., 190.

[315] Ibid., 195–198.

[316] Ibid., 199–200. Cozzens, *This Terrible Sound*, 97; OR XXX vol. 2, 106.

The terrain would have an effect upon the Battle of Chickamauga. Chickamauga Creek was not particularly deep or swift, but the banks of the creek were steep and rocky, thus preventing much east-west movement except at the five bridges and nine fords. The land was mostly flat, and scattered farm fields were laid out haphazardly and poorly cleared. Tree stumps were everywhere, and farm animals fended for themselves in the forests. There were many cedar glades and pine forests in the area, and scrub brush was everywhere. Visibility was limited in the wooded areas, and knowledge of the location of the enemy was only vague.[317]

September 19, 1863, was becoming a splendid morning. The weather was cool, but would soon warm up. Scott's Battery, under the command of John Marsh, crossed Dalton Ford around 8:00 a.m. to the west side of Chickamauga Creek. Cheatham's division had been ordered to fall in behind Buckner's Corps and await developments. By 9:00 a.m., sporadic firing could be heard to the north at Reed's Bridge. The Battle of Chickamauga had begun.[318]

The battle had begun at Reed's Bridge, and for two hours the brigades of General Nathan Bedford Forrest and William H. T. Walker had taken on the Federals of Major General George Thomas. The slugfest would eventually leave both forces spent. At 11:00 a.m., Bragg ordered Cheatham to move to the aid of Walker, who was still engaged near Winfrey Field. As the men were moving at the double-quick, they passed by a body of troops who appeared much better dressed than anyone in Bragg's army. One cannoneer wrote in his diary, "Our first impression was partly caused by the color of their uniform, but more by its uniformity, and the superior style of their equipments, in haversacks, canteens and knapsacks. This contrast between them and Gen'l Bragg's motley, ragged troops was striking in the extreme." Lieutenant Lucius G. Marshall of Carnes' Battery described it this way: "The Army of Tennessee never looked worse, while at the same time it was never in better fighting order. But three weeks of maneuvering in the densest dust without washing had conferred the same uninteresting color upon everything—man, beast and material. If this command was a specimen of Lee's troops, they are certainly superior to the troops of the Army of Tennessee, in dress."[319]

---

317   Ibid., 91.

318   Ibid., 128–131.

319   W. A. Brown, Diary, September 19, 1863, Greenwood Public Library, Greenwood, Mississippi; Lindsley, *The Military Annals of Tennessee*, 821.

These men had been part of Benning's brigade of Hood's division, and it was the first time the men knew anything about troops coming from Virginia. By noon Cheatham had his brigades ready to advance. General John K. Jackson's brigade on the right of the line went forward to support Walker. George Maney's brigade supported him in the second rank. To Jackson's left was Preston Smith's brigade with Scott's Battery coming up behind the infantry. General Otho F. Strahl's brigade supported Smith in the second rank. To the left of Smith was Marcus Wright's brigade.[320]

To the north of Brock Field, Jackson's troops ran into Colonel John Croxton's Federals, who had just finished fighting Walker's Confederates. Croxton's lines were split, and a charge by Jackson pushed the Federals back 300 yards where a static firefight evolved. Federal reinforcements under General Richard W. Johnson replaced the exhausted troops of Croxton. Jackson found his brigade up against a Federal division, and a Federal charge forced Jackson back.[321]

A short distance south of Jackson's fight was Brock Field. Federal General John M. Palmer of XXI Corps was advancing his men forward to support Johnson while Preston Smith's brigade was on a collision course planning to flank Johnson. Palmer had advanced in echelon making his left brigade of General William B. Hazen arrive at Brock field first. Looking north, Brock Field is shaped like a thick reverse *L*. Hazen halted his command in line with Johnson's division on his left on a small rise in the middle of the field at the top of the *L*.[322]

Coming to meet Hazen was the right of Smith's line made up of Dawson's Sharpshooters and the consolidated Thirteenth and One Hundred and Fifty-Fourth Tennessee Infantry Regiment. Dawson's Sharpshooters was made up of one company from each of the five regiments in Smith's Brigade, and the consolidated regiment was made because of the low numbers in each individual regiment. "A terrific contest here was added to the already severe battle on our left," as his men fell back to the tree line at the edge of the field, remembered Hazen.[323]

Scott's Battery was moving up behind Smith's line in a single column because of the underbrush and trees. Seeing the open field ahead and the

---

[320] Powell, *The Maps of Chickamauga*, 71.

[321] Ibid., 73.

[322] Ibid.

[323] Ibid; OR XXX vol. 1, 762.

infantry already engaging, Marsh ordered "From column into line, by the left, march!" The six-pound howitzers were in the lead and entered the field, turned about, and stopped with the guns at the edge of the woods. This was the left section. The right section made up of the Napoleon and twelve-pound howitzer did the same maneuver on the right. The guns were unlimbered, and Marsh commanded, "Action front! In battery!" Already the battery was taking fire from Hazen's men, and several men were wounded. Orders were given for spherical case with two-second fuse and canister when Marsh commanded "Commence firing!" The range was estimated at only 400 yards.[324]

Colonel Alfred J. Vaughan of the Thirteenth/One Hundred and Fifty-Fourth Tennessee explained:

> Scott's Battery ... advanced with the brigade and took a position as ordered, under a heavy and destructive fire of the enemy, so much so that a number of men and horses were disabled before the battery was placed in action. Immediately a rapid and well-directed fire was opened upon the enemy with telling effect upon his ranks. This fire was vigorously maintained until the brigade was relieved and ordered to the rear.[325]

Colonel William Watkins, who commanded the consolidated Twelfth/Forty-Seventh Tennessee on the left of Scott's Battery, described the situation with contact at "about 400 yards from the enemy, who seemed to [be] entrenched, having an open field between us, except a few yards of timber next to the enemy line." Actually, the Federals were not entrenched, but it appeared so because Brock Field was in the process of being cleared, and Watkins mistook piles of brush and felled trees as field works. Captain Alfred Fielder of the Twelfth Tennessee recalled that they "were engaged in an awful fight the enemy disputing every inch of the ground."[326]

---

[324]   Ibid., 117.

[325]   Ibid., 107.

[326]   Ibid., 111; Franklin, *The Civil War Diaries of Capt. Alfred Tyler Fielder*, September 19, 1863.

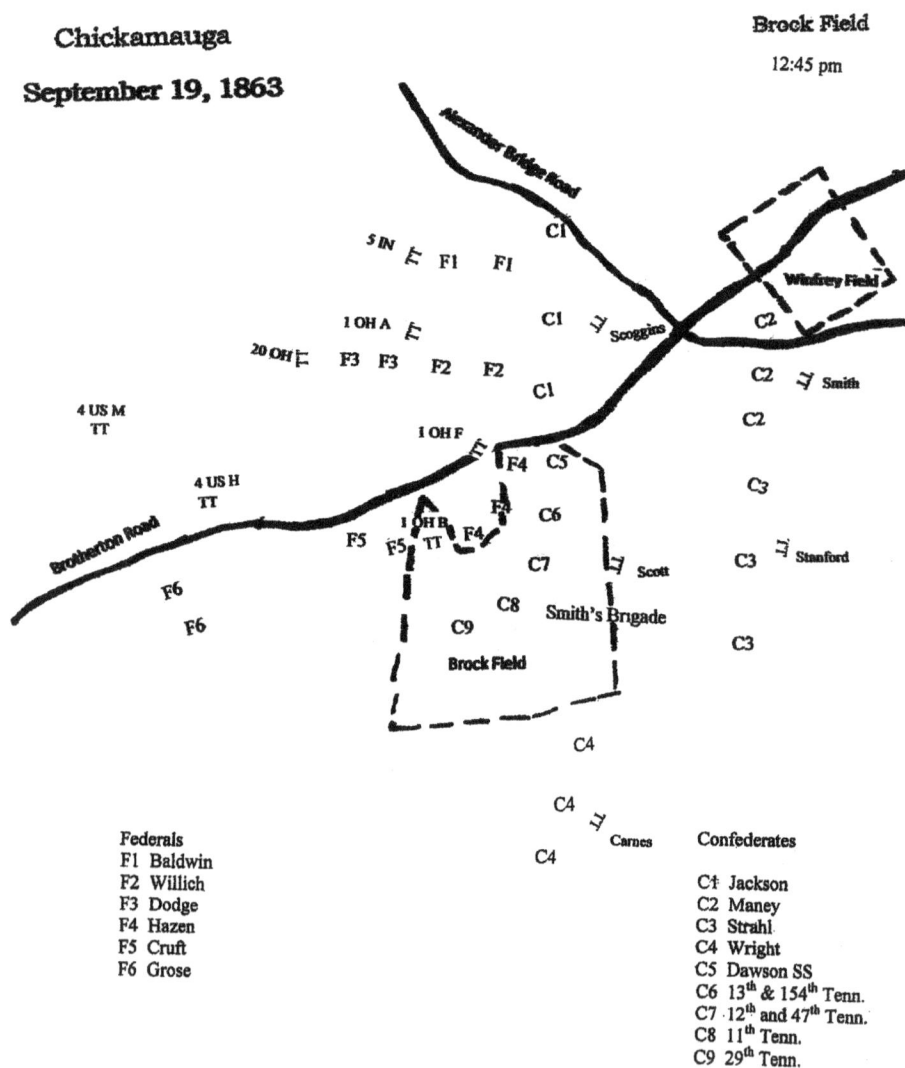

Chickamauga

September 19, 1863

Brock Field

12:45 pm

Federals
F1 Baldwin
F2 Willich
F3 Dodge
F4 Hazen
F5 Cruft
F6 Grose

Confederates
C1 Jackson
C2 Maney
C3 Strahl
C4 Wright
C5 Dawson SS
C6 13th & 154th Tenn.
C7 12th and 47th Tenn.
C8 11th Tenn.
C9 29th Tenn.

It was around 1:00 p.m. when Scott's Battery opened fire on Hazen's men. Alfred T. Watson reported it to be about 2:00 p.m. when they opened fire, but reports from all other sources dispute that. After firing only two rounds, the twelve-pound howitzer broke a cap square and was out of commission. A cap square is an iron strap that holds the cannon barrel onto the carriage. With only three serviceable guns, the battery continued to fire as fast as possible. Watson reported, "After fifteen or twenty minutes, First Lieut. John H. Marsh was severely wounded by a Minie ball passing through the left arm, and was taken from the field." Watson was now the only officer present with the battery. He reported, "I continued firing under a heavy fire from the enemy of musketry, shell and canister."[327]

The First Ohio Battery F was supporting Hazen, but no counter battery fire occurred. The closeness of the fighting meant that the infantry could easily shoot at artillery, and artillery could cause severe damage to infantry. Scott's Battery already had sustained several casualties, and many horses had also been hit. Smith's brigade was curving around Hazen's right flank only to be checked by the arrival of General Charles Cruft's brigade. Cheatham looked for a way to flank Palmer and ordered Wright's brigade, which was moving unopposed in the woods south of Brock Field, to wheel to the right and come up on Smith's left. Wright did that only to find that Palmer's reserve brigade, under Colonel William Grosse, had been sent to block him. Wright's left was now exposed, and he placed Carne's Tennessee Battery to guard his flank.[328]

Wright's line was stretched several hundred yards facing north. He was at a right angle to the rest of Smith's Brigade. As Wright became engaged, the rest of Smith's brigade was beginning to feel overmatched. The Twelfth/Forty-Seventh Tennessee had attacked the apex of the Federal line, but in doing so lost touch with the Thirteenth/One Hundred and Fifty-Fourth Tennessee, which had drifted across the front of Scott's Battery. On the west side of Brock Field, the Twenty-Ninth Tennessee under Colonel Horace Rice remembered, "Having double-quicked some distance over rough ground, studded in some places with short thick undergrowth, the line of the regiment was considerably broken and some confusion prevailed at the time we halted. A volley from the enemy at that moment added still

---

[327]   OR XXX vol. 2, 117.

[328]   Ibid., 118

more to the confusion." Smith now wisely ordered his brigade to fall back to the tree line with Scott's Battery.[329]

Scott's Battery continued to fire as Smith's infantry formed a line on the eastern and southern ends of Brock Field. It was now about 1:30 p.m., and the infantry were running low on ammunition. Cheatham ordered Strahl's brigade to replace Smith on the firing line with specific instructions to "make no attempt to advance." Unfortunately, Strahl's men went through Smith's men and into Brock Field taking many casualties before they replaced Smith, who took his brigade about half a mile to the rear to rest and regroup. The order not to advance did not get to Wright, who was still fighting on the extreme left. To the right of Smith, Maney's brigade replaced Jackson at about the same time. Scott's Battery remained in place with Strahl's men. Stanford's Battery, which was in Strahl's brigade, was unable to come into line and remained in reserve.[330]

---

[329] Ibid., 111, 114.

[330] Ibid., 78, 107.

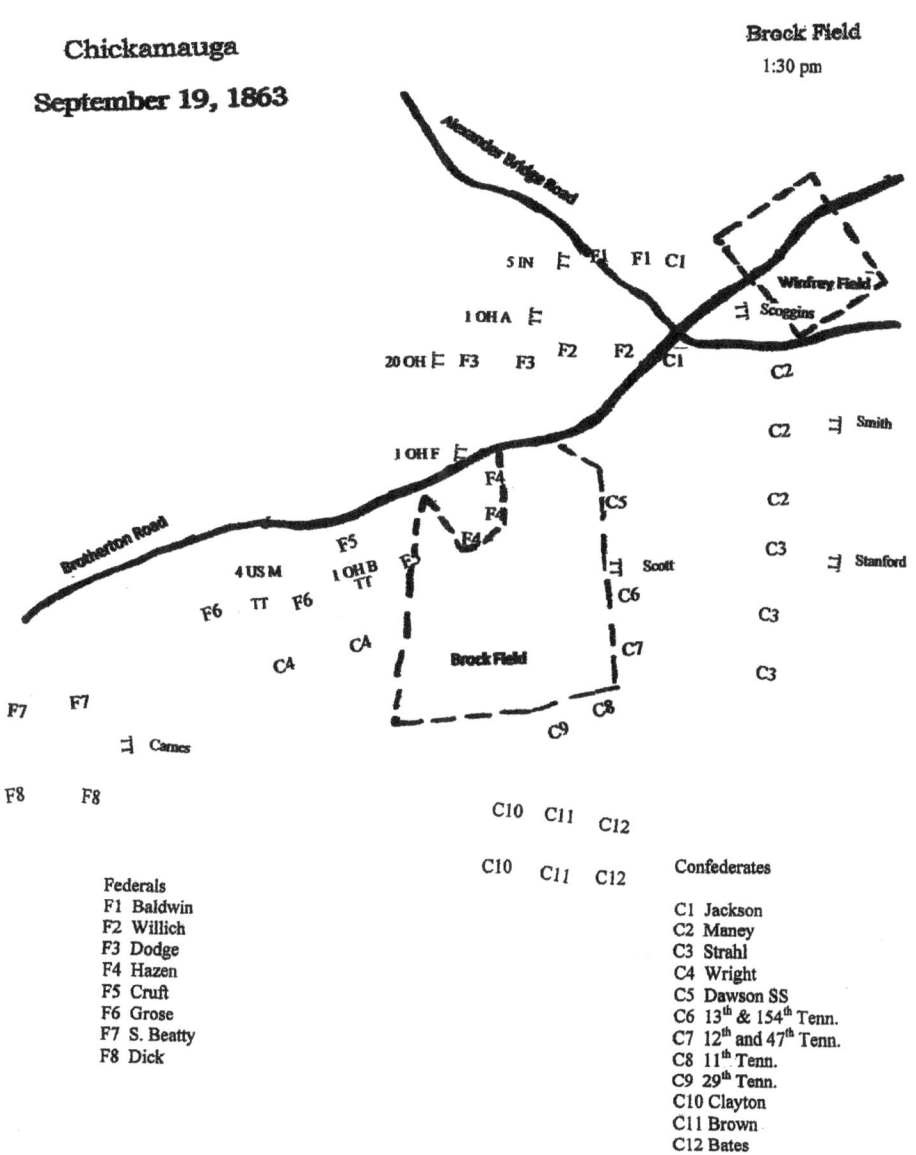

Chickamauga

September 19, 1863

Brock Field

1:30 pm

Federals
F1 Baldwin
F2 Willich
F3 Dodge
F4 Hazen
F5 Cruft
F6 Grose
F7 S. Beatty
F8 Dick

Confederates
C1 Jackson
C2 Maney
C3 Strahl
C4 Wright
C5 Dawson SS
C6 13th & 154th Tenn.
C7 12th and 47th Tenn.
C8 11th Tenn.
C9 29th Tenn.
C10 Clayton
C11 Brown
C12 Bates

As Wright engaged Palmer to his front, a large Federal force appeared on his left. Two brigades of infantry of Brigadier General Horatio P. Van Cleve supported by four artillery batteries entered the woods with only Carnes' Battery available to challenge them. What happened to Carnes' Battery is worthy to report, as it shows what happens to a battery of guns unsupported by infantry. It would also have an effect upon Scott's Battery.[331]

First Lieutenant Lucius G. Marshall of Carnes' Battery described what happened:

> Wright's brigade, at a double-quick the last four hundred yards, approached within perhaps three hundred yards of the enemy works, and swiftly drew into line of battle, not leaving room for the battery to form in the center of the line as they were supposed to ... After three of the cannoneers were killed in this awkward position ... the Captain, on his own responsibility, ordered the battery forward till it should pass the left flank of Wright's brigade.[332]

The limbers then turned to the left in front and unlimbered. Without turning the limbers around, the men immediately brought ammunition forward. Marshall continued, "Four times a minute for the first three or four minutes, at least, each gun was discharged at very short range." Double charges of canister held the enemy in check. Men and horses were being shot down, enemy infantry were moving in the woods at angles to the battery, and Wright's brigade had disappeared. "The battery now stood alone ... only two [men] of the right piece had escaped death or severe wounds. The battery was clearly overpowered." After about ten minutes Captain Carnes ordered the survivors to escape as best they could. Carnes' Battery lost all of its horses except two. Forty-nine men were killed or captured, and only thirty-five men escaped with the captain and the lieutenants.[333]

The Federal infantry then swarmed over the position and cut up the limbers and began to drag the guns back to their own lines. Although it

---

[331] Powell, *The Maps of Chickamauga*, 79.

[332] Lindsley, *The Military Annals of Tennessee*, 821–822.

[333] Ibid.

was too late for Carnes, help was on the way. Bragg had ordered Stewart's division to support Cheatham, and his arrival around 2:00 p.m. would save the day. Stewart's men drove the Federals back to near the Lafayette road, immobilized and then overran five Federal guns, and recaptured Carnes' guns. Stewart's arrival also helped take pressure off of Cheatham's men at the Brock Field.[334]

Meanwhile at Brock Field, the Federals were bringing up the fresh brigade of Colonel Joseph B. Dodge. Dodge came through Hazen's brigade and charged across the northern end of Brock Field. Coming up behind Dodge was John B. Turchin's brigade of Ohio troops. The chaplain of Turchin's brigade, William Lyle, was riding up behind the brigade and remarked about the sound up ahead:

> I had heard the roar of battle at Bull Run, had felt the earth quiver under the fierce conflicts of South Mountain and Antietam, but the incessant roar of artillery and musketry on this terrible day seemed to exceed all three battlefields combined. The musketry was neither in distinct shots nor in repeated volleys, but … was one mighty fearful, continuous roll.[335]

Scott's Battery was still firing along the line of infantry of Strahl's brigade. Ammunition was running low, as the battery had been in continuous action for almost two hours. On the right the Nineteenth Tennessee was unable to stop Dodge and withdrew into the woods. Strahl ordered his brigade to fall back, and Scott's Battery pulled their guns by hand into the woods and then limbered up and withdrew about half a mile to the rear. Scott's Battery had been in action for about two hours and twenty minutes and had fired 146 rounds with three guns. The losses were two men killed and thirteen wounded. Additionally, fourteen horses were lost.[336]

---

[334]   OR XXX vol. 2, 362, 370–371.

[335]   William W. Lyle, *Lights and Shadows of Army Life* (Cincinnati: R. W. Carroll, 1865), 289–290.

[336]   Ibid, 117; Powell, *The Maps of Chickamauga*, 81; Daniel, *Cannoneers in Gray*, 110.

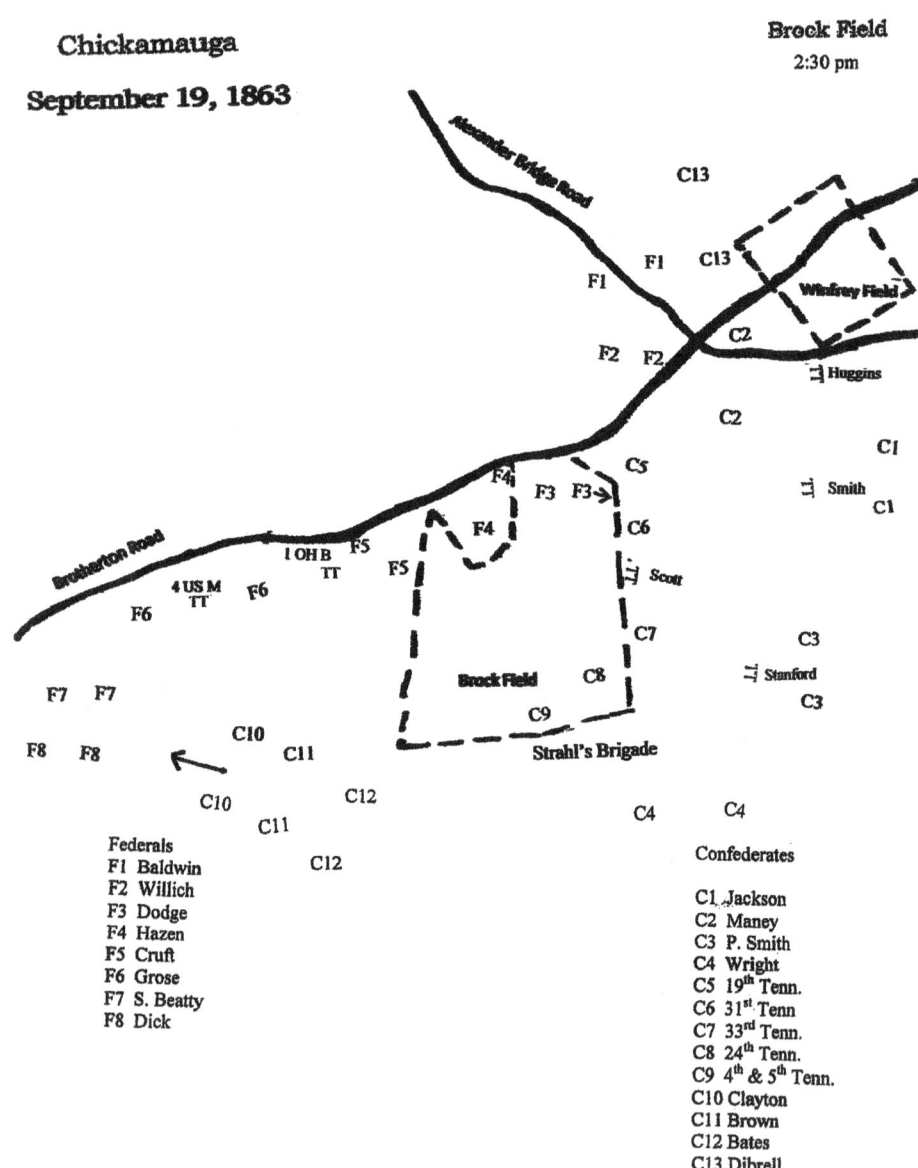

Chickamauga

September 19, 1863

Brock Field

2:30 pm

Federals
F1 Baldwin
F2 Willich
F3 Dodge
F4 Hazen
F5 Cruft
F6 Grose
F7 S. Beatty
F8 Dick

Confederates
C1 Jackson
C2 Maney
C3 P. Smith
C4 Wright
C5 19th Tenn.
C6 31st Tenn.
C7 33rd Tenn.
C8 24th Tenn.
C9 4th & 5th Tenn.
C10 Clayton
C11 Brown
C12 Bates
C13 Dibrell

While the men rested, Captain Carnes arrived with orders from Preston Smith to take charge of the battery. Not only did Carnes come to command Scott's Battery, but also he brought two lieutenants and thirty-five men with him. Stewart's division made further success against the Federals, and Longstreet's men also got involved south of Brock Field. Cheatham's division went back into action later in the day and participated in driving the Federals back north of Brock Field. Scott's Battery did not take part in this action due to its losses. Turner's Battery supported Smith in this action. It was during this time that General Preston Smith was killed by a ragged volley after dark. With his loss, Alfred J. Vaughan took over as brigade commander.[337]

Many things happened over the night. The Federals could be heard in the distance chopping trees and improving their defenses while the Confederate command was disorganized. Historian David A. Powell put it this way: "All of the frustrations, rivalries, personal dislikes, and general bad luck that were the hallmarks of the ill-used and frequently unlucky Army of Tennessee coalesced in one night of command dysfunction." The next morning the soldiers were ready to fight even if the generals were not.[338]

Cheatham's division, including Scott's Battery, was drawn up in battle line ready to advance shortly after sunrise. The broken cap square had been replaced, and all four guns were ready for action. It was a bright sunny day, and thoughts of repeating the bloodbath of the previous day were on everyone's mind. Captain Carnes stated, "I well remember that for nearly two hours I sat on my horse in front of the battery with drivers mounted ready to move forward at a moment's notice." No orders came to advance. Whether the blame goes to Bragg, Polk, or someone else, the battle would start late. When things got straightened out, it was discovered that Stewart's division was extended too far to the right in front of Cheatham. So Cheatham's division was placed in reserve.[339]

At around 11:00 a.m., Captain Scott arrived from his sickbed in Lafayette and relieved Carnes of his duty. Carnes would serve the remainder of the day as an aid to General Polk scurrying orders to various commands.

---

[337] Lindsley, *The Military Annals of Tennessee*, 822; Vaughan, *Personal Record of the Thirteenth Regiment Tennessee Infantry C.S.A.*, 30.

[338] Powell, *The Maps of Chickamauga*, 138.

[339] Major W. W., Carnes, "Chickamauga," 401.

Cheatham ordered Lieutenants Marshall and Cockrill and the men from Carnes Battery to retrieve the guns of their battery and the almost fifty guns captured from the Federals the day before. They were ordered to haul them to Dalton station for shipment to Atlanta and then report to Scott's Battery.[340]

No orders were given to Scott's Battery during the last day of battle. Ultimately the Federals were routed in the late afternoon, and only a bold stand by General Thomas at Snodgrass Hill saved the Federal army. The Federals retreated into Chattanooga, and a victorious Confederate army followed them. By September 24, Scott's Battery was on Missionary Ridge looking down upon Chattanooga and a demoralized Federal army.

The Officers

William L. Scott had maintained control over the battery in the hot months of the Carnes, "Chickamauga," summer. He had maintained discipline and built the camaraderie amongst the men. The retreat from Shelbyville, the drill, and the constant marching in the heat of early September had taken a toll on the captain, and he was in his sick bed when the Battle of Chickamauga began. Hearing of the wounding of Marsh, he returned to take command and remained with the battery after the Federal retreat.

John Henry Marsh helped make Scott's Battery a distinguished unit. Taking command at Brock Field, he advanced the men and went into battery in textbook style. Colonel Alfred J. Vaughan of the nearby Thirteenth/One Hundred and Fifty-Fourth Tennessee described Marsh as commanding "gallantly [while] encouraging his men and inspiring them by his own distinguished coolness and heroism." Scott would later say of Marsh, "His gallantry on the battle-field was of the noblest type. He embodied the very spirit of chivalry." Marsh's wound in the left arm was very severe. He spent six weeks in a field hospital and refused to allow the doctors to amputate it. He then was transferred to the hospital in Marietta, Georgia, where he remained for six months.[341]

Alfred T. Watson was an able lieutenant having worked his way up the ranks. After Marsh was wounded, he took control of the battery as

---

[340] Lindsley, *The Military Annals of Tennessee*, 823–824.

[341] Ibid, 793; OR XXX pt. 2, 107.

the only remaining officer. He fulfilled his duty maintaining a constant fire upon the enemy and was responsible for withdrawing the battery in good form. Vaughan said, "throughout the engagement [he] acted with commendable bravery." Watson turned over the command of the battery to William Carnes as ordered and reported to Brigadier General Maney on the night of September 19. He returned to the battery the next day as did Captain Scott and wrote the after-action report as requested by Vaughan on October 3.[342]

Scott's Battery had been short on officers during the fight at Brock Field. Lieutenant Peters had not returned from furlough even though his time to return was past due. Lieutenant Phillips was still on detached service in Texas. Neither of these men would return in time for the next action. Lieutenants Marshall and Cockrill would be with Scott's Battery for only three weeks and would be transferred to Atlanta to help Captain Carnes rebuild his battery. The thirty-five men from Carnes' Battery would go with them.[343]

The Enlisted Men

Scott's Battery, while camped at Chattanooga, received pay on August 31. There were eighty-seven officers and men present and fourteen absent. One of them was Private Edward W. Blease, who had been recruited from Rome, Georgia, on August 14. Several units were having trouble with desertion. The battery lost only J. Lightner and Joseph Hardin as deserters, and they were never seen again. Both of them were from Georgia and had decided to go home, while others were also doing the same. It is a tribute to the camaraderie of the unit that no one else left. Twenty-year-old Nathaniel Holmes from Mississippi was recruited and added to the roster later in September. There were no changes in the men's rank except that L. A. Ellis was promoted from ordnance sergeant to sergeant major. This occurred on August 21.[344]

Sickness was the main problem confronting the men. T. L. Rickerson, who had been in the Fairground Hospital No. 1 since July 2, was furloughed home on September 18. He did not return to the battery. William Saunders

---

[342] Ibid., 117.

[343] CCSR m268 roll 98; Carnes, "Chickamauga," 401.

[344] CCSR m268 roll 97–98.

was medically discharged in early September. Edward Toland returned from the hospital in late July after having high fevers. Edward Ford was sick and returned on September 24, after the Battle of Chickamauga, and received his pay of $48 including extra pay as artificer. William W. Weems died on August 14 while a patient at Cherokee Hospital in Ringgold, Georgia. He had $2.50 to his name.[345]

There is no question that the men in Scott's Battery did their duty in the Battle of Chickamauga. With courage they did not flinch from their duty. In spite of casualties, the men served "gallantly," working their pieces until relieved. Watson's official report showed "two privates were killed, 3 seriously wounded, and 10 slightly." Several of the men were wounded as the guns were unlimbered. Those killed were Privates George Bassett and Robert King. Private William Dowdy was severely wounded in the hip. The other wounded men were F. M. Davis, Lewis Davis, Charles Gravett, T. J. Heath, Michael Kinney, John Kirby, Joseph Kirby, J. M. Kirwin, James T. Morris, and William Powers. Two others were slightly wounded but not reported. The battery was not disabled as some have suggested. Even if those slightly wounded were removed to the rear, the battery fired throughout the engagement at Brock Field. The loss of fourteen horses equaled the loss of the howitzer; thus, there were enough horses for the other three guns. Carnes' men joined the unit by evening, and the unit was ready for action on the next day. Scott's Battery remained with Cheatham and was with him when they arrived on Missionary Ridge overlooking Chattanooga on September 24, 1863.[346]

---

[345] Ibid.

[346] OR XXX vol. 2, 107, 117.

CHAPTER 9

———◦◦⟨◉⟩◦◦———

CHATTANOOGA
SEPTEMBER–DECEMBER 1863

Army of Tennessee	Scott's Battery
General Braxton Bragg	Captain William L. Scott
	First Lieutenant John Doscher (November)
Hardee's Corps	Second Lieutenant Alfred T. Watson
Lieutenant General William Hardee	Quartermaster Sergeant T. E. Watts
Second Division (Hindman's)	Ordnance Sergeant L.A. Ellis
Brigadier General Patton Anderson	Sergeant John Purcell
Artillery Battalion	Sergeant John Watts
Major Alfred R. Courtney	Corporal J.D. Echols
Dent's Ala. Battery	Corporal John Halbert
Captain S.H. Dent	Corporal William Martin
Garrity's Ala. Battery	Corporal J.G. Westbrook
Captain James Garrity	68 privates
Water's Ala. Battery	11 absent
Lieutenant William B. Hamilton	
Scott's Tennessee Battery,	
Captain William L. Scott	

Scott's Battery arrived on Missionary Ridge on September 24. The 500-foot height provided a commanding view of Chattanooga. The Ridge got its name from the mission church that had been started on the east side of the ridge by Spanish missionaries in the 1770s. Civil War soldiers often called it Mission Ridge, but the name has been corrupted today to Missionary Ridge. Soon all of Bragg's army would arrive and try to infest the city. Cheatham ordered Vaughan's Brigade off the ridge and onto the plain to the east of the city. Stephenson's division, recently paroled from Vicksburg, would be assigned the occupation of Missionary Ridge, while Cheatham's division would occupy the valley of Chattanooga Creek.[347]

In Chattanooga, the Federals were making the old Confederate works stronger. In a few days the works would be too strong to attack. Cheatham's men were now busy building works opposite the Federals, and the men of Scott's Battery took their turn manning the defenses. Bragg did not appear to be too interested in the enemy's defenses, but instead would attack the enemy within his ranks. Not having a complete victory at Chickamauga, Bragg blamed Leonidas Polk, and this developed into a morale strike on Scott's Battery and a disaster for the Army of Tennessee.[348]

Bragg's attack upon his generals was poorly timed with all of the confusion following Chickamauga. Bragg blamed Polk for the command failures on the night of September 19, and on September 28 he suspended Polk and Major General Thomas Hindman and sent them to Atlanta. Nearly all of the corps and division commanders turned against Bragg, and soon President Davis was on his way to solve the issue. To summarize the results, it is plain to say that Bragg would remain as the commander of the Army of Tennessee, and Polk would be transferred to Mississippi.[349]

Bragg made a complete change in the command structure and in the unit dispositions. Hardee, who returned from Mississippi, took over Polk's corps, Breckenridge, who replaced D. H. Hill, had not quarreled with Bragg after Chickamauga, and commanded the second corps. Longstreet, who despised Bragg but could not be removed because of his connection with Robert E. Lee, commanded the third corps.

---

347   James Lee McDonough, *Chattanooga—Death Grip on the Confederacy*, 73.

348   Connelly, *Autumn of Glory*, 232, 234.

349   Ibid., 235–254. Readers are encouraged to read Thomas Lawrence Connelly's description of the events.

On November 12, the new organization took effect. Bragg was determined to break up the commands of the Kentucky and Tennessee units, which he felt had caused a large portion of the problems. Scott's Battery would no longer serve under Cheatham. Their new division commander would be Thomas Hindman, who had been reinstated. The artillery would be grouped into a battalion commanded by Major Alfred R. Courtney. Scott's Tennessee Battery would be grouped with three Alabama batteries commanded respectively by Samuel H. Dent, James Garrity, and William B. Hamilton. How the men felt about this can be seen in the words of Lieutenant Neal of Rowen's Battery when he said, "I do not care to leave this [brigade], as we have fought together and I know them to be good and excellent troops." The unit's many friends in Vaughan's Brigade were the only other Tennesseans in the division.[350]

The officers who had kept the battery focused now seemed to be gone when they were needed the most. Captain Scott was absent in late October and was not be present at the next battle. It is unclear if he was still sick or on furlough, but records show that eleven of the twenty-eight battery captains were absent at Missionary Ridge. Two of these absences were a result of promotion. Second Lieutenant Alfred T. Watson was the only officer present for duty with Scott's Battery on November 12 when he signed a requisition for forage as commanding the battery. First Lieutenant John Doscher was assigned to command the battery only a few days before the upcoming battle, giving him hardly enough time to get to know the men. Twenty-three-year-old Doscher was the son of German immigrants who had settled at Augusta, Georgia. He had previously served in Girardy's Georgia Battery until it was disbanded. More recently he had served in Pritchard's Battery, which had been disbanded before Chickamauga. Thus Scott's Battery did not have its usual corps, division, brigade or battery commanders for the test ahead.[351]

If the change in command wasn't bad enough for the camaraderie, the lack of supplies and the change in the weather had its effect upon every individual. Most of the men in Scott's Battery were beginning to feel disillusioned and disheartened. As September became October, the

---

[350] Ibid., 250–251; McDonough, *Chattanooga—Death Grip on the Confederacy*, 271–272; Neal to his father, November 20, 1863, Neal Letters, Emory University.

[351] McDonough, *Chattanooga—Death Grip on the Confederacy*, 271–272; CCSR m268 roll 98, m266 roll 17.

weather became cold and rainy. One soldier in the Seventh Florida wrote, "Some of the boys that were lucky enough to steal some ears of corn from the horses last night are busy grating it and making mush out of it, for we are almost starved to death. We draw enough in two days to make one good meal." He went on to say that it "was so cold I had to sit by the fire half the night." Many of the men were getting sick from poor drinking water, and many more had little sleep, because they stayed up all night around the fire. How did this compare to previous times? Lieutenant Neal of Rowen's Battery answered the question by saying, "the company complain but little but they certainly have a harder time than they have ever seen before." Sam Watkins of the First Tennessee supported Neal when he wrote, "I cannot remember of more privations and hardships than we went through than at Mission Ridge." [352]

There are no indications in the records that any of the men deserted from Scott's Battery, although this was the case in many units. Colonel Brent, of Bragg's staff, reported 2,929 desertions by the end of October. Most of the men merely continued to suffer, which led to thinking and then talking about the bloody triumph at Chickamauga, and they vented their feelings against General Bragg. One Tennessean wrote, "Everyone here curses Bragg ... [and his removal] will put our troops in much better spirits." The blame for the bad times and the Federals still sitting in Chattanooga was placed on Bragg. This sentiment was prevalent in the ranks of the battery.[353]

The camp of Scott's Battery was at the base of Missionary Ridge, and when it rained, water rushed down the slopes and flooded the camp. There were heavy rains in late September, and continuous rain began in mid-October. The roads were quagmires, and moving the guns proved impossible. To make matters worse, the horses had no forage, and the sacks

---

[352] McDonough, *Chattanooga—Death Grip on the Confederacy*, 63; Robert Watson diary, pt. 2, October 11, 1863, Chickamauga-Chattanooga National Military Park; Neal to his father, October 12, 1863; Samuel L. Watkins, *Co. Aytch, Maury Guards, First Tennessee Regiment*, (Chattanooga: Times Printing Company, 1900), 100.

[353] McDonough, *Chattanooga—Death Grip on the Confederacy*, 64; Harris letters, October 13, 1863; Peter Cozzens, *The Shipwreck of Their Hopes: The Battles for Chattanooga* (Urbana and Chicago: University of Illinois Press, 1996), 28.

of corn provided by the quartermaster were inadequate. Often guards had to be placed to prevent soldiers from stealing the horses' grain.[354]

With so much of the command structure in flux, the men often did not have direction. The Federals were only a mile or two away, yet there was no drill, just picket duty. This gave the men free time like they'd had at Columbus and Shelbyville. Games of cards and games of chance could be found in every camp. Camp followers arrived once the army had settled in. It was known that a "house of ill repute" was located at the base of Missionary Ridge. Yet there was a sense of despair. How many times had the Army of Tennessee won a battle only to have it given away?[355]

Never had Scott's Battery stayed in one place and not drilled. It was in a soldier's routine to be marching, drilling, or fighting. Here there was only free time.

One exception occurred on October 5. Cannoneers had been firing from Lookout Mountain for a week, and Bragg wanted to see if all of the artillery could force Rosecrans out of Chattanooga. A general bombardment was ordered, and Scott's Battery went into action with the rest of the Confederate artillery. After a short spell, the command "Cease fire!" rang out. The firing had been a dismal failure. One cannoneer wrote, "They are too well posted to be shelled and this business is all foolishness." Edward Porter Alexander, Longstreet's artillery chief, who commanded the guns on Lookout Mountain complained, "This army is far inferior to the Army of Northern Virginia in organization and spirit, and I regret very much that I ever left the latter." He may have said this in frustration over the effort or because of the overall observance of the situation. Alexander also complained of the poor quality of the ammunition compared to what he was used to.[356]

---

[354] Cozzens, *The Shipwreck of Their Hopes*, 18, 21, 30.

[355] McDonough, *Chattanooga—Death Grip on the Confederacy*, 66.

[356] Cozzens, *The Shipwreck of Their Hopes*, 34; Neal to his father, October 12, 1863; E. Porter Alexander, *Fighting for the Confederacy* (Chapel Hill: University of North Carolina Press, 1989), 304.

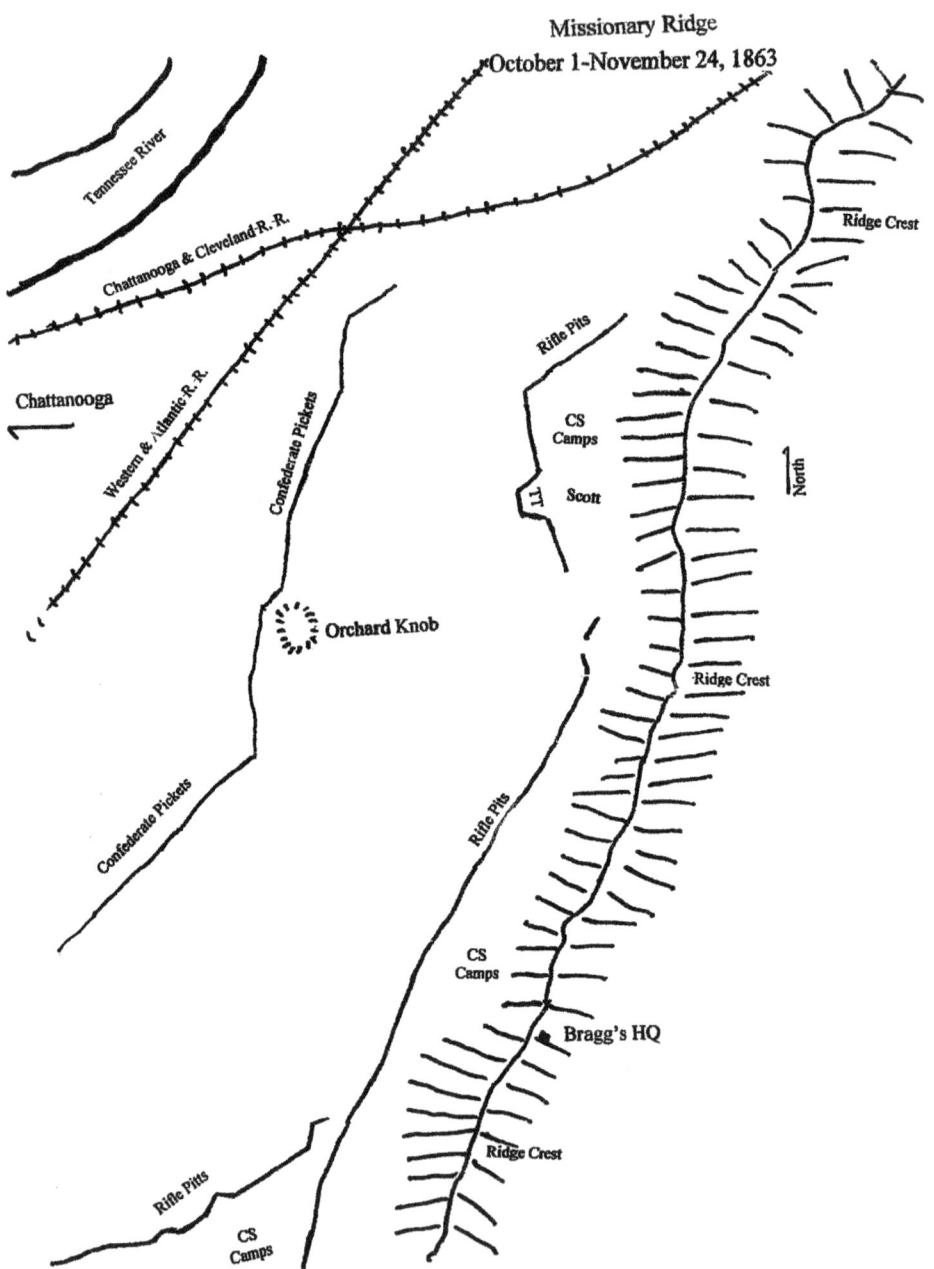

Missionary Ridge
October 1–November 24, 1863

Bragg's lack of planning was about to show disastrous results. First Bragg had failed to stop the supplies to the Federal troops in Chattanooga, and by October 28, the Federals had a direct link into the town, and reinforcements were arriving. Even the daily firing of artillery into the town from Lookout Mountain was futile. Soon 80,000 men would be available for Grant. Second, the personal feuds cut deep into the commanders as well as the rank and file. Bragg had changed many commanders and shuffled the brigades. Then, on November 4, he got rid of Longstreet's corps and sent it to Knoxville. The Army of Tennessee now stood at only 36,000, and commands had to be stretched to cover the defenses. Stevenson's Division would now cover Lookout Mountain, and Breckenridge would cover Missionary Ridge. Scott's Battery still remained on the plain at the base of Missionary Ridge.[357]

Never had the Army of Tennessee been able to see the entire presence of the enemy. As Brigadier General Arthur Manigault later wrote:

> Most of the timber on the ridge had been, by this time, cut away, used for fuel, building purposes, and breastworks at the foot of the hill. Such trees as were left standing had completely lost their leaves, and in the valley or level land below, the same condition of things existed, so that our view was uninterrupted … At night just after dark, when all the campfires were lighted, the effect was very grand and imposing, and such a one as seldom been witnessed.[358]

The increasing number of campfires was disheartening to the men, as many had deserted. Yet, the men of Scott's Battery continued to remain devoted to their cause.

On Monday, November 23, Grant put his plan of attack in motion. Sherman would get his army in position to cross the Tennessee River at the northern end of Missionary Ridge. Hooker would begin to attack the left side of Bragg's army by attacking Lookout Mountain. These two flank movements should force Bragg to retreat. In the center, Thomas would demonstrate in front of Missionary Ridge. The distance from the Federal

---

[357] Connelly, *Autumn of Glory*, 254–263.

[358] R. Lockwood Tower. *A Carolinian Goes to War* (Columbia, South Carolina, 1983), 128–129.

defenses at Chattanooga to the base of Missionary Ridge was about a mile and a half. Halfway between were several hundred Confederate pickets defending a large hill called Orchard Knob and a string of rifle pits going several hundred yards both north and south of the knob. They had marched out around 1:15 p.m. and made the assault at 1:30, catching the entire Confederate army off guard. Lieutenant Watson and many cannoneers were watching, from behind the breastworks, what appeared to be a dress parade. Once the Confederate pickets started firing, a few guns to the south opened fire. Watson, fearing a general Federal attack, shouted to the men, "In battery!" The men then scrambled to the guns and prepared to open fire.[359]

Posted at the bottom of Missionary Ridge about 2,000 yards from Orchard Knob, the battery came into action only to be ordered to cease fire. It was of no use. Other batteries also ceased fire, as there was no plan for any counterattack. What remained of the two Alabama regiments on the knob scurried back to the Confederate lines at the base of the ridge while the Federals dug in on the knob bringing up reinforcements, including several batteries of artillery.[360] General Thomas, with 25,000 troops, put on a great military show. In full view of the Confederate army, Thomas quickly and decisively captured Orchard Knob and many prisoners. The Federals now were much closer to Missionary Ridge and had an excellent observation point.[361]

Everyone was surprised at the result. At Fort Wood, near Chattanooga, Grant and many of his generals watched an amazing display. At the same time on Missionary Ridge, Bragg and many of his generals did the same. One Federal staff officer recorded the scene:

> It was an inspiriting sight. Flags were flying; the quick, earnest steps of thousands beat equal time. The sharp commands of hundreds of company officers, the sound of drums, the ringing notes of the bugles, companies wheeling and counter-marching and regiments getting into line, the bright sun lighting up ten thousand polished bayonets till they glistened and flashed like a

---

[359] Cozzens, *The Shipwreck of Their Hopes*, 129–131.

[360] Ibid.

[361] McDonough, *Chattanooga—Death Grip on the Confederacy*, 110–113; Cozzens, *The Shipwreck of Their Hopes*, 128–129.

flying shower of electric sparks-all looked like preparations for a peaceful pageant, rather than the bloody work of death.[362]

At around 4:00 p.m., Scott's Battery received orders to bombard Orchard Knob again. Bragg had decided to use his artillery to drive out the Federals. For nearly two hours, eleven batteries fired on Orchard Knob. One Federal soldier described the twilight bombardment:

> Such a spectacle I shall never forget. The dusky form of the mountain, encircling our position for three miles, seemed in the dim twilight like some dense thundercloud looming against the heavens, and shooting forth-unceasing flames of lightning. While its thunder made the earth tremble beneath our feet innumerable shells fell, bursting above and around our lines. I have not learned that any considerable injury was received from this terrific bombardment of the enemy.[363]

Meanwhile, General Manigault was preparing a single brigade to make a night attack. This would have been suicidal due to the number of Federals on Orchard Knob, and the attack was finally cancelled. The bombardment was ineffective, and Federal casualties were very light. The cease-fire brought out a dull silence.[364]

Tuesday, November 24, was a cold, rainy day with heavy fog covering the Chattanooga area in the morning. In front of Missionary Ridge, the Army of the Cumberland remained stationary at Orchard Knob. At 10:00 a.m., Hooker's Federals attacked Lookout Mountain in what became known as the Battle in the Clouds. Stevenson was unable to hold back the Federals, and by 2:30 p.m., Bragg ordered the Confederates off the mountain. Meanwhile, Sherman's Federals had crossed the Tennessee River at the northern end of Missionary Ridge and were poised to attack Bragg's right flank.[365]

---

362 OR XXXI pt. 2, 129.

363 Lynn S. Widney to his sister, November 27, 1863, Widney Letters, Chickamauga and Chattanooga National Military Park.

364 Cozzens, *The Shipwreck of Their Hopes*, 135.

365 Ibid., 199

This had been a unique day for Scott's Battery. The cannoneers had played the role of bystander with no activity from the enemy on Orchard Knob. Yet they found themselves in the bottom of an amphitheatre watching a drama on Lookout Mountain. This day they were treated to a battle from a safe distance; not like the usual battles they had participated in with deep forests, suffocating smoke, deafening racket, and gore. Instead, there were harmless gun flashes, puffs of smoke like clouds, and muted booms and crackling. It had a surreal quality similar to what they had experienced in their early days of recruitment back in 1861 and early 1862. The fog also created some mystery that only gave way to reality once the outcome was determined. By mid afternoon faint cheers could be heard on the mountaintop, and then cheering from Orchard Knob. The Federals had taken Lookout Mountain, and despair came over the men. What would tomorrow bring?[366]

That evening, Bragg held a conference of his generals. Hardee called for an immediate retreat, but others wanted to make a stand on Missionary Ridge. For two months Missionary Ridge had not been prepared to receive an attack. Now Bragg decided to hold the ridge. Breckenridge would command the left, and Hardee would command the right where Cleburne's division was already fortifying in front of Sherman. Cheatham's division was ordered to march to the ridge immediately, and Anderson would come up behind him. Thus Scott's Battery would proceed to a new battle position and arrive only a few hours before the upcoming battle.[367]

Wednesday, November 25, was a cold but sunny day. Sleep had eluded most of the men of the battery as they prepared to leave camp. Lieutenant Doscher, replacing the absent Captain Scott, gave orders before sunrise for the men to break camp and proceed up Missionary Ridge. The clapboard shanties that the men had constructed for the winter were abandoned. The camp baggage was moved behind Missionary Ridge where a new camp would be set up in the evening. Meanwhile, the men worked hard to get the guns up the ridge.[368]

Although the ridge was crisscrossed with small roads, the horses were feeble and had difficulty pulling up hill. With the help of infantry companies, the guns were finally brought up the hill. Scott's Battery

---

[366]   Ibid.

[367]   Ibid., 196; Daniel, *Cannoneers in Gray*, 119: Connelly, *Autumn of Glory*, 272.

[368]   Cozzens, *The Shipwreck of Their Hopes*, 194.

position was to be located at the right end of Anderson's division. At this location was a narrow ravine that cut into the ridge about 200 feet. The section of six-pounders was placed at the head of the ravine under the command of Doscher. At the angle of the ridge to the ravine, the other section was placed under the command of Watson. To Watson's left were the familiar Tennesseans of Vaughan's brigade. To the right of Doscher was Jackson's brigade of Cheatham's division. Skirmishers from the Twentieth Tennessee were placed between the two sections.[369]

From the top of Missionary Ridge, the cannoneers had a beautiful view of the valley below. About one and a half miles due west was the Federal Fort Wood on the outskirts of Chattanooga. South of the battery, about a mile and a quarter away, was Bragg's headquarters. It is unclear who had given the order to divide the battery into sections, but this seemed to be the general rule along the entire line of defenses. In Courtney's battalion, only Water's Battery kept their guns together.[370]

Perhaps it was a result of topography, but two things were different about this battle. One, the guns would not be massed as had proved successful at Shiloh and Murfreesboro; rather, they were dispersed. Two, the entire Confederate line would be on the tactical defensive for the first time. Bragg placed ninety-six artillery pieces along four miles of ridge crest. Attackers would have to cross a 1,200-yard plain swept by artillery fire and then ascend a 500-foot height that had been cleared of trees and brush. In Bragg's mind, this ridge could not be taken by assault. Hardee "observed that the natural strength of the position would probably deter such an (attack)."[371]

The real problem was time for preparation. Scott's Battery did not reach its position until after 2:00 p.m. There were few earthworks prepared at this position, and those that were prepared were poorly constructed. Morale was also at an all-time low because of the command changes, but also because of the toll taken by the cold weather and lack of rations. In the valley was a full panorama of Federal power. To the north, the men could hear the gunfire of Sherman's attack upon the right flank of the

---

[369] Ibid; Daniel, *Cannoneers in Gray*, 120; Edward E. Betts, Map of the Battlefields of Chattanooga and Wauhatchie, Chickamauga and Chattanooga National Park Commission, 1896.

[370] Ibid; Daniel, *Cannoneers in Gray*, 119–120.

[371] Ibid; McDonough, *Chattanooga—Death Grip on the Confederacy*, 127.

Confederate position. In the front, they could see 23,000 Federals of the army of the Cumberland. To the south, they could see Hooker's Federals slowly pushing across Chattanooga valley toward Rossville, which was the southern end of the Confederate line.[372]

Grant had planned to turn the two flanks of the Confederate line. Sherman, with the Army of the Tennessee, veterans of the Vicksburg campaign, would attack the right flank of the Confederate line. Hooker, with his troops from the Army of the Potomac, would attack the left flank of the Confederate line at Rossville. General Thomas held the center with his Army of the Cumberland. Grant planned only a limited role for Thomas, as he did not have enough faith in the soldiers who had been routed at Chickamauga. Hooker's move at the Confederate left was very slow because of having to cross the swollen Chattanooga Creek, but he would reach Rossville by the end of the day. Sherman began his attack at 10:30 a.m., only to be repulsed by Cleburne. This battle raged all day with no progress being made.[373]

By midafternoon it was clear that Cleburne's defense was sound, as Sherman could not advance. Sherman already had more men than he could use, but needed some help. Grant, who had placed himself on Orchard Knob, observed that Sherman was bogged down. He told Brigadier General Thomas J. Wood, his old roommate at West Point, now commanding a division of the Army of the Cumberland, "I think if you and Sheridan were to advance your divisions and carry the rifle pits at the base of the ridge it would so threaten Bragg's center that he would draw … troops from the right … and insure the success of General Sherman's attack." Wood responded that he would try. Wood later said, "It was conceded that a direct frontal attack of the enemy's works on Mission Ridge could not be made with reasonable prospect of success." Grant gave the order to form up for the advance around 3:00 p.m.[374]

At about 3:40 p.m., a signal was fired from Orchard Knob, and the Federal assault on Missionary Ridge began. Scott's Battery opened fire as did the rest of the Confederate line. The firing continued. In front of the battery was Brigadier General Absalom Baird's division with Colonel Edward Phelps's brigade on the left of the Federal line. In the center of the

---

[372]   Ibid., 121; Connelly, *Autumn of Glory*, 274.

[373]   McDonough, *Chattanooga—Death Grip on the Confederacy*, 133–135, 157–159.

[374]   Ibid., 162; OR XXXI pt. 2, 748–749.

division was Colonel Ferdinand Van Derveer's brigade, which formed the spearhead of the attack along with Brigadier General John B. Turchin's brigade on the right. Lieutenant Colonel Judson Bishop of the Second Minnesota described the situation: "Our own brigade was formed for battle in two lines of three regiments each, with the Second Minnesota regiment about three hundred yards in advance and covering the entire brigade front, with two companies deployed as skirmishers and six companies as reserve."[375]

As the attackers advanced, the fire from Scott's Battery and the guns to the north was so heavy that Phelps's brigade veered to the right and came up partly behind Van Derveer. Colonel Gustave Kammerling, commanding the Ninth Ohio, described the fire from the ridge: "As soon as the line moved forward it met with a most galling fire from the enemy's batteries posted on the ridge in front and on the left of our position, but notwithstanding this heavy artillery fire which we had to pass through, I succeeded in gaining the ridge." The rifle pits were easily taken as the defenders scampered up the ridge seeking safety at the crest.[376]

The Federals were not in a good position at the bottom of the ridge. As reported in *The Review*, published in Mankato, Minnesota, "It was at once evident to the Union soldiers who had won the entrenchment that they could not stay there. They were without protection from the fire … up the slope. [They] must either relinquish what they had won or they must go forward to the rest of the rebel position." Some of the men had gone beyond the entrenchment where they felt a little more secure among the Confederate. Watson was having difficulty getting the range, but the longer the Federals lay on the ground at the breastworks, the better were his chances of getting it right.[377]

One Federal officer called the artillery fire "harmless but annoying." It was Captain John Reed Beatty of Baird's staff who gave the order to advance and ordered bugler Billings J. Sibley to sound the advance. Within minutes, the entire Federal line began to ascend the Ridge. Grant had not

---

[375] Ibid., 527–529; Judson W. Bishop. *The Story of a Regiment* (St. Cloud: North Star Press, 2000), 135.

[376] OR XXXI pt. 2, 536 McDonough, *Chattanooga—Death Grip on the Confederacy*, 168.

[377] "Tribute to Late Capt. Beatty," *Mankato Review,* Mankato, Minnesota, May 9, 1916.

ordered the attack up the ridge, and Beatty could have been charged with insubordination. The men who knew this swore to be silent. It wasn't until 1916, after the death of most of the participants, that the truth was told.[378]

It was 4:10 p.m. when Baird's division began the ascent of Missionary Ridge. Coming up the ridge near the ravine in front of Scott's Battery was the Ninth Ohio regiment. The gunners and the small number of infantry had them pinned down. Colonel Edward Phelps, the third brigade commander of Baird's division, was stalled clinging to the ridge. It was a few minutes before 5:00 p.m. The sun had gone down, and a chill was setting in when, suddenly, from the left flank and rear, the Second Minnesota, supported by the Thirty-Fifth Ohio, fired into Watson's section killing several horses and hitting two men. Private Wiley Smith was killed, and Private Charles Dinkins was wounded. Then the Minnesotans charged into the section, capturing eight men and Lieutenant Watson. Other men fled, and Doscher ordered his section to withdraw. It was too late. As the sun set, so did it set on Scott's Battery. Doscher and most of the men retreated into the darkness behind the ridge, saving only one gun.[379]

Historians have debated the defenses of Missionary Ridge and the poor Confederate stand made by many units. The Federals actually pierced the Confederate line in several places. About 400 yards south of the Scott's Battery position was Tucker's brigade of Mississippians. Tucker's brigade were the first to run. The Federals had gathered a large group of men just below the breastworks; they were unseen by the defenders. Suddenly the Federals dashed over the works and surprised the Forty-First Mississippi. They panicked and ran, and Tucker's brigade soon fell apart. Water's Battery was then overrun, and some of the guns turned on the retreating Confederates. It was the first breech in the Confederate line.[380]

As the Federals moved north atop Missionary Ridge, Baird's second brigade, led by Lieutenant Colonel Judson Bishop of the Second Minnesota, finally reached the Confederate defenders. Having rested and gathered his men below the breastworks, Bishop ordered the men over the top. Bishop described the situation as follows:

---

[378] McDonough, *Chattanooga—Death Grip on the Confederacy*, 162; OR XXXI vol. 2, 530; Cozzens, *The Shipwreck of Their Hopes*, 273.

[379] OR XXXI vol. 2, 534-545; Cozzens, *The Shipwreck of Their Hopes*, 281, 291, 331; CCSR m268 Roll 97–98.

[380] OR XXXI vol. 2, 513, 538; Cozzens, *The Shipwreck of Their Hopes*, 291, 296.

My regiment moved forward with the others of the brigade, assembling on the colors as far as was possible on the way, until in ascending the steepest part of the slope, where every man had to clear his own way through the entanglement, in the face a terrible fire of musketry and artillery, the men of the different regiments of the brigade became generally intermingled, and, when the brigade finally crowned the enemy's works at the crest of the ridge, the regimental and even the company organizations had become completely in a crowd of gallant and enthusiastic men, who swarmed over the breastworks and charged the defenders with such promptness and vigor that the enemy broke and fled.

Without orders, and working under a broken command structure, individual officers of the Second Minnesota and other regiments moved north of the breakthrough to roll up Missionary Ridge. Confederate General Alfred J. Vaughan saw what was happening. He ordered some of his regiments to face left, and ordered an immediate counterattack. Bishop continues his story:

Hardly had a lodgment been gained in the works when the enemy reserves made a furious counterattack upon our men, yet in confusion. The attack was promptly met by a charge *en masse* by the crowd, which, after a few minutes of desperate hand-to-hand fighting, cleared the ridge, leaving the place in our undisputed possession, with between two and three hundred prisoners captured in the melee.[381]

Vaughan had sent in the Eleventh Tennessee and the Thirteenth/One Hundred and Fifty-Fourth Tennessee (consolidated) and now was almost out of ammunition. Realizing that he could not hold, as he was now being flanked on his right, he ordered his men, in an organized fashion, to withdraw off the ridge into the valley to the east. The word was passed to his men fighting near Scott's Battery, but in the heat of action, either the cannoneers did not see the infantry withdraw or they ignored their departure, as only a few seconds remained before the Second Minnesota

---

[381] Bishop, *The Story of a Regiment*, 137–138; Betts, Map of the Battlefields of Chattanooga and Wauhatchie; McDonough, *Chattanooga—Death Grip on the Confederacy*, 200–201;

fired into Watson's section. As historian Peter Cozzens stated, "It was a brave act but a grave miscalculation."[382]

Seeing Watson's predicament, Doscher called up the limbers only to have some of the men break to the rear while shots from the Federals took out some of the horses. One gun escaped into the darkness just before the Minnesotans captured the other. The drivers later cut the traces and used the horses for their own getaway, abandoning the last gun. After passing through Scott's Battery, the Federals proceeded north along the ridge, but were met by Jackson's brigade of Cheatham's division. They overran a section of McCant's Battery and were stopped from going any further. The sun had set, and fighting went on until about 6:00 p.m.[383]

---

[382] Vaughan, *Personal Record of the Thirteenth Regiment Tennessee Infantry C.S.A.*, 31; Cozzens, *The Shipwreck of Their Hopes*, 329–331.

[383] Daniel, *Cannoneers in Gray*, 128–129; OR XXXI vol.2, 538; Cozzens, *The Shipwreck of Their Hopes*, 329–331.

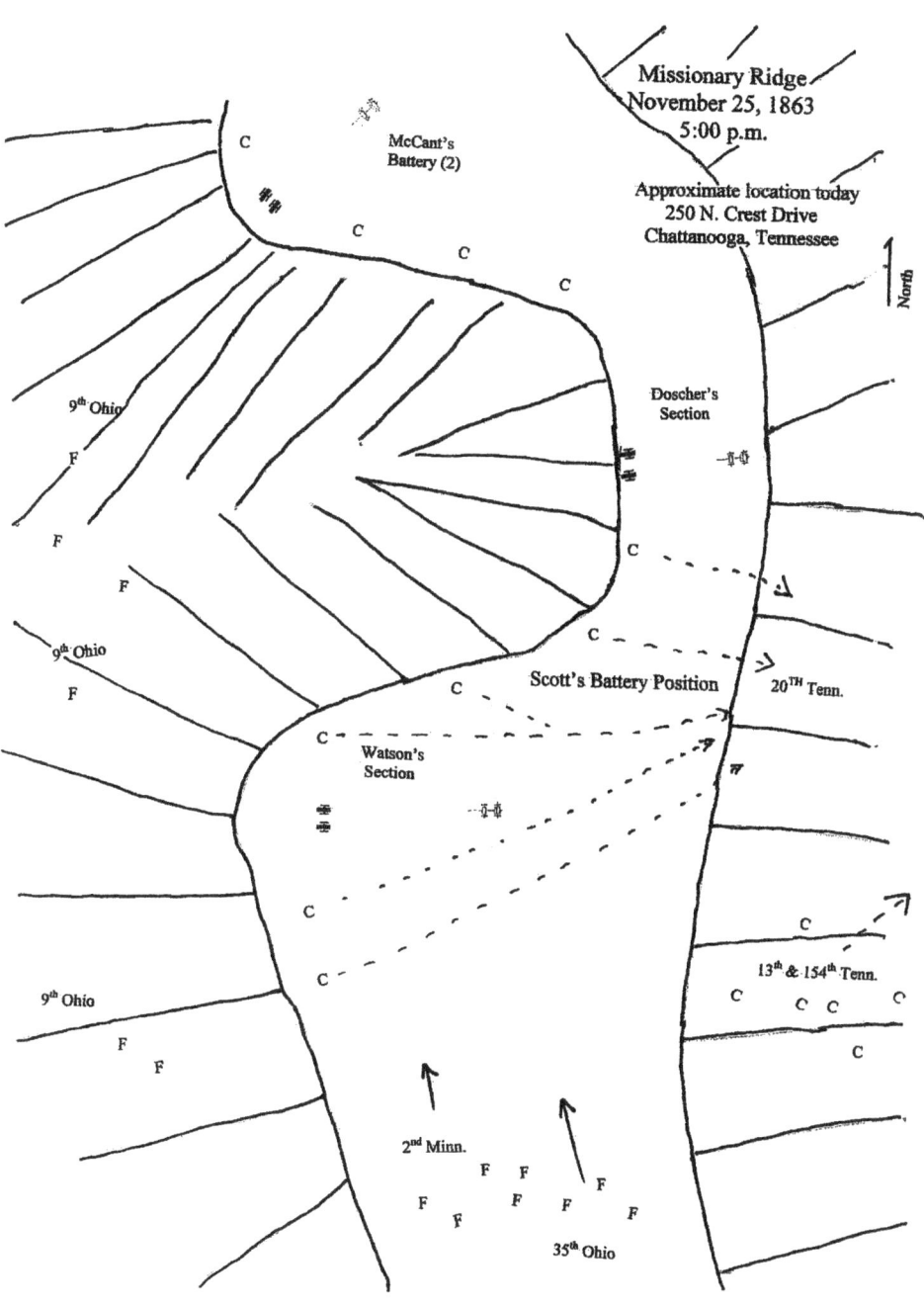

Missionary Ridge
November 25, 1863
5:00 p.m.

Approximate location today
250 N. Crest Drive
Chattanooga, Tennessee

North

McCant's
Battery (2)

Doscher's
Section

9th Ohio

F

F

F

9th Ohio

F

Scott's Battery Position

20TH Tenn.

C

Watson's
Section

13th & 154th Tenn.

9th Ohio

F

F

2nd Minn.

F   F   F

F   F   F   F

35th Ohio

All along the center of Missionary Ridge, the Federal soldiers were cheering and congratulating themselves for achieving the impossible. General Grant couldn't believe his good fortune. Down behind Missionary Ridge was chaos. The men of Scott's Battery were scattered in the dark. "The loss of Scott's Battery was the pathetic denouement to the battle," wrote one historian. Lieutenant Watson was captured, and Lieutenant Doscher could not rally any of the men. In fact, Doscher hardly knew his men. He made his way to Chickamauga Station on his own.[384]

General Manigault described the disaster: "I have on several occasions been repulsed and driven back when taking part in an attack, but never before or since have I been one of a routed army, where panic seemed to seize upon all, and all order, obedience, and discipline, were for the time forgotten and disregarded." He went on to say, "To stop the men in their mad flight, even after leaving the enemy hundreds of yards in their rear, was almost impossible." The men of Scott's Battery were scattered, and there was no Captain Scott to put them back together.[385]

Cheatham and Cleburne remained on Missionary Ridge until about midnight and then withdrew. Cleburne commanded the rear guard as the Federals made a light pursuit for a few days. The defeat was humiliating, and many men deserted after the disaster. Bragg could not remain after the defeat; he turned over the command of the Army of Tennessee to William Hardee and left on November 30. Hardee pulled the army south toward Dalton, Georgia, and tried to restructure the many broken units. Scott's Battery had no command structure and could not be put back together. The battery was disbanded on December 9, 1863. The men were reassigned to other units, but where were they?[386]

The Officers

Captain William L. Scott was unable to come to the rescue of his battery. It is unclear where he was. He had been ill in September and may have had a furlough. Alfred T. Watson did much of the daily battery staff work. One letter, written on October 17, 1863, had the heading "In the Field Near Missionary Ridge." And it was signed "W. L. Scott, Capt.

---

[384] Ibid., 212, 331.

[385] Tower, *A Carolinian Goes to War*, 143.

[386] Connelly, *Autumn of Glory*, 276–277; CCSR m268 roll 97.

Comd'g Light Artillery." Thus we know Scott was present in mid-October, but like several battery captains in the Army of Tennessee, he was absent when most needed. With the decision to disband the battery, Scott was transferred to Major General Joseph Wheeler's cavalry division where he became chief of artillery.[387]

Second Lieutenant Thomas Peters had been given a sixty-day furlough on June 8, 1863, and had never returned to the battery. The battery was in need of an active officer, so in a letter written by Scott to Colonel George Brent, the adjutant to General Bragg, on October 17 he wrote:

> On the 3rd of January 1863 Second Lieutenant Thomas Peters was assigned to duty in my Battery as Chief of section. From that time until the present he has not performed more than two weeks duty in the company owing to ill health. On the 8th of June last, he obtained sixty days leave of absence based upon Surgeon's certificate; since this time he has not been officially heard from, and has been reported absent without leave as required by law. I respectfully make application for the appointment of an examining board as required in such cases by the Act of Congress "to relieve the Army of disqualified, disabled, and incompetent officers."

General Bragg received the letter and responded by writing, "No board is necessary. This officer is absent without leave. He can be gotten rid of by Genl. Order No. 15 current series."[388]

Peters was already in the process of resigning. He was living at his father's plantation at Council Bend, Arkansas, when he penned a letter to General Samuel Cooper in Richmond. It was not precisely dated, merely saying October 1863. He said, "I have the honor to offer my resignation as Second Lieutenant Scott's Battery, Cheatham's Division, Polk's Corps, Army of Tennessee" His friend, William M. Polk, also sent a letter to Cooper asking him to accept the resignation. The next letter, dated October 29, 1863, from Memphis better explains the situation:

> We the undersigned practicing physicians of the city of Memphis certify that Lieut Thomas Peters formally of Scott's

---

387   CCSR m268 roll 98.

388   CCSR m268 roll 97–98.

Battery, Army of Tenn. A young man 21 years of age called on us this day to consult us relative to the state of his health. He has been laboring under intermittent fever for several months past at this time occurring daily, his health is likewise suffering from disease of the genital system requiring medical treatment and probably a surgical operation. In view of the actual condition of his health and the intense mental anxiety under which he labors, we are of the opinion that he should be relieved of duty by resignation or by furlough until his health can be restored.

Three doctors signed the letter. Captain Scott was asked to provide records of Peters on December 28, which he did. Meanwhile Peters was transferred to Marshall's Battery.[389]

Second Lieutenant Alfred T. Watson bore the burdens of the company. After the lieutenants from Carne's Battery left to return to their command, Watson remained the only officer other than Scott. Watson took over all of the duties and. in the captain's absence, held command only to have John Doscher supersede him just before the battle. Watson had the misfortune to be captured with the left section at Missionary Ridge. As an officer, he was separated from the other prisoners. He was sent to Louisville, where he changed trains to be sent to Fort Delaware. He never arrived, as he escaped somewhere along the way. He was transferred to Swett's Mississippi Battery on December 9 even though no one seemed to know where he was. He did report for duty at Dalton, Georgia, in January.[390]

First Lieutenant John Doscher had the misfortune to be the commander in the disaster at Missionary Ridge. He failed to rally the men as darkness and the enemy overtook their position. Doscher was transferred on December 9 to Swett's Battery but never served there. The circumstances that transferred him to Scott's Battery may have been only temporary, because he was already signing reports for Major Thomas R. Hotchkiss as acting adjutant.[391]

---

[389]   Ibid.

[390]   Ibid.

[391]   Ibid.

The Enlisted Men

The two months spent around Chattanooga in the fall of 1863 were the toughest times the battery had ever experienced. Shortages of food, cold weather, and a changed command structure had hurt the men's pride in what they had done at Chickamauga. The growing Federal strength in the town did not help the men think about the upcoming confrontation. There were no reported cases of desertion in Scott's Battery until the debacle at Missionary Ridge. J. R. Brinkley and John Shirey missed the battle, as they were admitted to Ocmulgee Hospital in Macon, Georgia. Shirey went in on October 2 with a fever and soon had chronic diarrhea. He was furloughed home in March. Brinkley complained of rheumatism on September 28 and was still hospitalized in January 1864. William Dowdy died on October 30 at Medical College Hospital in Atlanta from his wound at Chickamauga. He had twenty dollars in cash and nine dollars' worth of effects.[392]

Captain Scott, in his 1886 description of the battle, said that the battery was "overwhelmed by numbers, and completely surrounded by the enemy, the battery was captured. Its men stood to their guns to the last, and were literally hewn down at their pieces, dying at their post while attempting to discharge their guns." He went on to say that "the greater portion of the men were killed or so badly wounded they afterward died of their wounds. Many were taken prisoner but few escaped." This statement was an exaggeration. Only two men died fighting on Missionary Ridge. Wiley W. Smith was killed outright while serving the piece. Charles A. Dinkins was wounded at the same time and died of his wounds on December 5 at a Federal hospital in Chattanooga. Seven men were taken to Rock Island Prison. The rest of the men (about sixty-five of them) fled and made their escape. We can forgive Scott for his description, because he really didn't know. He wasn't there. He merely wanted the memory of his battery to have some meaning for the lost cause. The inscribed Napoleon, given to Captain Scott by Alfred J. Vaughan at Murfreesboro, was captured on Missionary Ridge. It was a symbol of the earlier success of the battery. After the war, this cannon barrel was kept by the Federal government and given to the Stones River National Military Park where

---

[392] Ibid.

it was on display in the late twentieth century in the museum. It was put into storage in 1990.[393]

One of those captured was Sergeant Charles Purcell, who had been recruited by Bankhead in Memphis on May 18, 1861. Also from Memphis were Charles Cooley, Edward Ford, Michael Kinney, and Daniel O. D. Brennan. The others captured were Edward Toland, originally from Girardy's Battery, and Nathan Holmes, recruited only two months before. Michael Kinney died of smallpox on December 20 at Rock Island Prison.[394]

It was not possible to assemble the men from Scott's Battery, because there simply was no officer remaining. Scott was still absent, Doscher had a new assignment, and Watson had been captured. On December 9, the battery was disbanded, and the men were assigned to new commands. This was done merely by taking the rolls and dividing the men to fill the losses of other commands. Carne's Tennessee Battery was in need of men after refitting after Chickamauga, and thirty-seven men were transferred from Scott's Battery. This included all seven men taken to Rock Island, along with two officers, Watson and Peters. No one knew where anyone was, as the missing men were promptly declared deserters. Within days, William Carnes, who was a graduate of Annapolis, was transferred to the Confederate Navy, and his battery became Marshall's Tennessee Battery.[395]

Forty-seven men were transferred to Swett's Mississippi Battery. This battery had been so heavily engaged at the northern end of Missionary Ridge that, by the end of the day, a corporal was in charge of the battery, and infantry were used to help man the guns. They had been badly mauled in their manpower but had not lost a gun. Not all of the men showed up. Some had merely drifted away after Missionary Ridge, fed up with the war.[396]

One case in point is James T. Morris, who was assigned to Swett's Battery, but he had already deserted. Somewhere in the confusion around Chattanooga Station, Morris teamed up with two brothers from the Second Tennessee, Walter and William Taylor. Morris had no family and had joined Bankhead at New Madrid at the age of seventeen. The Taylor brothers took Morris with them and made their way to their home

---

[393] Ibid; Lindsley, *The Military Annals of Tennessee*, 793.

[394] CCSR m268 roll 97–98.

[395] Ibid; Lindsley, *The Military Annals of Tennessee*, 824. See Appendix 12.

[396] CCSR m268 roll 97–98. See Appendix 13.

in Dyersburg, Tennessee. The Taylors had been a wealthy slave-holding family before the war and gladly took Morris in. Morris married the brothers' sister, Mary Francis Taylor, on August 28, 1864. He said that he had been wounded and was furloughed after Missionary Ridge. Actually he had been slightly wounded at Chickamauga and had fully recovered.[397]

Men who had left the war after Shiloh were members of Bankhead's Battery, but those who fought beyond Shiloh were members of Scott's Battery. The men who served in Marshall's or Battery Swett's Battery remained members of Scott's Battery. This is what many of them put on their parole papers and pension forms. Some would always carry the name of Scott's Battery. They were the men at Rock Island or Lewis F. Cook in prison in Delaware. Some men on detached service were not transferred. These included Neil Finney, serving as a nurse in Atlanta, and Marion Humphries, making shoes for the quartermaster department.[398]

Scott's Battery came to an end on December 9, 1863. The war was not over, and many of the men would fight to the end. William L. Scott, in his 1886 description of the battery that bore his name said, "it was so engaged in many a skirmish and artillery duel, in which the same cheerful courage and devotion were displayed." This group of men showed the courage to fight for their rights and was certainly devoted to the unit and to the cause. The mental and physical endurance against overwhelming odds had finally overtaken them. Their story does not end on December 9, 1863, but still lives as it is retold.[399]

---

[397] Billie Masters (Descendant of James T. Morris), personal correspondence with the author, December 24, 2010–January 12, 2011.

[398] CCSR m268 roll 97–98.

[399] Lindsley, *The Military Annals of Tennessee*, 793.

CHAPTER 10

———◈———

ROCK ISLAND, ATLANTA, HOME
JANUARY 1864–JUNE 1865

Rock Island Prison	Army of Tennessee
Lieutenant A.T. Watson (Ft. Delaware)	Swett's Miss. Battery Lieutenant John Doscher (absent) 48 men
7 men 1 man Ft. Delaware	
	Marshall's Tennessee Battery
	Lieutenant Thomas Peters (absent) 37 men
Home: Many of the Men are at Home	

Rock Island Prison

The seven men of the battery captured at Missionary Ridge, along with hundreds of others, were taken by boat to Bridgeport, Alabama, and then by rail to Nashville and Louisville destined for Camp Douglas near Chicago. However, on November 15, a fire destroyed some of the barracks where 1,000 men had been housed, so they were diverted to Rock Island Prison, which had been under construction since August 1863 and was nearing completion. This was to be the new home of 5,000 Confederate prisoners.[400]

The prison was built on an island in the Mississippi River. It was made up of eighty-four buildings. The prison was:

> … arranged 6 rows of 14 streets, 100 feet wide, 40 feet between barracks. The barracks were one story raised 1 to 3 feet off the ground, 82 X 22 X 12 feet, 10 windows, cook house at each end of the barracks, 2 ventilators, 4 X 2 feet on roof, 60 double bunks in each barracks, sinks 2 to 6 feet deep.

A stockade was constructed around the buildings 1,300 feet long and 900 feet wide with a boardwalk around the top and sentry boxes every one hundred feet. There was an artesian well inside the camp and a reservoir to collect water and to wash away drainage.[401]

The first train arrived at the prison at about 4:30 p.m. on December 3, 1863. The men were assigned to barracks, and each one selected one of the 120 beds available. One of the seven men from Scott's Battery who arrived at Rock Island Prison was Sergeant Charles Cooley. He had always been present for duty, had never been absent, and had served as sergeant throughout the war. He was twenty-seven years old. Daniel Brennan identified himself to the federal authorities as a sergeant. He had received that rank on December 13, 1861, after only six weeks in the service. Actually he was serving as a private during the Battle of Missionary Ridge,

---

[400] CCSR m268 roll 97–98; Benton McAdams, *Rebels at Rock Island* (DeKalb: Northern Illinois University Press, 2000), 23, 34.

[401] Ibid. 22; Lafayette Rogan, *Diary of Lafayette Rogan, Prisoner of War at Rock Island Prison Barracks 1863–1865*, n.p. 34.

having lost his stripes on September 29, 1862. He was twenty-eight years old. A third man, John Purcell, also identified himself as a sergeant.[402]

Four privates joined these men at prison: Edward Ford, age twenty-nine; Michael Kinney, age thirty-six; Edward Toland, age thirty-nine; and Nathaniel Holmes, age eighteen. Holmes had been with Scott's Battery for only two months before his capture.[403]

Although they lived in plank buildings, there were only two stoves in each building to keep warm. The temperature on January 1, 1864, was minus thirty degrees. There were large cracks between the boards and a shortage of blankets and coats. As prisoner W. J. Minnick relates, "I was captured in my shirt sleeves, a light cotton undershirt, with a captured knit woolen overshirt, and many were no better off." There were no proper medical facilities when the prison opened and only two doctors present. Smallpox, mumps, and measles were prevalent, and a hospital was not ready until February 1864. Many men died of disease the first few months, but after the hospital was built, the death rate from disease declined dramatically. Ten prison barracks in the southeast corner were set aside for the sick. Michael Kinney died of smallpox on December 20, 1863. He was buried in the prison cemetery.[404]

Life in prison was not particularly harsh. There was a prison library stocked with books and newspapers by local townspeople. Particularly, Charles Buford and Kate Perry of Rock Island were known to be Confederate sympathizers and would deliver mail for the prisoners. Sunday church services were held by local ministers and were well attended. There was no lack of money in the camp. Prisoners made buttons and ornaments from shells to sell, and poker games were quite common. Some guards were known to join in the games with prisoners.[405]

To relieve boredom, prisoners could work for ten cents a day cutting wood and repairing buildings. Although the civilian wage was $1.75 per day, the men would not work for nothing since they considered the work to be government work. One prisoner wrote his wife:

---

[402] McAdams, *Rebels at Rock Island*, 34; CCSR m268 roll 97–98.

[403] Ibid.

[404] J. W. Minnick, *Inside of Rock Island Prison* (Nashville, Tennessee: Publishing House of the M. E. Church, 1908), 22; Rock Island Arsenal Museum, Prison Files on display; CCSR m268 roll 97.

[405] McAdams, *Rebels at Rock Island*, 96.

I am happy to inform you that my health had been good since I have been here for which I feel very thankful. I have been kindly treated since a prisoner. I enjoy myself as well as could be expected. We have a nice prison the beautiful Mississippi River surrounds us nearly … we read and talk on scripture and pass off our time profitable to us … and sometime we talk over our courtship's & family trial. [406]

A sutler named Dart came to camp every day to sell items to the prisoners, and he did a lively business. Rations were satisfactory at first. The men received fourteen ounces of bread and twelve ounces of meat per day and bought other food items from Dart.[407]

Men were often punished for infractions of the rules. They could be made to march in place for hours. Sometimes they would be tied by the thumbs to a fence and made to stand on their tiptoes, or ride "Morgan's mule," which was made of a one-inch board nailed between two posts. Another punishment was to be chained to a thirty-two-pound cannon ball. None of the remaining six soldiers from Scott's Battery was ever disciplined for rules infractions.[408]

On June 10, 1864, life at the Rock Island Prison changed. In retaliation for news about Andersonville, it was decided to treat the Confederate prisoners in a similar manner. Rations were cut in half. Soon corn bread and salt pork were the only food to be found. Scurvy became a problem by late summer until potatoes were added to the diet. Dart was no longer allowed to sell items from his sutlery, and guards no longer played cards with the prisoners. Elijah Hall, a prisoner wrote home saying, "I have been her[e] eight months I seen a very hard time."[409]

In September 1864, the One Hundred and Eighth U.S. Colored Infantry became the guards at the prison. This was an insult to the prisoners, some of whom were slave owners. As Lafayette Rogan remarked on September 15, "The Yanks appear to have lost all care for humanity except so far as the Negro is concerned. During this time 12 prisoners were

---

[406] 406. Elijah Hall letter to Father, June 9, 1864, Hall Letters n.p., in author's possession.

[407] Rogan Diary.McAdams, *Rebels at Rock Island*, 96.

[408] Rock Island Arsenal Museum, Prison Files on display; CCRS m268 roll 97–98.

[409] Elijah Hall letter to father, October 24, 1864.

murdered by guards." Minnick states that one guard was even promoted to corporal. None of the men in Scott's Battery was a slave owner, but surely shared this concern.[410]

Some men tried to escape. None of Scott's men was involved. Lafayette Rogan stated, "If my government cant effect anything for me I must begin to devise some way of escape from prison." Although there were forty-two successful escapes from the prison, many men who got out often came back when they couldn't get off the island, especially in the winter.[411]

Another way to escape prison was to swear allegiance to the Union. A man would then be assigned to the navy or the frontier army to fight Indians. These men were moved to other barracks and given full rations. This area was called the calf pen, and those who remained loyal to the Confederacy were said to be in the bullpen. The men in the calf pen—the name came to mean those who were being fattened up for the slaughter—never actually left the prison. Charles Cooley joined the U.S. Army in October 1864. He received better food and privileges. That same month Daniel Brennan and Edward Ford joined the navy. The will to continue the Confederate cause had weakened within these men.[412]

Some prisoners were upset that their comrades would go over to the other side. So a secret club called the Seven Confederate Knights was formed. These men took an oath to stand together. Their emblem was C7K. They had secret handshakes and passwords and discussed the possibility of storming the walls. Eventually 1,767 prisoners joined the calf pen, including Edward Toland and John Purcell in January 1865.[413]

The bribe of better conditions was what disgusted many Confederate veterans. The last member of Scott's Battery, Nathaniel Holmes, finally joined the navy on January 24, 1865. The combination of cold winters and short rations had become too much to bear on the battery members. More likely these men saw the futility of continuing the struggle and wanted to go home. Two months after Lee surrendered, the prison was empty. There

---

[410] Rogan Diary, September 15, 1864; Minnick, *Inside of Rock Island Prison*, 45.

[411] Rogan Diary, November 7, 1864; Rock Island Arsenal Museum prison files.

[412] CCSR m268 roll 97-98; McAdams, *Rebels at Rock Island*, 140.

[413] Ibid; CCSR m268 roll 97–98; W. J. Bohan, "C7K" *Confederate Veteran*, 1904, 455.

were 12,412 men confined to the prison at one time or another, seven from Scott's Battery. Of them, 1,960 died, one from Scott's Battery.[414]

The Atlanta Campaign

Swett's Mississippi Battery had fought with distinction on Missionary Ridge. The unit had repelled numerous attacks on the north end of Missionary Ridge, taking many casualties. Forty-seven men from Scott's Battery were assigned to fill out Swett's company, which was commanded by First Lieutenant Harvey Shannon. Lieutenant John Doscher was listed on the transfer, but was serving on the staff of Major Thomas R. Hotchkiss. Not all of the forty-seven men reported for duty with Shannon. The list did not take into account men who were in the hospital or at home on furlough or on detached duty. It is doubtful that any of the men missing ever showed up for duty. One example was James T. Morris, who had deserted after Missionary Ridge.[415]

Swett's Battery was involved in all of the battles and skirmishes from Resaca (May 14–15, 1864) to Jonesboro (September 1, 1864). Killed in the actions of this campaign were Sergeant William Fowler, Corporal J. C. Mitchell, and Privates Clem C. Smith and Frank B. Culberson, all formally of Scott's Battery. At the Battle of Jonesboro on September 2, 1864, Swett's Battery was overrun by an overwhelming Federal force led by the Sixteen Illinois Infantry. All of the guns were captured, and the unit was disbanded. Gabriel M. Crabtree and Jacob Herberger were captured at the Battle of Jonesboro. They arrived at Camp Douglas on November 1, 1864. Shannon took the remainder of the battery to Macon, Georgia, where he would command the remaining men in a unit called Shannon's Scouts. The scouts did not engage in combat, but were used to gather information about Federal locations. They were not involved in any action until the Carolina campaign in early 1865. Several Scott's Battery men such as Calvin Fish, Calvin C. Hall, Burrill B. Battle, Oliver M. Bigbee, Isaac Cooper, and Hiram Campbell, served to the very end as scouts. Some

---

414   CCSR m268 roll 97-98; Rock Island Arsenal Museum prison files.

415   CCSR m268 roll 97-98.

of them surrendered with General Joseph Johnston at Greensboro, North Carolina.[416]

Marshall's Tennessee Battery was to receive thirty-seven men and two officers from Scott's Battery. Captain Marshall would never see many of the men. All seven men sent to Rock Island Prison were marked as deserters. Also men on detached duty, such as Patrick Joyce, James Fitzpatrick, Neil Finney, and Marion Humphries, were listed as deserters even though they were serving the Confederacy in another capacity. Lieutenant Thomas Peters never reported to duty either. He was still on furlough, but no one informed Marshall. Second Lieutenant Alfred Watson reported for duty after escaping from his captors and served loyally with Marshall's Battery as a section commander. Even with men from Scott's Battery added to Marshall's Battery, Captain Marshall faced a manpower shortage. With barely sixty men in his battery, infantry was often pushed into the ranks to help serve the guns.[417]

Like Swett's Battery, Marshall's Battery fought in all of the battles and skirmishes involved in the Atlanta campaign. As General Hardee said, "For ninety-three days the armies never lost their grapple." It was a campaign unlike previous campaigns, as the men dug entrenchments every time they moved. Captain Marshall described the constant fortifying:

> The mere labor of fortification was beyond what prudent masters would demand of robust slaves. Physical and mental powers were tested to the utmost degree of endurance. The strain of constant vigilance was perhaps harder to bear than the digging, marching, and fighting all combined; but neither could be relaxed for an hour.[418]

After the Battle of Jonesboro, the battery was pulled out for rest as Hood and Sherman parted and Atlanta fell to the enemy. Throughout the campaign, Marshall's Battery lost about thirty-five men, and they were replaced with infantrymen. The losses came from all categories: killed,

---

[416] Ibid., m232 roll 9, 14, 37; Rowland, Dunbar, *Military History of Mississippi 1803–1898*, Mississippi Department of Archives and History, 1908, 399–410.

[417] CCSR m268 roll 97–98; Lindsley, *The Military Annals of Tennessee*, 824.

[418] Ibid.

wounded, sick, and deserter. Thomas Cluin was captured at Dalton on May 13, 1864. He was sent to Camp Morton Prison near Indianapolis.[419]

Marshall's Battery traveled with the Army of Tennessee in Hood's invasion of Tennessee in the fall of 1864. The battery remained at Columbia, Tennessee, while the army fought at Franklin and then at Nashville. Hood's defeat at Nashville was a Confederate disaster, and Marshall's Battery served as part of a rear guard as Hood retreated into Alabama. So many artillery units had been destroyed at Nashville that all artillerymen without commands were ordered to Mobile to man the defenses of that city. This order did not affect Marshall's Battery, but men had left Marshall's Battery through desertion, as Captain Marshall had to add "twenty to thirty men from the infantry." Two deserters were Corporal William Martin and Private William Powers, who deserted on December 23, 1864. They were captured outside of Columbia, but were released after taking the oath of allegiance on December 28. The number of Scott's men who remained with Marshall is unknown.[420]

In February 1865, Marshall was ordered to North Carolina to join up with the Army of Tennessee. They arrived at Salisbury, North Carolina, on April 3. On April 12, Marshall's Battery was engaged against General George Stoneman's cavalry, and all of the artillery was captured. About half of the men escaped, but a total of 700 men of all branches were captured, including Captain Marshall and Lieutenant Watson. Also captured were Privates John Lundy and L. A. Davis. These men were marched to Knoxville, Tennessee, where they boarded trains to be sent to prison. They arrived at Camp Chase, near Columbus Ohio, on May 4, but were released on parole on June 14, 1865.[421]

The Officers

After the disaster on Missionary Ridge and the disbanding of Scott's Battery, William L. Scott was without a command. He was transferred to General Joseph Wheeler's cavalry where he became the chief of artillery. After a short time, he became Wheeler's ordnance officer. His old friend, W. Y. C. Humes, was also serving in Wheeler's corps. He had been promoted

---

[419]   Ibid. 827, 829; CCSR m268 roll 97.

[420]   Ibid; Lindsley, *The Military Annals of Tennessee*, 831–835.

[421]   Ibid., 842, 845.

to general and commanded a division of cavalry. Scott soon became an aid on his staff. In November of 1864, William L. Scott married Susan Washington Elder in Knoxville, Tennessee. Humes married Sallie E. Elder at about the same time in Memphis. Sallie and Susan were sisters, thereby making Scott and Humes brothers-in-law. How they got through enemy lines to get married and then return to their post is unknown.[422]

Scott was relieved from duty in Humes Cavalry division on January 22, 1865, and took a position at army headquarters in Tupelo, Mississippi. As the war came to an end, Scott signed the "Parole of Honor" on May 11, 1865, at Meridian, Mississippi. He signed the document "W. L. Scott, Captain Light Artillery P.A.C.S."[423]

Officially there were four lieutenants assigned to Scott's Battery at the time of Missionary Ridge. They were John H. Marsh, Joseph Phillips, Thomas Peters, and Alfred T. Watson. Watson was the only officer present in late November, so John Doscher was assigned to command the battery, as a battle seemed imminent. After the battle, Doscher returned to staff duty for Major Thomas Hotchkiss and did not attempt to keep Scott's Battery together. On February 4, 1864, he was granted a leave of absence while a court-martial was called to look into Doscher's conduct at Missionary Ridge. The court determined that he was "reported as very inefficient." He was allowed to return to his post as assistant adjutant to Major Hotchkiss, but would never hold a command again. He served to the end of the war and swore his oath on June 5, 1865, in his hometown of Augusta, Georgia.[424]

John H. Marsh had been severely wounded in the left arm at Chickamauga and was not released from the hospital until April 17, 1864. He had refused to have his arm amputated and kept his useless arm in a sling. He was furloughed home but refused to accept a discharge. He joined the staff of his old teacher, General Otho Strahl, and was with the Army of Tennessee at the Battle of Franklin. Marsh was riding a white horse on that fatal day as William L. Scott described it many years later:

> While his comrades were falling thick and fast around him on
> that terrible night when horse and rider were … pressed on into

---

[422]   CCSR m268 roll 98; Family Data Collections, Scott and Humes Records.

[423]   CCSR m268 roll 98.

[424]   OR XXX vol. 2, 692; CCSR m268 roll 97–98.

the holocaust of death as he rode. And then on foot—his horse being shot from under him—dealing death with his revolver … he pressed forward until he fell as the ball went crashing through his brain. He fell there, swelling the already swollen heap of the dead … No nobler spirit ever went up to the God of battles than that of this brave soldier, born on Tennessee soil, and offering up his life-blood for his native land in what he believed to be the defense of her most sacred rights.[425]

Bishop Charles Quintard carried Marsh's body to Ashwood, the church of Leonidas Polk near Columbia, Tennessee, for burial.

Lieutenant Joseph Phillips had been on detached duty with Smith P. Bankhead since February 1863. He served in Texas as Colonel Bankhead's post adjutant in San Antonio until he was reassigned on July 1, 1864, to Lieutenant General Richard Taylor where he became the assistant chief of artillery for the Department of Alabama, Mississippi, and Eastern Louisiana. On November 11, 1864, he was posted to Selma, Alabama. Phillips requested that he be relieved from staff duty and be assigned to the ordnance department. This transfer was approved on December 5, 1864, and he served with the ordnance department until the end of the war.[426]

Thomas Peters remained on furlough pending his resignation. His resignation was refused, and he was ordered to report to Captain Marshall. Marshall was serving as the battalion commander and appointed Peters to be the ordnance officer for the battalion. It is not known when he returned for duty, but on December 28, 1864, he was transferred to Chalmer's Cavalry Division. He served in that capacity until the end of the war.[427]

Alfred T. Watson served valiantly with Marshall's Battery to the very end. He served as the left section commander and became a close friend of Captain Marshall. Captured for a second time at Salisbury, North Carolina, Watson remained a prisoner until he signed his Oath of Allegiance on June 14, 1865.[428]

---

[425] Lindsley, *The Military Annals of Tennessee*, 794.

[426] CCRS m268 roll 98.

[427] Ibid.

[428] Lindsley, *The Military Annals of Tennessee*, 840–842; Roll of Prisoners of War 465 sheet 2.

Enlisted Men

The men of Scott's Battery returned home by various means. Those who had been wounded or sick often were furloughed home to recover. One such man was John Shirey, who left Ocmulgee Hospital in Macon, Georgia, on March 5, 1864. Others merely walked away from their unit, like Corporal William Martin. Another who walked away was Philip Sullivan, who gave himself up to Federal troops outside of Nashville on December 27, 1865. Another deserter was Daniel McKenzie, who avoided Confederate, as well as Federal, authorities. He came forward on May 5, 1865, near Chattanooga to sign the Oath of Allegiance. About forty-three men were deserters after Missionary Ridge. They left at various times and were never accounted for.[429]

Some of the forty-three deserters may have done their duty in the ranks, but when the war ended they simply went home. Some signed the Oath of Allegiance. Those who survived in North Carolina merely walked home or swore allegiance with General Johnston. Neil Finney and Marion Humphries walked away from their assignments to avoid capture when the Federals were near enough.[430]

Some of the men swore the oaths of allegiance after the war ended. Patrick Joyce, who had lost both hands at Shiloh, served at Mobile, Alabama, and signed his oath on April 25, 1865. Calvin Fish signed his oath on April 26 at Columbus, Mississippi. Isaac Cooper, Hiram Campbell, Calvin C. Hall, and Oliver M. Bigbee signed the oath at Greensboro, North Carolina, on April 28. Burrill B. Battle signed the oath in Selma, Alabama, on May 4, as he was traveling home to Arkansas. The six men held at Rock Island Prison were released on May 16. Lewis F. Cook was held by Federal forces longer than anyone. He swore his oath on June 10 and was released from Fort Delaware after being captured on June 28, 1863. Watson and those captured at Salisbury were released on June 14.[431]

---

[429]   CCSR m268 roll 97–98.

[430]   Ibid.

[431]   Ibid. See appendix 14.

Epilogue

The men went home to their wives and sweethearts and returned to their former occupations. Some moved to other towns or states and raised their families, often not saying much about the war. A few joined Confederate veterans' organizations, and some lived to receive a pension. A total of 252 men served at one time or another in Bankhead's/Scott's Tennessee Light Artillery Company. Thirteen men (5 percent) were killed in battle, and thirty-six (14.3 percent) were wounded and survived the war. Thirteen men died of sickness. That was only 5 percent of the men who served, and a lower percentage than average Civil War statistics.[432]

Twenty-five men (17.5 percent) were captured. Lewis F. Cook and Alfred T. Watson were captured twice. In 1862 those captured were the sick or wounded left behind in the hospital. In 1863 and afterwards, the men captured were those performing their duty at the guns.[433]

There were 116 men classified as deserters. This was 46 percent of the men, a number that demonstrates the weakness of almost half of the men's loyalty. Some of these men were not really deserters. They were forgotten in hospitals or furloughed home without a proper accounting, but they did not return to duty. When considering this, the desertion rate was more like 20–25 percent, which is higher than the 10–15 percent applied to the Confederate Army. [434]

Although some had stayed until the very end, only four could say they surrendered with General Johnston on April 28, 1865, when the Army of Tennessee gave up the cause. They were Oliver M. Bigbee, Hiram Campbell, Isaac Cooper, and Calvin C. Hall. These men demonstrated the most courage and devotion of them all. Of course it goes without saying that the thirteen men killed in action paid the highest price in their courage and devotion.[435]

---

[432] CCSR m268 roll 97–98.

[433] Ibid.

[434] Ibid.

[435] Ibid.

CHAPTER 11

—⟫•(⊙)•⟪—

A SELECTION OF BIOGRAPHIES

Officers
    Smith Pyne Bankhead 1823–1867
    John Doscher 1836–1891
    William Bowden Greenlaw 1841–1907
    William Young Conn Humes 1830–1882
    John Henry Marsh 1839–1864
    James Clare McDavitt 1834–1900
    Thomas McNeal Peters 1842-1866
    William Mecklenburg Polk 1844–1918
    William Luther Scott 1836–1891

Enlisted Men
    Burrill Bunn Battle 1838–1917
    Isaac Washington Cooper 1841–1902
    Elijah Fawbush 1833–1905
    Calvin Celsor Hall 1845–1924
    James Thomas Morris 1843–1920
    Lorenzo R. Richardson 1840–1918
    Talty Brothers:
        Patrick 1829–1910
        Simon 1831–1919
        George 1835–1913
        John 1842–1917

The selected biographies in this chapter are representative of the officers and men who served in Bankhead's/Scott's Tennessee Battery. Some of the information has been was covered in the previous chapters, but has been repeated here to make a more complete biography.

The Officers

Smith Pyne Bankhead came from a noble family in early American history. He was a descendent of Robert Bankhead, who was born in Scotland in 1663. Two generations later, his great-grandfather, James Bankhead, emigrated to Virginia in the 1740s. His father, Brigadier General James Bankhead, was a career army officer who was stationed in South Carolina at the time when he was born on August 20, 1823, at Fort Moultrie, South Carolina. His mother was Anne Pyne. He grew up in Virginia and attended Hampden Military School before attending Georgetown University and the University of Virginia. During the Mexican War, Bankhead was a captain of artillery with the Virginia Volunteers, and he passed through Memphis en route to Vera Cruz, Mexico, to serve under his father who was commanding the American troops stationed there after the city had been captured. After the Mexican War, Bankhead was presented an engraved dragoon officer's sword for "gallant service." He migrated to California during the gold rush, but found life hard there and decided to settle in Memphis in 1851.[436]

In Memphis, Bankhead became involved in politics and was well known as a Mexican War hero. He married Susan Adeline Garth in 1851, and they had one daughter, Ada, who was born in 1852. He founded and edited the Memphis *Whig*, a party newspaper. He soon sold the newspaper and was elected the city attorney of Memphis in 1852. He built up a reputable private law practice throughout the decade before the Civil War.[437]

On May 15, 1861, Bankhead began recruiting an artillery company in Memphis. Attached to General Gideon Pillow and then General Leonidas

---

[436]   1. Nigel Bufton, *A Complete Genealogy Report for Smith Pyne Bankhead* (http://www.myheritage.com. 2007): Civil War Preservations, *Swords of Honor*, (www.civilwarpreservations.com.) (accessed March 12, 2013); Daniel, *Cannoneers in Gray*, 218.

[437]   Lindsley, *The Military Annals of Tennessee*, 792.

Polk, Bankhead's Battery trained at Fort Pillow and then saw action at Columbus, Kentucky, and New Madrid, Missouri. Just prior to the battle of Shiloh, Bankhead was promoted to chief of artillery for Polk's corps. Oddly, though, he served with his own battery at Shiloh, fighting at no less than six different locations including Ruggles' artillery line. After Shiloh, the battery was reorganized at Tupelo, Mississippi. Bankhead served as artillery chief for Cheatham's division in the Kentucky campaign. After the Battle of Perryville, he transferred to the Trans-Mississippi Department at the request of his first cousin, John Bankhead Magruder, and became his colonel of artillery. Bankhead served in the Trans-Mississippi Department throughout the rest of the war.[438]

During the occupation of Memphis, General Sherman ordered the exile of twenty-three prominent families whose male members were fighting for the Confederacy. Ada Garth Bankhead, wife of Smith P. Bankhead, was among those who received such orders. The fiery southern lady sought out General Sherman. "General, I won't go," she announced. "Madam," Sherman replied, "we'll have to put you out then at the point of bayonets." "I wish my grandmother was here," she reported. "She'd spank you. To think you were my Grandfather's adjutant in the Mexican War and trying to put me and my daughter out of our home. I'll not have it, and when you try to force us you had best drag along a cannon instead of a bayonet." General Sherman modified his order of exile.[439]

Bankhead served under Major General John Bankhead Magruder, who had been transferred to Texas following his dogged defense at Yorktown in the Peninsula Campaign in Virginia. He was promoted to colonel on November 13, 1862. However, the Confederate Senate did not confirm Bankhead's promotion papers. Evidently the promotion papers were mislaid in the Confederate War Office, and the Senate never saw them. This oversight was not made good until January 14, 1865, to rank from June 15, 1864.[440]

In the summer of 1863, Bankhead commanded the Third Military Sub-District of Texas at San Antonio. He was promoted to acting brigadier general on May 30, 1863. His tenure as commander of a district was not very successful. Deserters and cotton speculators overran his district while

---

[438] Ibid.

[439] OR XXVI vol. 2, 25; Ada Bankhead Collection, Manuscript 316.

[440] OR XXII vol. 2, 1026, XXVI pt. 2, 25.

he was trying to organize his forces. He was ordered into Indian Territory (Oklahoma) in command of Mann's Cavalry Brigade to link up with Confederate forces. He had only three regiments of cavalry and skirmished with Federal patrols, but failed in his mission. In his absence, he was replaced (August 29, 1863) as district commander and soon was replaced as brigade commander of his cavalry. It was believed that a Texan should actually command any military district. Besides, he had left Texas and was no longer under the command of Magruder. He returned to San Antonio and reverted to his substantive rank of colonel, but did not see field service again. He was removed of his command position in November 1864 and again became chief of artillery, District of Texas.[441]

On March 1, 1865, Brigadier General Smith P. Bankhead passed through the Union lines near New Orleans. The war was not quite over, but Bankhead was going home. Major General Canby had given him a pass of safe conduct and protection with the assurance that he would not fight against the United States again. Under these circumstances, Bankhead returned to Memphis where he became a prominent figure in the Reconstruction government that was harsh on the Memphis area. He was appointed deputy city attorney and trustee of the navy yard.[442]

On Saturday, March 31, 1867, General Bankhead was assassinated near the corner of Main and Washington in Memphis. The *Memphis Appeal* reported, "Gen. Smith P. Bankhead, who is well known as a prominent citizen, high toned gentleman, an emulent lawyer, an affectionate husband and father was the victim of a senseless blow." It was 11:00 p.m. when he was struck down from behind and beaten to death by persons never identified, and the crime is now famous in Memphis as the oldest unsolved murder. The funeral was held on April 1 at the Calvary Episcopal Church. He was buried in the family plot, lot 67, Chapel Hill Area of Elmwood Cemetery. Although he held the rank of general at the end of the war, he is not considered one of the twelve Confederate generals buried in this cemetery. A Bankhead letter dated September 24, 1863, mentions that he was appointed brigadier by order of General Edmund Kirby Smith. Kirby Smith actually approved Magruder's assignment to duty pending action

---

[441] Bruce Allardice, *More Generals in Gray* (Baton Rouge and London: Louisianna State University Press, 1995) 26; OR XXII vol. 2. 921–922, 976–978, XXV vol. 2, 1066–1067, XXVI vol. 2, 1014–1015; Casdorph, *Prince John Magruder*, 262.

[442] CCSR m268 roll 97.

by the War Department. The Confederate congress never approved this promotion.[443]

Bankhead's wife died in 1872 while in Charlottesville, Virginia, and was buried beside her husband. Two of his brothers served on the Union side during the war. Captain John Bankhead was the commander of the *Monitor* when it sank, and General Henry Bankhead served on General Don Carlos Buell's staff. On July 14, 1924, Miss Ada Payne Bankhead, the only child of General and Mrs. Bankhead, died at the family home. Bankhead had no other children, but there are over 700 direct descendents of Robert Bankhead.[444]

John Doscher was born in Prussia in 1836 and came to America with his immigrant parents as a child. Raised in Augusta, Georgia, he joined the Washington Light Artillery of Augusta in 1861 as a private. He rose to the rank of first lieutenant serving in Girardy's Battery and finally on the staff of Major Thomas Hotchkiss. Due to the lack of officers in Scott's Battery during the siege of Chattanooga, he was assigned the command of the battery just before the Battle of Missionary Ridge. It was his misfortune that he was in command on that fateful day, and the failure to rally the men afterwards led to his court-martial in February 1864. He remained on the staff of Hotchkiss but was no longer allowed to have a command position.[445]

After the war, Doscher returned home and worked in the family grocery store. He married after the war and was blessed with three children. By 1880 his parents had died and he became the sole proprietor of the grocery business. His wife also had died, and he and the three children lived with his in-laws. He served on the August city council and was a member of the Confederate Survivors Association as well as several other civic groups. He ran the grocery business until his sudden death of a heart attack on May 4, 1891. The Augusta Chronicle described him as "quiet and unostentatious in manner, and whom many knew as most kind, liberal and true. His hand and purse were ever ready to aid the distressed and needy, and only those

---

[443] OR XXII vol. 2, 285; *Memphis Appeal*, April 2, 1867.

[444] Bufton, *A Complete Genealogy Report For Smith Pyne Bankhead*, 23.

[445] CCSR m266 roll 17; OR XXX pt. 2, 692; *Augusta Chronicle* May 5, 1891.

who knew him most intimately were acquainted the deeds of kindness which he so quietly performed."[446]

William Bowden Greenlaw Jr. was the son of Memphis business tycoon William B. Greenlaw, who had made a fortune in investments before the war. Greenlaw was born in May 1841 and grew up in Memphis. His father employed him as a lawyer in his business. When the war broke out in 1861, Greenlaw became an officer in Bankhead's Battery. In the fall of 1861, Greenlaw was the only officer of the battery who did not sign on to fight until the end of the war. He was therefore passed over for promotion, and because of that he resigned his commission in February 1862.[447]

Returning to Memphis, Greenlaw worked with his father, but with Federal occupation of the city, business opportunities declined. Federal authorities denied to him "the right to appear in court." This order was later dismissed, but his practice of law in Memphis was over. Greenlaw married Fannie Jennett Brown on April 8, 1863, in Mississippi. They had three daughters. The war ruined the Greenlaw family business. Young Greenlaw went into real estate after the war, but after the yellow fever epidemic in 1873, he moved his family to Texas. He lived in the Dallas area, selling real estate until his death on January 27, 1907. Many of his descendents still live in Texas.[448]

William Young Conn Humes was born in Virginia on May 1, 1830. His great-grandfather had immigrated to America from Ireland in the 1770s and settled in Pennsylvania. William graduated second in his class of 1851 from the Virginia Military Institute. After studying law, he moved to Knoxville, Tennessee, where he married Margaret Rhea White in 1854. Their son, Newton, was born in 1859. William had been working in Memphis, intending to move there, when the war began. Leaving his wife and child in Knoxville, he joined with Smith P. Bankhead to form an artillery company. After the Battle of Belmont, Humes was promoted to

---

[446] Ibid; John Doscher. Family Data Collections, Individual Records, Ancestry. com.; U.S. Ninth Census.

[447] CCSR m268 roll 97.

[448] William Greenlaw, Family Data Collections; Robert A. Lanier, "The Memphis Legal Community Under Federal Occupation 1860–1870," *The West Tennessee Historical Society Papers*, Vol. LXVI, 2012, 43.

Winston's Battery, but it became known as the Belmont Battery. He was placed in charge of all of the artillery at Island Number Ten and was taken prisoner after Island Number Ten surrendered on April 7, 1862. Taken to Johnson's Island, he was eventually exchanged and sent to Mobile where he was promoted to major. He became chief of artillery for General Joseph Wheeler. He spent the rest of the war in the cavalry rising to the rank of brigadier general on November 16, 1863. He commanded a cavalry brigade and eventually a division, and gave his old friend William L. Scott a position on his staff after Missionary Ridge. During this time he received word that his wife had died in Knoxville. He campaigned throughout 1864 with Wheeler's cavalry, raiding Sherman's supply lines and later harassing Sherman's march to the sea. He was wounded at Monroe's Crossing, North Carolina, on March 10, 1865.[449]

Humes married Sallie E. Elder in 1864 in Memphis. How he accomplished this while Memphis was under Federal control is amazing. After the war, Humes raised four children and continued his law practice in Memphis. He was a member of the law firm of William K. Posten, Humes and Scott on Court Street. His old friend, William L. Scott, was not only his partner but also his brother-in-law, as Scott had married Susan Elder in 1864. Humes was a staunch defender of race segregation after the war. In court he argued the standard in the 1870s that would eventually become the Supreme Court decision of separate but equal established with *Plessy v. Ferguson* in 1896. While on a speaking engagement in Huntsville, Alabama, he died on September 11, 1882. He is one of the twelve generals buried in Memphis at Elmwood Cemetery.[450]

John Henry Marsh was born in Chatham, North Carolina, in 1836. His father, Daniel Marsh, moved to Hardeman County in Tennessee when he was just an infant. The family lived on a plantation about six miles from Bolivar. Marsh grew up with his brothers and sisters on the plantation with what has been described by Charles Quintard as "happy and contented slaves."[451] His father was very generous with many influential

---

449   W. Y. C. Humes. Family Data Collection; Daniel and Bock, *Island No. 10*, 137; CCSR m268 roll 97; John W. Cothern, *Confederates of Elmwood* (Bowie, Maryland: Heritage Books, Inc., 2001), 183.

450   Ibid.; Humes, Family Data Collections; Memphis City Directory 1866.

451   Quintard, "Tribute to Lieut. John Marsh," 599.

friends. On his mother's side, Marsh was related to the Perkins family of Middle Tennessee and to the Harstons and Daltons of North Carolina. His family line in America went back six generations. Robert Marsh settled in Connecticut in the 1630s. His father had fifteen siblings, and his grandfather had nine, so the Marsh clan in America is very large.[452]

As a boy, John Marsh attended New Castle Village School where he was described as high spirited, manly, and handsome. The teacher at the school was Otho French Strahl. Marsh and Strahl formed a lifetime friendship of respect, and they died together at the Battle of Franklin in 1864. Marsh had exceptional qualities that were seen by all who knew him. When Congressman F. P. Stanton visited the Daniel Marsh plantation, he was struck by these qualities and gave him an appointment as a cadet at the West Point Military Academy in 1860.[453]

Marsh never completed his education, because of the outbreak of the Civil War, and he left the academy and returned home. In Bolivar, Marshall T. Polk was forming an artillery battery, and Marsh joined him as a second lieutenant on April 25, 1861. Marsh served with the battery with distinction through the Battle of Shiloh, where he received a promotion to first lieutenant and was transferred to Phillip's Battery. At the Battle of Perryville and Stone's River, Marsh served on the staff of General Leonidas Polk. In February 1863, Lieutenant Phillips of Scott's Battery requested a transfer to be with Colonel Bankhead in Texas. John Marsh was transferred to the Battery on February 23 to replace Phillips. Marsh became senior in command of the battery when Captain William L. Scott was gone. Scott was frequently absent from the camp near Shelbyville that spring, and it was Marsh who continued to drill and train the battery. It was during this time that General Bragg ordered an artillery contest between the batteries in the Army of Tennessee. Scott's Battery was well known for their drill and was considered the favorite for the contest. Unfortunately, the battery came in second and did not win the prize of a new banner.[454]

On September 19, 1863, Scott's Battery became engaged in the Battle of Chickamauga. Captain Scott was absent due to illness, and Marsh commanded the battery. On the first day of action, the battery was engaged

---

[452] John Marsh. Family Data Collection; Quintard, "Tribute to Lieut. John Marsh," 599.

[453] Ibid.

[454] Ibid.; Lindsley, *The Military Annals of Tennessee*, 792–793.

at Brock Field. Marsh was severely wounded in the left arm and was carried from the field. He was taken to a field hospital where he remained for six weeks before he was moved to Gilmer Hospital, Georgia, where he remained for six months. His arm was shattered, and it never healed. During this period of suffering, he became interested in religion and became a close friend to Bishop Charles T. Quintard. He was furloughed and went home to visit his mother, his father having passed away since he joined the army. There his mother and friends begged him to stay and be discharged from the army. His left arm was useless and shrunken, and he could easily have gotten an exemption from service. He replied, "*No*; my country needs me now more than ever, and I must go."[455]

Just before the fall of Atlanta, Marsh reported for duty. General Johnston, upon seeing Marsh's condition, offered him a discharge from service, but Marsh refused it. He then took a position as chief of artillery on General Strahl's staff of Cheatham's Division. By November, General Hood commanded the Army of Tennessee and re-entered the state, pushing back the Federals toward Nashville. On November 30, 1864, Marsh was killed at the Battle of Franklin. William L. Scott had this to say about Marsh:

> No braver soldier than John Marsh ever went upon a battlefield; Tennessee soil was never wet by the blood of a nobler son than when John Marsh poured out his life-blood in defense of the Lost Cause at the carnival of death, the bloody field of Franklin. His gallantry on the battle-field was of the noblest type. He embodied the very spirit of chivalry. It was with feeling of exaltation that he rushed into the very thickest of the battle. His face then beamed with joy, and his carriage was proud and peerless as that of Henry of Navarre. Upon seeing him as he rode amongst the smoke, in the din and the roar of battle, one was instinctively reminded of Ney, "the bravest of the brave." In him was exhibited not merely courage, but a lofty disdain of danger. He went in to the thickest fight not only with that high resolve which is born of an exalted since of duty, but with an enthusiasm which invested the battle-field with the charm of a festive occasion. To him it was the field of glory. No nobler spirit ever went up to God of battles than that of this brave soldier, born on Tennessee soil, and offering up his

---

[455] Quintard, "Tribute to Lieut. John Marsh," 599.

life-blood for his native land in what he believed to be the defense of her most sacred rights[456].

Marsh was riding a white horse and wore an artillery jacket, as he always did, on that fateful day. First his horse was shot from under him, and he continued forward on foot to within 300 yards of the breastworks when he took a bullet in the brain. Dying with him that day was his friend and mentor General Strahl as well as Generals Cleburne and Jackson. Bishop Quintard recovered Marsh's body and removed it to Ashwood Cemetery west of Columbia, Tennessee. There he was buried only yards away from the grave of General Leonidas Polk. After the war, Bishop Quintard sold Marsh's horse and with the funds erected a memorial window in St. James Church, Bolivar, to the memory of John Marsh, whose descendents still live in Hardeman County today.[457]

"IN MEMORY OF OTHO FRENCH STRAHL AND
JOHN HENRY MARSH DIED NOV. 30, 1864"

James Clare McDavitt was born in Shelby County, Kentucky, on November 25, 1834. He was of Scottish extraction. James McDavitt,

---

456 Lindsley, *The Military Annals of Tennessee*, 793–794.

457 Ibid; Quintard, "Tribute to Lieut. John Marsh," 599; Historical Data Systems, comp. *American Civil War Soldiers*. (ancestry.com/search/db.aspx?dbid+1565). Provo, UT, USA.

his great-grandfather, had come from Scotland in 1760, and settled in Charleston, South Carolina. At Charleston, James McDavitt, his grandfather, was born in 1769 and served as captain of a company in the famous Kentucky Rifles in the War of 1812. His father, Dr. George McDavitt, was a prominent physician of Shelby County. James C. McDavitt received his education in the schools of Richmond, Indiana, and at Asbury (now DePauw) University at Greencastle. He studied law under Judge T. W. Brown of Shelbyville, Kentucky, and in 1856 he was admitted to the bar. He moved to Memphis in 1857 and practiced law at Kortrecht & McDavitt until he enlisted as a first lieutenant in Bankhead's Battery.

At Shiloh he was slightly wounded and independently commanded a section on the second day of the battle. After Shiloh, he was transferred to ordnance, and in the fall of 1862, Lieutenant McDavitt was ordered to Mobile as instructor of artillery on the staff of General Maury. The following summer he was in command of the floating ironclad battery in Mobile Bay. Later he commanded Battery McIntosh, and in June 1864, was recalled to the army under General Polk, reporting the day that Polk was killed at Pine Mountain, Georgia. Subsequently he served as adjutant and inspector of artillery under Generals Loring and Stewart. In the Atlanta campaign and at Mobile he served with Lieutenant-Colonel John Quattlebaum. He surrendered with Quattlebaum's command at Meridian, Mississippi.[458]

After the war, McDavitt returned to Memphis and went into law with his friend Lewis Bond. They had served together briefly while at Columbus, Kentucky. Their law office of McDavitt & Bond was located at 274 Second Street. In 1870 he became a member of the law firm of Estes, Jackson & McDavitt. In 1882 the law firm was closed, and he became the manager of The Memphis Abstract Company. In 1866 he married Flora R. Dobyns, and their daughter, Martha, married William E. Hoshall of Memphis. McDavitt died on May 28, 1900.[459]

Thomas McNeal Peters was born on May 21, 1842, in Bolivar, Tennessee. He was the first son of Dr. George Peters, who was a distinguished physician in Bolivar. Dr. Peters served on various medical boards and had been a state senator in Tennessee before the war. His third wife, Jesse, with

---

[458] James McDavitt, Family Data Systems.

[459] Ibid; Memphis City Directory 1866.

whom he had five children, stayed in Spring Hill, Tennessee, where she was raised and is known for her affair with General Earl Van Dorn. Dr. Peters murdered Van Dorn on May 7, 1863, after catching him visiting his wife. George's brother, Thomas Hill Peters, served on the staff of General Leonidas Polk, and his son James Arthur Peters was a midshipman in the Confederate navy. [460]

Thomas Peters graduated first of his class from the University of Mississippi in 1861. He enlisted in Marshall Polk's Tennessee Battery and was placed as first sergeant. He was a friend of John Marsh, also of Bolivar, who enlisted in the same battery as a second lieutenant. Peters was promoted to second lieutenant on September 1, 1861. Polk's Battery was broken up after Shiloh, and Peters was placed on General Polk's staff. On February 17, 1863, he was transferred to Scott's Battery as senior second lieutenant on the same day his friend, John Marsh, was made senior first lieutenant. On March 20, 1863, Peters asked for a thirty-day furlough. He went to Memphis where his father was staying. Under the cover of being treated for a wound, Peters was in great pain for a genital disease, probably gonorrhea. He received an extension on his furlough, but his father had killed Van Dorn and fled to Nashville. Other doctors treated him and advised him to have surgery and resign from the army. It is not known whether he ever had the surgery. His resignation was never approved, and he never returned to Scott's Battery. He was transferred to Marshall's Battery, but served in the ordnance department. He was transferred to Chalmer's Cavalry Division on December 28, 1864. [461]

After the war Peters studied to be a lawyer. He visited his father's plantation in Arkansas and stopped in Memphis. On April 9, 1866, Thomas Peters put on his Confederate uniform, lay on his hotel bed, and fired a pistol just behind his ear. His suicide was never expected by anyone who had seen him that day. His body was taken to Bolivar, Tennessee, where he is buried in Polk's Cemetery near his mother. [462]

William Mecklenburg Polk was the youngest son of General Leonidas Polk. His family affectionately called him Meck. He was born

---

[460] David Wake, Peters family notebook compiled by David Wake; Thomas Peters. Family Data Collection.

[461] Ibid; *University of Mississippi Yearbook*, 1861, 136; CCSR m268 roll 98.

[462] David Wake, Peters family notebook.

in Ashwood, Maury County, Tennessee, on August 15, 1844. He grew up on his father's plantation in Louisiana and was positively influenced by the house slave called Mammy Betsey. He was a cadet at the Virginia Military Institute in Lexington, Virginia, and helped train Confederate troops under the guidance of Major Thomas J. Jackson (Stonewall) when he entered the Confederate army in April 1861. He was then assigned similar duty for General Felix Zolicoffer. He was commissioned a first lieutenant and joined Bankhead's Battery in November 1861, his father placing him there. He served under Bankhead and Scott until February 17, 1863, when he was assigned assistant chief of artillery in his father's corps, joining his brother Alexander Hamilton Polk who was an aid on his father's staff. After his father's death, he served as adjutant to the artillery regiment of Stewart's corps, ending the war as a captain and adjutant in the inspector general's department.[463]

Polk married Ida Lyon on November 14, 1866. They had four children, but only two grew to adulthood. After the war, he attended the New York College of Physicians and Surgeons and graduated in 1869. He practiced medicine in New York City, and from 1875 until 1879, he was professor of therapeutics and clinical medicine at Bellevue College. He then accepted the chair of obstetrics and the diseases of women in the medical department of the University of the City of New York. He was also a surgeon in the department of obstetrics in Bellevue hospital. Dr. Polk has also contributed to medical literature, writing a number of articles. In addition, he wrote a biography of his father, which was published in 1893. His wife Ida died in 1912, and he married his second wife, Maria Dehon, in 1914. He died on January 3, 1918. His son, Frank Lyon Polk, had several children, and Meck's descendents live in the New York City area today.[464]

William Luther Scott was born in 1834 in Knoxville, Tennessee. His great-grandfather had come from England and settled in North Carolina in the 1750s. The Scott clan in America is very large, as each generation had many children. Scott became a lawyer in Knoxville, and when his friend, William Y. C. Humes, invited him to join the staff of Bankhead's Battery, he finished his law business and reported for duty on June 4, 1861. At the Battle of Shiloh, Scott's horse was shot from under him, and was

---

[463] Polk, *Leonidas Polk*, vol. 1, 16–165, Vol. 2, 32; CCSR m268 roll 98.

[464] William M. Polk, Family Data Collection.

wounded severely in the neck. He was hospitalized for several weeks, and when he returned, Bankhead had been promoted to major and had left the battery. McDavitt was reassigned to ordnance, and Scott found himself in charge of the battery and promoted to captain. Scott commanded the battery throughout the campaigns of 1862 and 1863. At Missionary Ridge, the battery lost all of its guns and was broken up. McDavitt's old friend, Humes, took him into his division as artillery inspector. He later was assigned to headquarters in Tupelo, Mississippi.[465]

Scott had married Susan Washington Elder in 1864, and they were blessed with four children. After the war, Scott went practiced law in Memphis with the firm William K. Preston, Humes and Scott. He was later appointed a chancellor of the Second Chancery Court of Shelby County. In 1875, after his son was born, Scott moved his family to St. Louis, Missouri, where he practiced law until his death on March 26, 1891. An old friend of his once said of him, "His life was austere and severe." He went on to say, "He had no taste for wit and humor," and "I never saw him laugh."[466]

The Enlisted Men

Burrill Bunn Battle was born in Hinds, Mississippi, on October 28, 1838. He was the seventh generation after John Battle, who was one of the original colonists to settle in North Carolina in the 1680s. He was the oldest son of eleven siblings. When he was six, his family moved to Lafayette County, Arkansas, and he attended the local country school. He went to Arkansas College, and by 1858 had attained a law degree from Cumberland University in Lebanon, Tennessee. He set up a law office in Lewisville, Arkansas, but closed it when he joined Bankhead's Battery. On December 6, 1861, Captain G. W. McCown enlisted Battle and thirty-nine other men into Bankhead's Battery. Also enlisting with him was his brother, Napoleon O. Battle (1841–1902). He had a third brother, Sydney, who later joined the infantry and was killed at Shiloh. The group of recruits marched together to join the battery, which was then

---

[465] William Scott, Family Data Collection; Lindsley, *The Military Annals of Tennessee*, 790–792.

[466] Ibid 793; William Scott, Family Data Collection; John Hallum, *The Diary of an Old Lawyer* (Nashville: Southern Publishing House, 1895), 233.

located at Columbus, Kentucky. Battle served through the entire war and was never sick or wounded. It was noted later that the war "impaired his hearing for the remainder of his life."[467] After Missionary Ridge he served in Swett's Battery and finally with Shannon's Scouts. Even though he was well educated, he never was promoted and finished the war as he started, a private. He did not surrender with Shannon's Scouts, but signed a separate parole at Selma, Alabama, on May 5, 1865.[468]

After the war, Battle set up his law practice in Washington, Arkansas. In 1871 he married Josephine Cannon Whitherspoon, and he was elected to the Arkansas State Legislature. In 1879 he moved his law practice to Little Rock. In 1885, he was elected to fill a vacancy in the State Supreme Court and held that post until he retired in 1910. He was highly regarded as a jurist and was considered a man of high "mental and physical caliber." He was "always cautious in forming and giving opinions, and with a well-balanced and discerning mind." He died on December 21, 1917 and was buried in the Mount Holly Cemetery in Little Rock. He had no children.[469]

Isaac Washington Cooper was born in Hall, Georgia, in 1841. His great-great-grandfather, William Cooper, settled in Pennsylvania in the early eighteenth century, and Isaac had many cousins. When Captain McCown came to Camden, Arkansas, in December 1861, Cooper and many of his neighbors joined Bankhead's Battery. He had been working as a saloonkeeper. Cooper served in every battle and was never absent from duty. After Missionary Ridge, he was transferred to Swett's Battery, serving there until that battery was disbanded after the Battle of Jonesboro. He continued to serve with Shannon's Scouts and was one of only four members of Bankhead's Battery to surrender with the Army of Tennessee in North Carolina on April 28, 1865.[470]

After the war, Cooper married Lovie Telissie Nix in Monroe, Mississippi. Together they had ten children. His family lived in Arkansas.

---

[467] Robert L. Taylor, "Men of Affairs," *Bob Taylor's Magazine*, vol. IV no. 2, November 1906, 163–164

[468] Ibid., Burrill B. Battle, Family Data Collection; CCSR m268 roll 97.

[469] Taylor, "Men of Affairs," 163–164; Burrill B. Battle, Family Data Collection.

[470] Randy Cooper, personal correspondence with the author, February 2003; CCRS m268 roll 97; Isaac Cooper, Family Data Collection.

After his wife died, he married Racilla Anderson. He died on June 24, 1902, a common man who had served the lost cause to the very end. He is buried in Peytonville Cemetery near Ashton, Arkansas. Many of his descendents live today.[471]

Elijah M. Fawbush was born in Tennessee in August of 1833. His parents moved to Lafayette (today Miller) County, Arkansas, in the 1850s where his youngest brother, James, was born in 1856. He had seven other siblings. That same year, Fawbush married Mary E. A. Muse. Their son, Richard, was born just two years before Fawbush joined Bankhead's Battery in 1861. They would have three other children after the war. The Fawbush family farmed at the border near Texarkana, Texas. They also operated a ferry on the Sulpher River.[472]

Fawbush joined the Confederate service with his friends and neighbors on December 6, 1861, and faithfully served in Bankhead's/Scott's Battery throughout the war. He was transferred to Swett's Mississippi Battery after Missionary Ridge. He joined Shannon's scouts, but left them to return home before the surrender of the Army of Tennessee.[473]

After the war, Fawbush returned to farming for the rest of his life. The ferry near Texarkana provided supplies to the merchants across the river and served as an additional means of income. Fawbush died in 1909. In 1924 the Fawbush Ferry was no longer operating, and a bridge was authorized to be built on the ferry site. That bridge was washed out in the 1940s and was not replaced.[474]

Calvin Celsor Hall was born on October 21, 1843, in southwest Arkansas. His grandfather, Richard Hall, was born in Kentucky in 1783, one of the first pioneer families of that state. Hall had eight other siblings. When Captain McCown came recruiting in Camden, Arkansas, on December 6, 1861, Hall eagerly joined the Confederate service with many of his friends and neighbors. After Missionary Ridge, he was transferred to Swett's Battery. Hall served throughout the entire war and was never absent until he was wounded in the leg at Kennesaw Mountain. After

---

[471]   Ibid.

[472]   Elijah M. Fawbush, Family Data Collection; U.S. Seventh Census.

[473]   CCSR m268 roll 97.

[474]   Cheryl Clark, personal correspondence with the author, April 2013.

being discharged from the hospital, he served in Shannon's Scouts where he reached the rank of corporal. It was this kind of devotion that led him and only three others from Scott's Battery to fight until the very end and surrender with Joseph Johnston in North Carolina on April 28, 1865. His neighbors, Oliver M. Bigbee and Isaac Cooper, were with him on that final day. Also with him was Hiram Campbell of Mississippi County, Missouri.[475]

After the war, Hall lived in Lewisville, Arkansas, where he married Tabitha Baker in 1868. Together they had five children. He lived in Lafayette County for the rest of his life where he was a member of the United Confederate Veterans, Sam H. Hill Camp No. 444. After his death on May 17, 1924, his wife applied for a Confederate Pension. Hall had been too proud to request a pension himself. His descendants still live in Arkansas today.[476]

James Thomas Morris was born in Georgia in 1843. His parents died of yellow fever when he was four or five years old, and he was raised by an aunt or at an orphanage. He didn't know his real birthday, so he chose December 24. In 1861, at the age of seventeen, he was living in southeastern Missouri. Not having had much of a home during his childhood, Morris found a home in Bankhead's Battery. Morris fought without distinction at Shiloh, Murfreesboro, and Chickamauga. He endured the Kentucky campaign and felt the discomfort of the war, but remained devoted to his new family. At Chickamauga he fought with courage and was slightly wounded. Morris never missed a day of Confederate service and was not promoted. On November 25, 1863, Scott's Battery was overrun, and the danger of death or capture became all too real. The fortunes of the Confederacy did not appear good, and Morris ran into the darkness of the night. He was transferred to Swett's Battery, but he never showed up. He was already walking away from the war.[477]

Morris had fled from Missionary Ridge and found the brothers Walter and William Taylor heading home. They had had enough of the war. The

---

[475] Calvin C. Hall, Family Data Collection; CCSR m268 roll 97.

[476] Calvin C. Hall, Family Data Collection; U.S. Ninth Census; Arkansas History Commission, state.archives@arkansas.gov.

[477] Billie Masters (descendant of Morris), personal correspondence with the author, December 2010.

Taylor brothers had been in the infantry and invited Morris to come home with them to Dyersville, Tennessee. The Taylors came from a wealthy, slave-owning family, and Morris was accepted into their home. In Dyersville, Morris met the brothers' sister, Mary Francis Taylor, and they were married on August 24, 1864. They stayed in Dyersville until about 1880 when they moved to Texas and then to Oklahoma in 1888. Morris died April 17, 1920, at Rush Springs, Oklahoma, and is buried in Rush Springs Cemetery. He had eleven children and over one hundred grandchildren and great-grandchildren. His Confederate uniform remained in the family until 1940 when it was borrowed for a parade but was not returned.[478]

Lorenzo R. Richardson was born in Benton County, Tennessee, on April 30, 1840. He was known as Ranz. It is believed that he was orphaned, since he was living with William A. and Lewellen Sweaney in Mississippi County, Missouri. The names of his parents and the relationship with the Sweaneys are unknown. When Bankhead's Battery arrived in New Madrid, Richardson and six neighbors walked twelve miles to join up. His two best friends, Andrew (1842–1911) and Francis Marion Oliver (1841–1940) joined with him. Richardson participated in the Battle of New Madrid, but he may have lost heart when Bankhead withdrew from Missouri heading for Corinth. He may have been wounded at Shiloh. His Texas pension record says, "I was captured by the enemy at Corinth, Miss. I was in hospital there at time of capture. Held prisoner for many months. Was turned out of prison at Alton, Ill., but never recovered." He may have been sick, but family lore is that he had been wounded. His friend Andrew Oliver was sick at Overton Hospital in Memphis at the same time.[479]

Richardson was eventually released and returned to live with the Sweaneys in Mississippi County, Missouri. He was then inducted into the Enrolled Missouri Militia Co. H, Seventy-Ninth Regiment. This was mandatory service, and he had no choice but to go into hiding or back to prison. The Seventy-Ninth Regiment was called up in August 1864 for

---

[478]   Ibid.

[479]   U.S. Seventh Census; State of Texas Pension Records, number 32774; Jerry Herd (descendant of Richardson), personal correspondence with the author, August 2006 and March 2013; Andrew Oliver, Family Data Collection.

emergency service, and he served until relieved from duty on November 28, 1864.[480]

Richardson was always poor. He married his best friend's sister, Elizabeth Oliver, in 1869. They had three children. After the Sweaneys died, he moved the family to Red River County, Texas, in 1883. At this time Richardson switched his initials from L. R. to R. L. He was a founding member of the United Confederate Veterans John C. Burkes Camp no. 656 in Clarkesville, Texas. He remained a poor farmer for the rest of his life. He died of Bright's disease on May 8, 1918, in Detroit, Texas, and is buried in Bluff Cemetery. He had twenty-three grandchildren, and many of his descendents still live in Texas today.[481]

Patrick Talty was the oldest son of six children born to Michael and Catherine Talty. All of the children were born in County Clare, Ireland: Patrick in 1829, Simon in 1831, George in 1835, and John in 1842. The Talty family came to the United States in 1853 and settled in Davenport, Iowa. Here they found work at the lumber mills and in the Mississippi River trade. Steamboats were making continuous runs between St. Paul and New Orleans. Michael worked as a laborer and often found work for his sons. In 1856, the first railroad bridge over the Mississippi was completed at Davenport, bringing more work opportunities to immigrants. The Talty brothers were very close. When one of them found work, he would help the others get work as well. By 1861, the four brothers had moved to Memphis, leaving their parents and two younger sisters in Davenport. Simon married Johanna Garash in 1857 and lived in a boarding house in the pinch area of Memphis with his brothers. They were working as laborers along the river when the war began.[482]

With the secession of several states, the Mississippi River business was drying up. The Talty brothers were unemployed when Smith P. Bankhead offered them rations, shelter, and a monthly income if they joined the

---

[480] Missouri State Archives' Soldiers Database, www.sos.mo.gov. (accessed September 23, 2013).

[481] Jerry Herd, personal correspondence with the author; Lorenzo Richardson, Family Data Collection.

[482] Phillip Talty (descendent of George Talty), interview with the author, March 4, 2003; James Carey (descendant of George Talty), personal correspondence with the author, March 2003. Memphis City Directory 1860.

battery he was forming. They joined the army on May 20, 1861, and Patrick was made a corporal that very day. The brothers trained on artillery at Fort Pillow that summer, and the work was not particularly dangerous. The men practiced artillery drill and occasionally engaged Federal gunboats at Columbus, Kentucky. The winter was not particularly comfortable. They lived in makeshift clapboard houses above the riverbank, and army pay was irregular. In December, Simon became ill and was sent to Memphis to recover. In March, Bankhead's Battery was ordered to New Madrid where the three brothers participated in the action there until ordered to retreat to Fort Pillow. Ultimately the unit was heading for Corinth and the Battle of Shiloh. As the men passed through Memphis, the three Talty brothers went to visit Simon and his wife. They did not return to Bankhead's Battery and were officially marked as deserters on June 24, 1862. Simon was not listed as a deserter, as he had been furloughed home.[483]

After the Federals had occupied Memphis, the Talty brothers returned to their parents in Davenport, Iowa. The brothers were subject to the military draft in 1863 but were not called up. Patrick became a stonemason and married Mary McMahon in 1865. They had two children. Simon took up farming. George married Bridget Meehan in 1862 in Davenport. They went on to have seven children. John married Margaret Rourick in 1876, and they had seven children. In 1871, the entire family moved to western Iowa and settled in the town of Atlantic. George's wife died, and he married his second wife, Margaret Ryan, with whom he had five children. Patrick died on April 17, 1910. George died on August 31, 1913. John died on January 22, 1917. Simon died on May 13, 1919, and is the only brother to have a Confederate military tombstone. All four brothers are buried in the Catholic Cemetery in Atlantic, Iowa, and are listed on a plaque in Des Moines at the State Historical Center as Confederate soldiers from the state of Iowa. Some of the Talty descendents still live in Atlantic. Others live in Nebraska, Wisconsin, South Dakota, Montana, and California.[484]

---

[483]   CCSR m268 roll 98.

[484]   Phillip Talty, descendent of George Talty, interview with the author, March 4, 2003; George Talty. Family Data Collection; Davenport City Directory 1863.

APPENDIX 1

---===◦((◦))◦===---

RECRUITS FROM MEMPHIS, ENLISTED MAY 1861

Day	Name	Age	Married	Born	Rank	Occupation
15	W. J. Harrison	23		Tennessee	Private	
	Michael Nason	17		Ireland	Private	
16	Samuel Brown	26		New York	First Sergeant	Laborer
	John Clooney	22		Ireland	Private	
	Lewis Merchant	39		France	Sergeant	Tailor
	John T. Thomas	22	Yes		Private	
18	Timothy Cavanaugh	37		Ireland	Private	Laborer
	John Connell	38		Ireland	Private	Laborer
	Richard Connell			Ireland	Private	
	Dennis Dailey	43		Ireland	Private	
	Patrick Joyce	26		Ireland	Private	
	James McLaughlin	28		Ireland	Corporal	
	Owen McPartlin	36		Ireland	Private	Laborer
	John Murphy	27		Ireland	Private	Drayman
	John Purcell			Ireland	Sergeant	
	Eugene Sullivan	21		Ireland	Private	
	Edward Tooney	28		Ireland	Private	Laborer
	James Welsh	27		Virginia	Sergeant	
20	Samuel Denton	26	Yes		Private	
	John Flynn	20		England	Private	
	John Hayes	27		Ireland	Private	RR work
	James McCarty	41		Ireland	Private	Laborer
	Lewis Putney	35		Virginia	Second Sergeant	Clerk
	John Rooney	25	Yes	Ireland	Private	
	Nicholas Schriner	25		New York	Artificer	
	Patrick Talty	32	Yes	Ireland	Corporal	Laborer
	George Talty	26		Ireland	Private	Laborer
	John Talty	19		Ireland	Private	Laborer
	Simon Talty	30		Ireland	Private	Laborer

21	Jerry Driscoll	29		Tennessee	Private	
	Miles Kehoe	27		Ireland	Corporal	
	Francis McShane	28		Ireland	Private	
22	John Dewire	27		Ireland	Private	
	Cornelius Layton				Private	
	Martin Lyon	25		Pennsylvania	Private	Steamboat Steward
	Patrick Murphy	25		Ireland	Private	Laborer
23	Edward Cearns	23			Private	
	Charles W. Cooley	26			Private	
	Neil Finney	40			Private	
	Michael Mahoney	21		Ireland	Private	
	William O'Donnell	21		Ireland	Private	Laborer
24	Thomas Clooney	30		Ireland	Private	
	Patrick Mathews	30		Ireland	Private	Col'D Holster
25	James Fitzpatrick	33		Ireland	Private	Laborer
	Thomas Fitzpatrick	21		Ireland	Private	
	William Kanary			Ireland	Private	
	John O'Donnell	25		Ireland	Private	
	Michael Shea	37	Yes	Ireland	Private	Laborer
	Philip Sullivan	45		Ireland	Private	
	Edward Swinney	36		Ireland	Private	Laborer
26	Robert King	42			Private	
	Dennis Leary	28		Ireland	Private	Laborer
28	Jerry Crowley	26		Ireland	Private	
	Albert Sailhorst				Private	
29	David Ennis	28		New York	Private	

Sources: Compiled Confederate Service Records; National Archives, Record Group 109, M231, Rolls 6, 9, 10, 12, 24, 27, 29, 30, 31, 35, 36, 38; National Archives microfilm group 268 rolls 97–98; James Carey correspondence (descendant of the Talty brothers), March 2003.

APPENDIX 2

————— ·«(❂)»· —————

PLANS OF ENCAMPMENT

The artillery camp at Fort Pillow was not set up according to regulations. Most of the time the guns were placed in battery, either in fortifications or in field works, and the camps were located a short distance away. This was the case in every long-term camp the battery set up with two specific exceptions. The camp at Tupelo, Mississippi, in June 1862, and at Camp Wright at Shelbyville, Tennessee, in the spring of 1863 had a large area where the guns were parked in the camp.

According to regulations, the plan of encampment called for an eighty-two-yard front and a one hundred ninety–yard depth for a six-gun battery. A four-gun battery would need only a fifty-eight-yard front. The officer's area took up the first thirty yards of depth and was separated from the enlisted men by a twenty-three-yard area where the enlisted men's mess area was. The enlisted men's tents were grouped with eight tents for each section of guns. These tents were in line with about eight yards distance separating the sections. Sixteen yards away from the enlisted tents was the picketing of the horses. Twelve yards beyond that was a parking area for the forge, battery wagon, and baggage wagons all in line. Sixteen yards from that was the line of caissons, and sixteen yards beyond the caissons were parked the line of pieces. A guard tent was then placed at the back of the encampment. During times of drill, the area used for the parking of all of the vehicles was used as the drill field.

Source: *U.S. Army Field Manual*, 1861, Plate 4.

Appendix 3

―――――⟨⟨⟨◉⟩⟩⟩―――――

Recruits June-July 1861

Day	Name	Age	From	Rank	Occupation
June					
5	Charles Campbell	30	Randolph, TN	Private	Laborer
6	John Ragan	22	Randolph, TN	Private	
July					
2	James E. Johnson		Memphis, TN	Artificer	Blacksmith
9	J.A.R. Gatch	25	Memphis, TN	Artificer	Blacksmith
9	William Powers	27	Memphis, TN	Private	
12	Michael Flynn	22	Memphis, TN	Private	Laborer
19	Edward Ford	25	Memphis, TN	Artificer	
23	Patrick McCarty*	35	Memphis, TN	Private	Gardener
24	Patrick McNamara	27	Memphis, TN	Private	Laborer
26	Issac Harrison	25	Memphis, TN	Farrier	Farmer
26	George McKenzie	20	Memphis, TN	Private	Laborer
29	Frank. A. Pfaffenschlager	47	Memphis, TN	Bugler	Music Teacher

*   Married

Sources: Compiled Confederate Service Records; National Archives, Record Group 109, M231, Rolls 7, 16, 17, 23, 28, 33, 35, 36; National Archives microfilm group 268 rolls 97–98; Historical Data Systems, comp, American Civil War Soldiers (ancestry.com/search/db.aspx?dbid+1565) (accessed March 12-13, 2013).

APPENDIX 4

RECRUITS JULY–SEPTEMBER 1861

Day	Name	Age	From	Rank	Occupation
July					
30	W. D. Jackson*	29	New Madrid, MO	Private	
	J. W. Campbell	25	New Madrid, MO	Private	
31	Joseph Byrd	22	New Madrid, MO	Private	Farmer
	John W. Cooper	22	New Madrid, MO	Private	Farmer
	William J. Cooper	26	New Madrid, MO	Private	Farmer
	Charles Gravitt	20	New Madrid, MO	Private	Farmer
	Andrew Oliver	21	New Madrid, MO	Private	Farmer
	F. Marion Oliver	20	New Madrid, MO	Private	Farmer
	L. R. Richardson	21	New Madrid, MO	Private	Farmer
August			New Madrid, MO		
3	Charles H. Jones	19	New Madrid, MO	Private	Teacher
	J. H. Jones		New Madrid, MO	Private	
8	Paleman C. Bush	19	New Madrid, MO	Private	
	Henry Kraps	26	New Madrid, MO	Private	
9	James Thomas Morris	17	New Madrid, MO	Private	
	T. Morris		New Madrid, MO	Private	
10	Washington Boren	19	New Madrid, MO	Private	
	Hiram Campbell	25	New Madrid, MO	Private	
	James Campbell		New Madrid, MO	Private	
	Thomas Liggett	25	New Madrid, MO	Private	
	William Turner	21	New Madrid, MO	Private	
14	Emile Huffmeister***		Nashville, TN	Private	
20	Louis Myers**			Bugler	
23	Michael Kinney#	22	Memphis, TN	Private	
September					
1	Frank Crosnow		Sikeston, MO	Private	

*   Married

**   Recruited by Colonel Hayes in Nashville to fill the need for musicians.

***   Transferred by order of Colonel McCown.

\# Transferred from the 4th Tennessee Infantry Regiment. He was an Irish immigrant.

Sources: Compiled Confederate Service Records; National Archives, Record Group 109, M231, Rolls 7, 16, 17, 23, 28, 33, 35, 36; National Archives microfilm group 268 rolls 97–98; Historical Data Systems, comp., American Civil War Soldiers (ancestry.com/search/db.aspx?dbid+1565) (accessed March 15, 2013).

APPENDIX 5

—➤◼️◀—

RECRUITS OCTOBER-DECEMBER 1861

Date	Name	Age	Where	Rank	Recruiter	Occupation
October 6	Alfred T. Watson	28	Columbus, KY	Private	Bankhead	Salesman
16	Edward Joseph Kinsella	19	Columbus, KY	Artificer	note 1	
	Laurence Gilfoil		Columbus, KY	Private	note 1	
	Owen McGrath	24	Columbus, KY	Private	note 1	
	Martin Mc-Namara	36	Columbus, KY	Private	note 1	Tailor
	J.P. Gilloughly	20	Columbus, KY	Private	note 1	Painter
	Edward Boyle		Columbus, KY	Private	note 1	Laborer
26	William B. Houston	26	Columbus, KY	Private	Bankhead	
November 1	D.O.D. Brennan	26	Memphis, TN	Private	Harris	
15	Thomas Cluin	25	Columbus, KY	Private	note 1	
	Michael Mason		Columbus, KY	Private	note 1	
16	Michael Culinen		Memphis, TN	Private		
25	James Hubbard	22	Nashville, TN	Private	Phillips	
	Wright Hubbard	21	Nashville, TN	Private	Phillips	Laborer
	G. W. Jennett	31	Nashville, TN	Private	Phillips	
	Joseph Kirkwood	19	Nashville, TN	Private	Phillips	Laborer
	Alf Ledbetter	28	Nashville, TN	Private	Phillips	
	William Moore		Nashville, TN	Private	Phillips	
	D. C. Tally	22	Nashville, TN	Private	Phillips	
??	A. G. Comstock		Columbus	Artificer	Bankhead	
December 1	?? Erlin		Memphis, TN	Bugler	Bankhead	
	William M. Fowler	19	Jackson, TN	Private	Caruthers	
	Stephen B. Irvin	24	Jackson, TN	Private	Caruthers	
	O. E. Williams	21	Milan, TN	Private	Caruthers	
2	William Dick-enson	26	Jackson, TN	Private	Caruthers	
	John C. Jones		Jackson, TN	Private	Caruthers	
	P. G. Kemp	26	Jackson, TN	Private	Caruthers	Farmer
	S. W. Adams		Jackson, TN	Private	Caruthers	
3	L. Roper		Jackson, TN	Artificer	Caruthers	
5	D. A. Kennedy	22	Jackson, TN	Private	Caruthers	

	W. C. Green	21	Jackson, TN	Private	Caruthers	
	W. J. Green		Jackson, TN	Private	Caruthers	
6	J. B. Cole	43	Jackson, TN	Private	Caruthers	Farmer
	Joseph R. Robertson	34	Jackson, TN	Private	Caruthers	Farmer
7	J. G. Westbrook	27	Jackson, TN	Private	Caruthers	
	James T. Maroney	24	Medan?, TN	Private	Caruthers	
8	Jacob Herberger	22	Columbus, KY	Private	Bankhead	
January 1	T. Goins	26	Columbus, KY	Private	Bankhead	
17	William Dowdy	27	Columbus, KY	Private	Bankhead	
February 5	W. P. Bradshaw	37	Columbus	Private	Bankhead	
March 1	A. L. Townsend		Memphis, TN	Cpl	Captain Street	
8	W. B. Chrisp	38	Memphis, TN	Private	Captain Cole	

Note 1: These men enlisted May 15, 1861, at Union City, Tennessee into the 4th Tennessee Infantry Regiment, Company E. They transferred to the Battery at Columbus, Kentucky

Sources: Compiled Confederate Service Records. National Archives, Record Group 109, M231, Rolls 1, 2, 5, 9, 14, 15, 16, 17, 20, 21, 24, 29, 37, 45, 46; National Archives microfilm group 268 rolls 97–98; Historical Data Systems, comp., American Civil War Soldiers (ancestry.com/search/db.aspx?dbid+1565) (accessed March 20, 2013).

APPENDIX 6

———❦———

RECRUITS FROM CAMDEN ARKANSAS DECEMBER 6, 1861

Captain G. W. McCown recruited all men as privates unless noted. Most men were probably farmers and some were landowners.

Name	Rank	Age	Occupation
H. F. Allen	Corporal	24	
Burrill Bunn Battle		23	Lawyer
Napoleon O. Battle		21	
Oliver M. Bigbee		23	
James M. Canada		19	
Lewis F. Cook		22	
W. H. Cook		20	
J. Cookson		22	
Isaac Cooper		20	Saloon keeper
Frank Culberson		20	
Francis M. Davis		22	
Oliver P. Davis		20	
Charles A. Dinkins		18	
James D. Echols		23	
Calvin Fish		22	Farmer
Robert M. Fish		20	Farmer
Elijah Fawbush		29	Farmer/ferryman
Calvin C. Hall		18	
B. R. Harrell	Sergeant	29	
James Kennedy	Sergeant		
J. M. Kirvin		21	

William Green Lee	17	
G. W. Long	41	
A. Maxey	30	
Daniel McKenzie	38	
C. Miller	21	
William Saunders	16	Farmer
John Shirrey	23	
H. Smith	17	
W. Tatum	30	
William B. Thompson	55	Mechanic
William W. Weems	25	
G. Weldon	24	
Thomas B. Wood	40	

Sources: Compiled Confederate Service Records; National Archives, Record Group 109, M231, Rolls 22, 24, 29, 39, 42, 46, 47; National Archives microfilm group 268 rolls 97–98; Historical Data Systems, comp., American Civil War Soldiers (data base online) (accessed April 4, 2013).

APPENDIX 7

———⊷◉⊶———

RECRUITED MARCH, 1862

The following men were all recruited in Arkansas by Captain D. W. Harris for Bankhead's Battery. Some records refer to this group of men as Harris' Battery but there was no such organization. Those recruited on March 1 were all from Ouachita County in the southwestern part of the state. Other places will be noted. They were all privates. Several were landowners and all were farmers unless noted.

Date	Name	Age	Married	Occupation
	F. W. Adams	39		Carpenter
	R. Archer			
	George Bassett	29		
	William Brown	28		
	Edward P. Burnett	31	Yes	
	J. Collier			
	James Collins	23		
	Gabriel M. Crabtree*	27	Yes	
	Oliver H. Edwards	40	Yes	
	L.A. Ellis	35		
	R. B. Harrison	36	Yes	
	Thomas J. Heath	29		
	John T. Herrin	24	Yes	
	James W. Hill	42		
	Hines Holt	23		
	John W. King	45		
	John Kirby	28		
	Joseph Kirby	29		
	Philip B. Land	40		
	J. C. Mitchell	32		
	Miles McCollum	22		Wagoner

James A. Owen	18		Student
Jason Paulk	28		
James H. Roach	45		
William F. Roberts	26		
T. M. Robertson	27	Yes	
S. Rose	37		
Thomas Smart	42	Yes	
Clem C. Smith	25		
Willis Smith	29		
Alexander W. Stinson	32	Yes	
David J. Vining	30		

March 27 at Camden, AR

J.E. Torrence	34	
T. E. Watts	29	

March 29 at Camden, AR

J. B. McRae	36	
R. G. McRae	32	
Washington McRae	37	

May 12 at Monroe, LA

John B. Watts	27	

*He owned two slaves.

Sources: Compiled Confederate Service Records; National Archives, Record Group 109, M231, Rolls 2, 9, 13, 44; National Archives microfilm group 268 rolls 97–98; Historical Data Systems, comp., American Civil War Soldiers (ancestry.com/search/db.aspx?d-bid+1565) (accessed April 11, 2013).

APPENDIX 8

━══◈══━

TRANSFERS TO SCOTT'S BATTERY
MAY 25, 1862

All of the men were members of Girardey's Georgia Battery. These men had enlisted in May 1861 in the First Confederate Infantry Regiment or the 36th Georgia Infantry Regiment and were transferred by Captain Isadore P. Girardey to his battery in December 1861 or January 1862. This battery was stationed at Pensacola, Florida until ordered on March 10 to Corinth, Mississippi. In the Battle of Shiloh the battery lost one gun and its caissons and had the rest of its guns disabled. General Leonidas Polk ordered the battery broken up. The following men were assigned to Scott's Battery as privates unless noted otherwise:

Name	Age	Infantry Regiment	Date of transfer
W. F. Brown	31	First Confederate	December 23, 1861
H. Coppel		First Confederate	December 23, 1861
W. L. Dail*		First Confederate	December 23, 1861
J. Halbert*		First Confederate	December 23, 1861
Alphonsus D. Hardin		First Confederate	December 23, 1861
Joseph D. Hardin*	31	First Confederate	December 23, 1861
Marion E. Humphries	21	First Confederate	December 23, 1861
J. Lightner	24	First Confederate	December 23, 1861
J. Lundy	21	First Confederate	December 23, 1861
Edward Martin	24	First Confederate	December 23, 1861
Marcus P. Maxwell	27	First Confederate	December 23, 1861
Edward G. W. Moon	28	First Confederate	December 23, 1861
J. R. Brinkley	19	36th Georgia	January 10, 1862

Patrick Jordan		36th Georgia	January 10, 1862
William H. Martin		36th Georgia	January 10, 1862
J. McGuire	25	36th Georgia	January 10, 1862
James T. Nethercut	22	36th Georgia	January 10, 1862
Edward Toland	38	36th Georgia	January 10, 1862
J. Johnson	21		February 3, 1862
B. Rickerson	28		March 1, 1862
T. Rickerson	30		March 1, 1862

*Had the rank of corporal.

Sources: Compiled Confederate Service Records; National Archives, Record Group 109, M231, Rolls 10, 11, 14, 23, 30, 44; National Archives microfilm group 268 rolls 97–98; Historical Data Systems, comp., American Civil War Soldiers (ancestry.com/search/db.aspx?dbid+1565). (accessed April 16, 2013). Whitham, George F. *Shiloh, Shells and Artillery Units* (Memphis, Tennessee: Riverside Press, 1980), 69–70.

APPENDIX 9

$\Longrightarrow\ggg\mathbf{(0)}\lll\Longleftarrow$

LAST RECRUITED AND MISCELLANEOUS

Name	Age	Rank	Where	Recruiter
May 1861				
William A. Miller*	19	Sergeant	Monroe, LA	Harris
Before July 1862				
J. F. Krindler	26	Private		
J. W. Horton ^	28	Private	Columbus, KY	Bankhead?
Aug. 14, 1862				
Edward W. Blease	24	Private	Rome, GA	Scott
Aug. 23, 1862				
Lewis A. Davis	18	Guidon	Tupelo, MS	Scott
April 14, 1863				
William E. McRae	18		Union County, AR	Williamson
Sept. 1863				
Nathaniel Holmes	20	Private	Mississippi	
Missing Records				
G.G. Pegram**	37	Private	Mississippi	
John Reynolds#				

*Miller claims to have been in Bankhead's command at Columbus through the Battle of Shiloh, but there are no records to confirm his rank or his story. He told his story in *Confederate Veteran* Vol. VI, 371.

**Pegram is not found in any battery records except that he claimed to be from Scott's Battery when he was captured near Knoxville, Tennessee, in May 1865. Actually, he belonged to Swett's Mississippi Battery and later to Shannon's Scouts where he fell in with former Scott's Battery members. Source: Harvey Shannon, *Confederate Veteran* 1904, 112.

#Appears on a list of soldiers but he is not in the records.

^Horton was from Marion, Kentucky. He was sick and was left behind after the Battle of Perryville in October 1862, and he died as a prisoner at a Federal hospital in Harrodsburg on November 5, 1862.

Bruce R. Kindig

Sources: Compiled Service Records; National Archives, Record Group 109, M231, Rolls 4, 21, 34, 36; National Archives microfilm group 268 rolls 97–98; Historical Data Systems, comp., *American Civil War Soldiers* (ancestry.com/search/db.aspx?dbid+1565) (accessed April 16, 2013).

Appendix 10

—◦«◉»◦—

Men over thirty-five years of age leaving Bankhead's Battery on June 22, 1862, because of the Conscription Act

Name	Age
F. M. Adams	39
Timothy Cavanaugh#	37
J. B. Cole	44
John Connell	38
James W. Hill*	42
John King*	45
Martin McNamara	37
James McCarty	42
Owen McPartlin	37
Lewis Merchant	37
James Roach*	45
J. R. Robertson	36
Edward Swinney	37
William B. Thompson*	55
Edward Toomey	37
Thomas B. Wood	40

*Stayed in the Battery as a teamster.

#Promoted to corporal and sergeant on day of discharge.

Sources: National Archives microfilm group 268 rolls 97–98; Historical Data Systems, comp. American Civil War Soldiers (ancestry.com/search/db.aspx?dbid+1565) (accessed April 20, 2013).

APPENDIX 11

―――◦《◦》◦―――

MEN WHO DESERTED FROM
BANKHEAD'S BATTERY
FEBRUARY 23–JUNE 24, 1862

Washington Boren

Edward Boyle

Paleman C. Bush

Joseph Byrd

Charles Campbell#

James Campbell#

J.W. Campbell

John Clooney~

Thomas Clooney~

A. G. Comstock

Richard Connell~

William J. Cooper

Frank Crosnow

Jerry Crowley~

Michael Culinen

John Dewire~

William Dickenson

Jerry Driscoll~

David Ennis~

?? Erlen

Thomas Fitzpatrick~

John Flynn~

Michael Foley*~

J. A. R. Gatch

J. R. Gillouly

W. J. Harrison*~

Isaac Harrison

John Hayes~

William Houston*

J. D. Hubbard*

Wright Hubbard*

W. Jennett*

John C. Jones*

J. H. Jones

Miles Kehoe~

P. G. Kemp

D. A. Kennedy

Joseph Kirkwood*

Joseph Kinsella*

Cornelius Layton~

Thomas Leggett*

Martin Lyon~

Michael Mahoney~

Patrick Mathews~

Owen McGrath*^

James McLaughlin*~

Francis McShane*~

George McKenzie*

Edward G. W. Moon*

William Moore

John Murphy

Patrick Murphy

Louis Myers

John O'Donnell~

Andrew Oliver*

John Purcell*~

John Ragan

L. R. Richardson*#

L. Roper

Nicholas Schriner*~

Eugene Sullivan~

D. C. Tally

George Talty*~

John Talty*~

Patrick Talty*~

William Turner

James Welsh~

O. E. Williams*

*Listed AWOL on the official report

227

\#Left in the hospital and not discharged

~Had served twelve months and could have been discharged if the Conscription Law had not been passed.

^Became a bounty jumper; served in other units.

Sources: National Archives microfilm group 268 rolls 97–98; Historical Data Systems, comp. *American Civil War Soldiers* (ancestry.com/search/db.aspx?dbid+1565) (accessed April 21, 2013).

APPENDIX 12

—⟫•⟪◈⟫•⟪—

MEN FROM SCOTT'S BATTERY TRANSFERRED TO MARSHALL'S BATTERY ON DECEMBER 10, 1863

Brenan, Daniel.O.D.*

Brinkley, J.R.

Brown, W.F.

Chrisp, W.B.

Cluin, Thomas

Cooley, Charles W.*

Davis, Lewis A.

Fitzpatrick, James[1]

Flynn, Michael

Ford, Edward*

Halbert, J.

Hardin, A.D.

Hardin, J.D.

Harrison, R.B.

Hayes, John

Jacob Herberger

Holmes, Nathan*

Humphries, Marion E.[1]

Johnson, J.

Jones, Charles H.

Jordan, Patrick

Joyce, Patrick[1]

Kinney, M.*

Lightner, J.

Lundy, John

Martin, William H.

McGuire, John

McLaughlin, James

Oliver, Francis Marion

Peters, Thomas[1]

Powers, William

Purcell, John*

Rickerson, B.

Sullivan, Philip

Thompson, William

Toland, Edward*

Turner, William

Watson, Alfred T.**

Westbrook, J.G.

*In POW camp

**Escaped before arriving at POW camp

[1]On detached service or furlough.

Sources: Compiled Service Records; National Archives, Record Group 109, M231, Rolls 4, 21, 34, 36; National Archives microfilm group 268 rolls 97–98; Historical Data Systems, comp., American Civil War Soldiers (ancestry.com/search/db.aspx?dbid+1565) (accessed April 22, 2013).

APPENDIX 13

———— ➤●(①)●◄ ————

MEN FROM SCOTT'S BATTERY TRANSFERRED TO SWETT'S MISSISSIPPI BATTERY ON DECEMBER 10, 1863

Adams, F.W.

Battle, B.B.
Battle, N.O.
Bigbee, Oliver M.
Burnett, Edward P.
Campbell, Hiram
Cook, W.H.
Cookson, John
Cooper, Isaac
Crabtree, Gabriel M.
Culberson, Frank
Davis, F.M.
Davis, O.P.
Doscher, John*
Echols, J.D.
Ellis, L.A.
Fawbush, Elijah
Fish, Calvin
Fish, Robert M.
Fowler, William M.
Hall, Calvin Celsor

Harrell, B.R.
Heath, T.J.
Herberger, Jacob
Herrin, J.
Welden, George

Ledbetter, A.
Maxey, A
McKenzie, Daniel
McRae, J.B
McRae, R.G.
McRae, Washington
McRae, William E.
Mitchell, J.C.
Morris, James Thomas
Pegram, G.G.
Roberts, William
Robertson, T
Rose, Samuel
Shirey, John
Smith, Clem C.
Smith, Hardy
Stinson, A.W.

Torrance, J.E
Watson, W.A.
Watts, John B.
Watts, T.E.
Kirby, John

*Served on the staff of Major Hotchkiss.

231

Bruce R. Kindig

Source: Compiled Service Records. National Archives, Record Group 109, M231, Rolls 4, 21, 34, 36; National Archives microfilm group 268 rolls 97–98; Historical Data Systems, comp., American Civil War Soldiers (ancestry.com/search/db.aspx?dbid+1565) (accessed April 24, 2013).

APPENDIX 14

SCOTT'S BATTERY MEMBERS WHO SWORE AN OATH OF ALLEGIANCE

Name	Date of Oath	Where Taken	Date of Capture
Charles Cooley#	October 10, 1864	Rock Island, IL	November 25, 1863
Daniel O.D. Brennan#	October 24, 1864	Rock Island, IL	November 25, 1863
Edward Ford#	October 24, 1864	Rock Island, IL	November 25, 1863
William Martin	December 28, 1864	Nashville, TN	December 23, 1864
William Powers	December 28, 1864	Nashville, TN	December 23, 1864
Philip Sullivan	December 28, 1864	Nashville, TN	December 27, 1864
John Purcell#	January 10, 1865	Rock Island, IL	November 25, 1863
Edward Toland#	January 10,1865	Rock Island, IL	November 25, 1863
Nathaniel Holmes#	January 24,1865	Rock Island, IL	November 25, 1863
Thomas Cluin	February 4, 1865	Camp Morton, IN	May 13, 1865
Patrick Joyce	March 25, 1865	Mobile, AL	
Calvin Fish	April 26, 1865	Columbus, MS	
Isaac Cooper*	April 28, 1865	Greensboro, NC	
Hiram Campbell*	April 28, 1865	Greensboro, NC	
Calvin C. Hall*	April 28, 1865	Greensboro, NC	
Oliver M. Bigbee*	April 28, 1865	Greensboro, NC	
Daniel McKenzie	May 5, 1865	Chattanooga	
Burrill B. Battle	May 5, 1865	Selma, AL	
James Fitzpatrick	May 11, 1865	Montgomery, AL	
William L. Scott	May 11, 1865	Meridan, MS	
William M. Polk	May 12, 1865	Meridian, MS	

John Doscher	June 5, 1865	Augusta, GA	
Lewis F. Cook	June 10, 1865	Ft. Delaware, DE	June 28, 1863
Alfred T. Watson	June 24, 1865	Camp Chase, OH	April 12, 1865
John Lundy	June 13, 1865	Camp Chase, OH	April 12, 1865
L. A. Davis	June 13, 1865	Camp Chase, OH	April 12, 1865
Robert Fish		Camp Douglas, IL	October 6,1864
Gabriel M Crabtree		Camp Douglas, IL	September 2, 1864
Jacob Herberger		Camp Douglas, IL	September 2, 1864

*Surrendered with the Army of Tennessee under General Joseph Johnston

#Released from prison on May 16, 1865

Source: Compiled Service Records. National Archives, Record Group 109, M231, Rolls 4, 21, 34, 36; National Archives microfilm group 268 rolls 97–98.

APPENDIX 15

———◦◦(◦)◦◦———

BANKHEAD/SCOTT'S
BATTERY FINAL TOTALS

Killed in Battle: 13

Shiloh	Two not recorded
Murfreesboro	A. L. Townsend
Chickamauga	George Bassett, Robert King
Missionary Ridge	Wiley Smith, Charles A. Dinkins
Jonesboro	Frank Culberson, William Fowler, J. C. Mitchell, Clem C. Smith
New Hope Church	William M. Fowler
Franklin	John Marsh

Wounded: 36

Columbus	Dennis Leary
New Madrid	two not recorded
Shiloh	Neil Finney, Patrick Joyce, Miles McCollum, James McDavitt, Ranz Richardson, William L. Scott, and ten others
Murfreesboro	Patrick Jordan, Washington McRae
Chickamauga	F. M. Davis, Lewis Davis, William Dowdy, Charles Gravert, T. J. Heath, Michael Kinney, Joe Kirby, John Kirby J. M. Kirwin, James T. Morris, William Powers, and two others
Kennesaw Mountain	Calvin C. Hall
Monroe's Crossing, NC	William Y. C. Humes

Died from Illness: 13

William Brown, J. Collier, John W. Cooper, William Dowdy (wounds), Thomas Goins, Hines Holt, J. W. Horton, Michael Kinney, James T. Maroney, Edward Martin, Albert Sailhorst, T.Thomas, William Weems

Deserters: 117

1861	Emile Huffmeister, Patrick Mathews (executed)
1862	67 men (see Appendix 11)
1863	Edward Cearns, Joseph D. Hardin, J. Lightner, James T. Morris, Michael Nason
1864–65	43 unaccounted for

Captured: 25

Bruce R. Kindig

1862	Lewis F. Cook, Patrick Joyce, Marcus P. Maxwell, Ranz Richardson (all in hospitals), Marcus P. Maxwell (Harrodsburg hospital)
1863	Murfreesboro: Patrick Jordan, James Kennedy (hospital)

1863
Shelbyville: Lewis F. Cook (hospital)
Missionary Ridge: Daniel O. D. Brennan, Charles Cooley, Edward Ford, Nathan Holmes, Michael Kinney, Charles Purcell, Edward Toland, Alfred T. Watson

1864	Thomas Cluin (Dalton), Gabriel M. Crabtree, Jacob Herberger (Jonesboro), William Martin, William Powers, Philip Sullivan (Columbia)
1865	L.A. Davis, John Lundy, Alfred T. Watson (Salisbury, NC)

Surrendered with the Army of Tennessee April 28, 1865: 4

Oliver M. Bigbee, Hiram Campbell, Isaac Cooper, Calvin C. Hall

Sources: Compiled Service Records. National Archives, Record Group 109, M231, Rolls 4, 21, 34, 36; National Archives microfilm group 268 rolls 97–98.

Bibliography

Government Publications

Davenport City Directory 1863.

Memphis City Directory 1860, 1865, 1866.

U. S. Sixth Census.

U. S. Seventh Census.

U. S. Eighth Census.

U. S. Ninth Census.

War of the Rebellion: *A Compilation of the Official Records of the Union and Confederate Armies.* 129 vols. Washington DC, 1880–1901. (Note: Labeled OR in footnotes with Volume and chapter noted.)

Government Archives

Arkansas History Commission, state.archives@arkansas.gov. 2013. (accessed June 12, 2013).

Consolidated Confederate Service Records. National Archives. Record Group 109.

Series 268 microfilm rolls 97–98. Series 231 microfilm rolls 1–50. (Note: These are labeled "CCSR" in Footnotes.)

DeBow, ed., *Statistical View of the United States: A Compendium of the Seventh Census.* 1962.

Dunbar, Rowland. *Military History of Mississippi 1803–1898.* Jackson, Mississippi: Mississippi Department of Archives and History, 1908.

Missouri State Archives' Soldiers Database. www.sos.mo.gov. (accessed July 12, 2013).

Shelby County Death Records 1842–1899 (Tennessee).

Shelby County Marriage Records 1842–1899 (Tennessee).

State of Texas Pension Records.

Manuscripts

Bankhead, Ada Collection. Alderman Library. University of Virginia, Charlottesville.

Blaisdell, Timothy M. Letters. Civil War Times Collection. Carlisle Barracks, Pennsylvania, United States Military History Institute.

Bluie, John. Papers. Duke University.

Brent, George. Diary. Bragg Papers. William Palmer Collection, Western Reserve Historical Society, Cleveland.

Brown, W. A. Diary. Greenwood Public Library, Greenwood, Mississippi.

Bush, Squire H. Diary. Filsen Club, Louisville, Kentucky.

Coleman, D. Diary. Southern Historical Collection, University of North Carolina, Chapel Hill.

Dillon, William S. Diary. John Davis Williams Library, University of Mississippi, Oxford.

Goelet, Ed. Goelet-Buncombe Papers. Southern Historical Collection, University of North Carolina, Chapel Hill.

Hall, James Iredell. Diary. Southern Historical Collection, University of North Carolina, Chapel Hill.

Harris, John A. Letters. Louisiana State University, Department of Archives and History.

Humes, W.Y.C. Letter to O. P. Temple, March 17, 1861. University of Tennessee, Digital Library Initiatives. (dlc.lib.utk.edu accessed February 5, 2013).

Jones, George W. Diary. Stanford Battery File, Chickamauga-Chattanooga Military Park.

Magee, John Euclid. Diary. Duke University.

Neal. Letters. Emory University.

Rosser, James. Diary. Gloria Gardner Collection, Jackson, Tennessee.

Semmes, Benedict J. Papers. Southern Historical Society, University of North Carolina, Chapel Hill.

Searcy, James. Letters. Alabama Department of Archives and History.

Street, John K. Correspondence. Southern Historical Society, University of North Carolina, Chapel Hill.

Watson, Robert. Diary. Chickamauga-Chattanooga National Military Park.

Warrick, Thomas. Letters. Alabama Department of Archives and History.

Widney, Lyman S. Letters. Thirty-fourth Illinois File, Chickamauga-Chattanooga National Military Park.

Wyman, Belser L. Letters, Alabama Department of Archives and History.

Newspapers
Augusta *Chronicle*, Georgia
Chattanooga Daily Rebel, Tennessee

Daily Confederate News, Columbus, Kentucky

Louisville Daily Courier, Kentucky

Mankato Review, Minnesota.

Memphis Appeal, Tennessee

Memphis Avalanche, Tennessee

Richmond Examiner, Virginia

Published Primary Sources

Alexander, E. Porter. *Fighting for the Confederacy: The Personal Recollections of General Edward Porter Alexander*. Edited by Gary Gallagher. Chapel Hill: University of North Carolina Press, 1989.

Beattie, John. *The Citizen Soldier: Or, Memoirs of a Volunteer*. Cincinnati, 1897.

Belknap, William W. *History of the 15th Regiment Iowa Veteran Volunteer Infantry from October 1861 to August 1865*. Keokuk, 1887.

Betts, Edward E. *Map of the Battlefields of Chattanooga and Wauhatchie*. Chickamauga and Chattanooga National Park Commission, 1896.

Billings, John D. *Hardtack and Coffee or The Unwritten Story of Army Life*. Williamsburg, Massachusetts: Corner House Press, 1984.

Bishop, Judson. *The Story of a Regiment: Being a Narrative of the Service of the Second Regiment Minnesota Veteran Volunteer Infantry In the Civil War of 1861 to 1865*. St. Cloud, Minnesota: North Star Press, 1890.

Civil War Preservations, *Swords of Honor*. http://www.civilwarpreservations. com/. (accessed March 12, 2013).

Cross, Reverend Joseph. *Camp and Field: Papers From The Portfolio of an Army Chaplain*. Macon, Georgia: Burke, Boykin & Company, 1864.

Douglas, Lucia R. Ed. *Douglas' Texas Battery, C.S.A.* Waco, 1966.

Family Data Collections, Birth, Individual Records. Ancestry.com Operations Inc., 1999.

Franklin, Ann Y., comp. *The Civil War Diaries of Capt. Alfred Tyler Fielder 12th Tennessee Regiment Infantry, Company B 1861–1865*. Louisville, KY: by Author, 1996.

Hallum, John. *The Diary of an Old Lawyer.* Nashville: Southern Publishing House, 1895.

Historical Data Systems, comp. *American Civil War Soldiers* Provo, Utah, 2009. (ancestry.com/search/db.aspx?dbid+1565).

Instructions for Field Artillery. Prepared by a board of officers. J.B. Lippincott & Co., 1861.

Keeling, E.A., secretary. *Annual Statement of the Trade and Commerce of Memphis, Tennessee.* Reported to the Memphis Merchants Exchange, Memphis, 1866.

Lindsley, John B. ed. *The Military Annals of Tennessee.* Nashville: J. M. Lindsley & Co., Publishers, 1886.

Lyle, William W. *Lights and Shadows of Army Life: or, Pen Pictures From the Battlefield, The Camp and the Hospital.* Cincinnati: R. W. Carroll, 1865.

Minnick, J. W. *Inside of Rock Island Prison, From December 1863, to June 1865.* Nashville, Tennessee: Publishing House of the M.E. Church, South Smith and Lamar, Agents, 1908.

Polk, William Mecklenburg M.D., LL.D. *Leonidas Polk: Bishop and General.* In Two Volumes, London: Longmans, Green, and Co., and New York: 15 East 16th Street, 1893.

Pullen, Eloise LaFont. hand-written family records in family Bible, 1822–1900.

Tower, R. Lockwood, ed. *A Carolinian Goes to War: The Civil War Narrative of Arthur Middleton Manigault, Brigadier General C.S.A.* Columbia South Carolina, 1983.

Vaughan, A. J. *Personal Record of the Thirteenth Regiment Tennessee Infantry C.S.A.* Memphis: S.C. Toof and Company, 1897.

Watkins, Samuel R. *Co. Aytch, Maury Guards, First Tennessee Regiment; or, A Side Show of the Big Show.* Chattanooga: Times Printing Company, 1900.

Welker, David A., ed. *A Keystone Rebel: The Civil War Diary of Joseph Garey, Hudson's Battery, Mississippi Volunteers.* Gettysburg, PA: Thomas Publications, 1996.

Woods, Earl C., ed. *The Shiloh Diary of Edmond Enoul Livaudais.* New Orleans, 1992.

Unpublished Primary Sources
Hall, Elijah. Letters. n.p.
Rogan, Lafayette, *Diary of Lafayette Rogan, C.S.A., Prisoner of War at Rock Island Prison Barracks 1863–1865.* n.p.

Post War Accounts
Bohen, W. J. "C7K," *Confederate Veteran.* vol. 14, 1904.

Carnes, Major W. W. "Chickamauga," Southern Historical Society Papers, 1883.

Cunningham, S. A. "General O. F. Strahl," *Confederate Veteran,* vol. 4, 1896.

Erwin, Joseph. "Swett's Battery at Jonesboro," *Confederate Veteran,* vol. 12, 1904.

Quintard, C. T. "Tribute to Lieut. John Marsh," *Confederate Veteran,* vol. 5, 1897.

Scarbrough, L. Alex Jr. Camp Journal of Corporal Lemuel.

Scarbrough, Sr. "Company E 'Dixie Rifles' 13th Tennessee Infantry Regiment," *The West Tennessee Historical Society Papers,* vol. LXVI, 2012.

Shoup, Francis A. "How We Went to Shiloh," *Confederate Veteran*, vol. 2, 1894.

Secondary: Books

Allardice, Bruce S. *More Generals in Gray*. Baton Rouge and London: Louisiana State University Press, 1995.

Bradley, Michael R. *Tullahoma: The 1863 Campaign for the Control of Middle Tennessee*. Chapel Hill and London: University of North Carolina Press, 1991.

Bufton, Nigel. *A Complete Genealogy Report For Smith Pyne Bankhead*. My Heritage, http://www.myheritage.com, 2007.

Casdorph, Paul. *Prince John Magruder: His Life and Campaigns*. New York: Wiley and Sons, 1996.

Cathern, John W. *Confederates of Elmwood*. Bowie, Maryland: Heritage Books, Inc., 2001.

Connelly, Thomas Lawrence. *Army of the Heartland: The Army of Tennessee, 1861–1862*. Baton Rouge: Louisiana State University Press, 1967.

Autumn of Glory: The Army of Tennessee, 1862–65. Baton Rouge and London: Louisiana State University Press, 1971.

Cozzens, Peter. *The Shipwreck of Their Hopes: The Battles for Chattanooga*. Urbana and Chicago: University of Illinois Press, 1996.

This Terrible Sound: The Battle of Chickamauga. Urbana and Chicago: University of Illinois Press, 1992.

Daniel, Larry J. *Cannoneers in Gray*. Tuscaloosa: The University of Alabama Press, 2005.

and Riley W. Gunter. *Confederate Cannon Foundries*. Union City, Tennessee: Pioneer Press, 1977.

and Lynn N. Bock. *Island No. 10: Struggle for the Mississippi Valley.* Tuscaloosa: The University of Alabama Press, 1996.

Shiloh: The Battle that Changed the Civil War. New York, New York: Simon and Shuster, 1997.

Soldiering in the Army of Tennessee: A Portrait of Life in a Confederate Army. Chapel Hill and London: The University of North Carolina Press, 1991.

The Battle of Stones River: The Forgotten Conflict between the Confederate Army of Tennessee and the Union Army of the Cumberland. Baton Rouge: Louisiana State University Press, 2012.

Davis, William C. *Encyclopedia of the Civil War.* "Life in Army Camp." The Civil War Society, 2002.

Elliot, Sam Davis. *Soldier of Tennessee: General Alexander P. Stewart and the Civil War in the West.* Baton Rouge: Louisiana State University Press, 1999.

Gleeson, David T. *The Irish in the South 1815–1877.* Chapel Hill: University of North Carolina Press, 2001.

Harkins, John E. *Metropolis of the American Nile.* Woodland Hills, California: Windsor Publishing, Inc., 1982.

Hughes, Nathaniel Cheairs Jr. *The Battle of Belmont: Grant Strikes South.* Chapel Hill: The University of North Carolina Press, 1991.

The Pride of the Confederate Artillery: The Washington Artillery in the Army of Tennessee. Baton Rouge: Louisiana State University Press, 1997.

McDonough, James Lee. *Chattanooga: A Death Grip on the Confederacy.* Knoxville: The University of Tennessee Press, 1984.

Noe, Kenneth W. *Perryville: The Grand Havoc of Battle.* Lexington, Kentucky: University of Kentucky Press, 2001.

Powell, David A. *The Maps of Chickamauga*. New York and California: Savas Beatie LLC, 2009.

Strickland, Colin A. and Timothy S. Huebner. *From Civil War Fort to State Park: A History of Fort Pillow State Historic Area*. Memphis, Tennessee: Rhodes College, n.d.

Ross, John Kelly Jr. *Confederate Columbus and the Story of the "Lady Polk."* Clinton, Kentucky: Hickman County Museum, 2003.

Wiley, Bell I. *The Story of Johnny Reb*. Indianapolis, 1962.

Witham, George F. *Shiloh, Shells and Artillery Units*. Memphis, Tennessee: Riverside Press, 1980.

Secondary Articles

Jones, James B. Jr., "Reign of Terror of the Safety Committee Has Passed Away Forever: History of Committees of Safety and Vigilance in West and Middle Tennessee, 1860–1862," *The West Tennessee Historical Society Papers*, vol. LXIII, 2009.

Lanier, Robert A., "Memphis Legal Community Under Federal Occupation 1860–1870," *The West Tennessee Historical Society Papers*, vol. LXVI, 2012, 27–64.

Long, John Mack, "Memphis Mayors 1827–1866: A Collective Study," *The West Tennessee Historical Society Papers*, vol. LII, 1998, 105-133.

Taylor, Robert L., "Men of Affairs," *Bob Taylor's Magazine*, Nashville: Taylor Pub. Co., vol. IV no. 2, November 1906.

Interviews and Correspondence with Descendents
Brady, Mike. April 2013. (Edward P. Burnett)
Carey, James. March 2003. (Talty Brothers)
Clark, Cheryl. March 2013. (Elijah Fawbush)
Cooper, Randy. February 2003. (Isaac Cooper)
Herd, Jerry. April 2004, March–April 2013. (Lorenzo R. Richardson)

Hill, Connie. April 2013. (J. G. Westbrook)
Kunis, Darlene. December 2012. (Thomas Smart)
Masters, Billie. December 2010–January 2011. (James Thomas Morris)

McCollum, David. March 2013. (Miles McCollum)
Richardson, James III. March 2013. (Lorenzo R. Richardson)
Robertson, Craig. March 2013. (T. Goins)
Shappell, Dee. October 2006. (William Miller)
Talty, Phillip. March 4, 2003. (Talty Brothers)
Wake, David. August 2010. (Thomas Peters notebook)

About the Author

Bruce R. Kindig is a retired teacher residing in Davenport Iowa. He has taught various history classes in his forty-six-year career spanning from junior high to community college. He earned his B. A. and M. A. degrees in history from the University of Northern Iowa. As an accomplished author, he has received several book review awards. All of his books can be found at Amazon.com.

ABOUT THE BOOK

———— ◦◉◦ ————

This is a regimental history of a Confederate battery in the American Civil War. The battery was originally recruited by Smith P. Bankhead in Memphis in 1861, and this book gives a breakdown of all of the members of the unit. This case study examines the reasons the men joined the unit and provides insight into their backgrounds. Although slavery is often given as a reason for the war, most of the men fought for other reasons, as few of them owned any slaves. The book touches on the trials of training and the difficulties of army life and addresses why some men deserted while others fought to the very end. After the battle of Shiloh, Bankhead was promoted, and William L. Scott assumed command. The history of the battery explains the part the men played in the battles and campaigns in the Western theater. When the battery was overrun at Missionary Ridge, many of the men continued to fight in other units, while others went home. All the men who served in Bankhead/Scott's Battery are accounted for in this book, with information about recruitment, occupations, deaths, wounds, illness, desertions, and discharges. Four men were still serving when the Army of Tennessee of Tennessee surrendered in April 1865.

OTHER BOOKS WRITTEN BY BRUCE R. KINDIG

Kindig has also authored ***George Washington Starts a War***, a primer on the French and Indian War with a focus on George Washington who has the distinction of starting a war in his youth and ending a war in his maturity.

The Origins of Military Theory in World War I is a scholarly look at a subject every history student has studied. The focus is not the typical diplomatic approach but instead an evaluation of military theorists from Clausewitz to Foch.

Peace Proposals of the First World War, is about the little know diplomatic attempts at peace from 1914 through the Treaty of Brest-Litovsk. It discusses why peace could not be negotiated and why; in spite of the seriousness of those who wanted a just peace.

Essays in Military Leaders is a collection of three essays. The first essay is about Hannibal and Scipio Africanus and the development of Roman tactics in the Second Punic War. With Julius Caesar, we develop his philosophy of war by examining the strategy and tactics of the Gallic Wars. Finally, we examine the philosophy of history from the author of *On War*, Carl von Clausewitz. The descriptions are all in their own words.

Bruce R. Kindig has written a non- historical work. Combining good advice with humor he writes under the pen name John H. Marsh, ***Words of Wisdom from Anonymous Wise Guys***. Through a question format he answers the dumb questions people often ask like "what are two things you should never ask in bed"?

Kindig has written a sequel to **The Anonymous Wise Guys** with **Is It True? Or Are You Being a Wise Guy?** He has authored it under his own name and continues to give it that wise crack advice, while adding some puzzles for you wise guys who think you are so smart. Go Ahead and see how smart you are. Realizing that humor can be good for the mind this book is a self-help to mental discipline.

Military Reformers and Turning Points in Greece and Rome Is a "Cliff Notes" type of book for those who know little about ancient warfare but would like to learn it quick and easy. Read the stories of Epaminondas,

Hannibal, Africanus, Caesar and Augustus or use the cliff notes in the back of the book for quick understanding.

The Evil Party is a history of the origins and practices of the American Democratic Party. Consider it a primer of the basics derived from a series of questions about our countries founding and how evil can take over a democracy (or Republic).

Easter, Time and Miracles is a history of time or more precisely why we need to know the exact time. Or, how do we know when Easter will be now and in the future. A blend of astronomy, science, history and mankind's conquest of time; including our errors.

INDEX

Dent, Samuel H. 153
Denton, Samuel 52, 207
Dewire, John 208, 227
Dobyns, Flora 197
Dodge, Joseph B. 145
Doscher, John 151, 153, 170,
    175, 180, 183, 187,
    191-2, 234
Douglas, James 123
Douglas' Texas Battery 84, 123,
    240
Dupree, Lewis J. 18-19

E

Echols, J. D. 94-5
Edwards, Oliver H. 128, 219
Eighteenth Indiana Battery 134
Eighth Indiana Battery 104
Elder, Sallie E. 183, 193
Elder, Susan Washington 125,
    183, 193, 200
Eleventh Tennessee 117, 165
Ellis, L. A. 77, 79, 95, 128, 149
Elmwood Cemetery 190, 193
Erlen 51, 227

F

Fawbusch, Elijah 187, 217, 245
Fielder, Alfred 98, 139
Fifteenth Iowa 63
Fifth Company, Washington
    Artillery 61, 64
Fifth Tennessee 43-4
Finney, Neil 92, 114, 173, 181,
    185, 208
First Ohio Battery F 141

First Tennessee 1, 4, 13, 24, 154
    242
Fish, Calvin 180, 185, 217, 233
Fish, Robert 217
Fitzpatrick, James 92, 181, 208
    233
Fitzpatrick, Thomas 208, 227
Ford, Edward 77, 93, 150, 172
    177, 179, 211, 233
Forrest, Nathan Bedford xi, 135
    137
Fort Bankhead 44-5, 47-8, 53
Fort Delaware 170, 185
Fort Donelson 42, 56
Fort Henry 42, 56
Fort Pillow vii, 4, 6, 13-6, 18,
    23-4, 27, 30, 44, 47-8
    56, 189, 206, 209, 245
Fort Thompson 43-5, 47
Fort Wright 14, 30
Forty-first Mississippi 164
Fourth Tennessee ix, 51, 63, 76
    82, 138-9, 141, 148, 165
Fowler, William 77, 95, 117, 131
    180
Fowler's Battery 133
Flynn, John 207, 227
Flynn, Michael 211
Franklin, Battle ix, 183, 194-5

G

Garey, Joseph 31, 242
Garrity, James 151, 153
Garth, Susan Adeline 188
Gatch, J. A. R. 227
Gayoso Hotel 19
Gilfoil, Laurence 215
Gilmer Hospital 195

Girardey's Battery 74, 77, 221
Goins, Thomas 128
Grant, U. S. 32, 39
Gravert, Charles 53, 213
Green, W. C. 52, 216
Green, W. J. 216
Greenlaw, J. Oliver 9
Greenlaw, William B. Jr. 5, 13, 29
Greenlaw, William B. Sr. 5, 8-9
Grenada, Miss. 80

H

Halbert, J. 221
Hall, Calvin Celsor 217, 231, 235
Hall, Elijah 178
Hall, Richard 202
Hallack, Henry 71
Hallonquist, James 81
Hamilton, S. D. H. 34
Hamilton, William B. 151, 153
Hampden Military School 7, 188
Hardee, William 81, 151, 168
Hardin, Joseph M. 92
Harrell, B. R. 52, 55, 77, 217
Harris, D. W. 52, 219
Harrison, Isaac 180, 216, 229, 234
Harrison, W. J. 207, 227
Hayes, John 11, 26, 29, 207, 227
Hazen, William B. 138
Heath, T. J. 150
Herberger, Jacob 180, 216, 229
    234
Hickman, Kentucky 32, 35, 41,
    245
Hill, Daniel H. 133
Hill, James 75, 114
Hindman, Thomas 152-3
Holmes, Nathan 172

Holt, Hines 94-5, 117, 128, 219
Hoshall, William E. 197
Hotchkiss, Thomas R. 170, 180
Houston, William B. 215
Huffmeister, Emile 52, 213
Humes, William Y. C. 4, 7, 182
    193, 199

I

Island Number Ten 32, 43, 47, 49
    56, 193

J

Jackson, John K. 138
Jackson, Thomas J. 199
Jackson, W. D. 52, 213
Jackson's Battery 37, 41-2, 50, 81
James, Fred R. 102
Jefferson Flying Artillery 68, 87
Jennett, G. W. 215
Johnson, J. 222
Johnson, James E. 52, 211
Johnson, Richard W. 138
Johnston, Albert Sidney 19, 42
    58
Johnston, Joseph 96-7, 181, 203
    234
Jones, Charles H. 52, 213
Jones, J. H. 213, 227
Jones, John C. 215, 227
Jonesboro, Battle 180-1, 201
Jordan, Patrick 106, 113, 222
Joyce, Patrick 66, 70, 75, 92,
    181, 185, 207, 233

K

Kammerling, Gustav 163
Kanary, William 208
Kehoe, Miles 11, 13, 29, 52, 55
    208, 227
Keiter, William 41
Kemp, P. G. 215, 227
Kennedy, D. A. 215, 227
Ketchem's Alabama Battery 65
King, John 75, 93
King, Robert 150, 208
Kinney, Michael 150, 172, 177
    213, 229
Kinsella, Joseph 215, 227
Kirby, John 150, 219
Kirby, Joseph 150, 219
Kirkwood, Joseph 215, 227
Kirvin, J. M. 217
Knoxville, Tenn. 5-6, 8-9, 84, 90,
    110, 125, 132, 134, 157,
    182-3, 192-3, 199, 223,
    244

L

Lady Polk 41, 49, 245
Land, Philip B. 219
Layton, Cornelius 208, 227
Leary, Dennis 36-7, 52-3, 76, 208
Lee, Robert E. ix, xi, 120, 134,
    152
Lee, William Green 218
Liggett, Thomas 213
Lightner, J. 135, 149, 221
Long, G. W. 128, 218
Longstreet, James 136
Lookout Mountain 155, 157, 159-
    160

Lundy, J. 221, 229
Lyle, William 145
Lyon, Ida 199

M

Magee, John 90, 97
Magruder, John Bankhead 91, 189
Mahoney, Michael 10, 208, 227
Maney, George 138
Manigault, Arthur 157
Maroney, J. T. 52
Marsh, Daniel 193-4
Marsh, John Henry ix-x, 102, 112
    117, 123, 126, 131, 137,
    141, 148, 183, 187,
    193-6, 198, 242
Marsh, Robert 194
Marshall, Lucius G. 137, 144
Marshall's Battery 170, 181-2,
    184, 198, 229
Mathews, Patrick 11, 51, 208, 227
Martin, Edward 128, 221
Martin, William 117, 128, 131,
    151, 182, 185, 233
Mason, Michael 215
Maxey, A. 93, 218
McCant's Battery 166
McCarty, James 207
McCarty, Patrick 211
McCook, Alexander 88
McCown, G. W. 51, 200, 217
McCown, J. P. 43
McDavitt, George 8, 197
McDavitt, James C. 4, 8, 13, 29,
    49, 55, 72, 187, 196-7
McGrath, Owen 215, 227
McGuire, J. 222

Tooney Edward 207
Townsend, A. L. 77, 79, 94-5,
    103, 113, 216
Trabue, Robert 64
Travis, William E. 43
Tullahoma, Tenn. 96, 106-7, 114,
    124-5, 132, 243
Tupelo, Miss. 71, 75-6, 80, 82, 91,
    93, 183, 189, 200, 209,
    223
Turchin, John B. 145, 163
Turner, William 213, 227
Turner's Battery 88, 133, 147

V

Van Cleve, Horatio P. 144
Van Derveer, Ferdinand 163
Van Dorn, Earl 70, 126, 198
Vaughn, Alfred J. 55, 61, 77, 79,
    89, 95, 107, 117, 139,
    147-48, 165, 171

W

Walker, William H. T. 137
Waterhouse, Allen C. 61
Water's Battery 161, 164
Watkins, William 139
Watson, Alfred T. 52, 55, 73, 79,
    95, 113, 117, 127, 131,
    141, 148, 151, 153, 168,
    183-4
Watts, John B. 94, 114, 220
Watts, T. E. 77, 79, 95, 117, 151
    220
Weldon, G. 218
Welsh, James 11, 13, 29, 55, 114
    207, 227

Westbrook, J. G. 52, 77, 79, 95,
    216, 246
Wheeler, Joe 88
White, Margaret Preston 8
White, Margaret Rhea 192
Wilder, John 134
Williams, O. E. 215, 227
Winslow, Henry 38
Winston's Battery 193
Wink, D. H. 93
Witherspoon, Josephine Cannon
    201
Wood, Thomas B. 114, 218
Wood, Thomas J. 162
Wright, Marcus 138